The Cuyahoga

BOOKS IN THE
RIVERS OF AMERICA SERIES

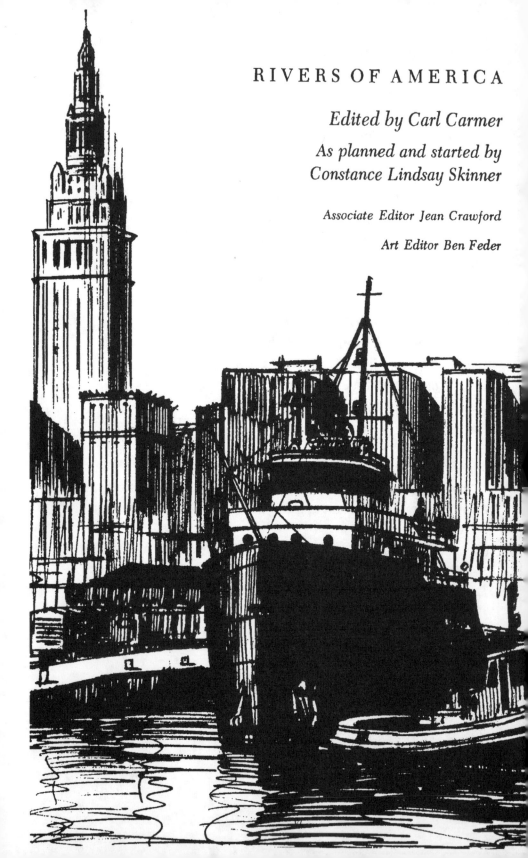

RIVERS OF AMERICA

Edited by Carl Carmer

As planned and started by
Constance Lindsay Skinner

Associate Editor Jean Crawford

Art Editor Ben Feder

The Cuyahoga

REVISED EDITION

BY WILLIAM DONOHUE ELLIS

Assisted by Nancy A. Schneider

Illustrated by Kinley T. Shogren

Landfall Press, Inc.
Dayton Ohio

The Cuyahoga
by William Donohue Ellis
Assisted by Nancy Schneider
Illustrated by Kinley T. Shogren

Revised Edition
Copyright © 1998 by William Donohue Ellis

ISBN 0-913428-81-7
Library of Congress Catalog Card Number: 98-075284

Original text copyright © 1966 by William Donohue Ellis
First Landfall Press, Inc. Edition March 1975
ISBN 0-913428-17-5
Library of Congress Catalog Card Number: 66-13558
Second Landfall Press, Inc. Printing December 1985

To Nancy A. Schneider and Marcia G. Siedel

Other Books
By The Author

Novels

The Bounty Lands Trilogy
The Bounty Lands
Jonathan Blair: Bounty Lands Lawyer
The Brooks Legend

Boomerang
with Raymond Q. Armington

Non-Fiction

Land Of The Inland Seas

Early Settlers Of The Western Reserve

Life on the Great Lakes - A Wheelsman's Story
with F. W. Dutton

Clarke of St. Vith

How To Win The Conference
with Frank Siedel

On The Oil Lands

For Reasons of the Heart
Yours In Scouting
both with Nancy A. Schneider

Something About Author's Debts And Acknowledgments

First — Alexander Kaye, President, Landfall Press, who decided it was time to update *The Cuyahoga*. It was also his idea that I should write and Landfall Press should publish *A Nation Begins. The Ordinance of 1787*, official book of the Bicentennial Commission for the Northwest Ordinance.

Next — my colleagues (at Editorial, Inc.) Nancy A. Schneider and Marcia G. Siedel. Nancy Schneider co-authored four books with me. Marcia Siedel handled research including print and taped interviews. Together we edit *Inland Seas®*, Great Lakes journal of record, published by the Great Lakes Historical Society.

Elaine Marsh chairs or coordinates several regional river organizations including the Crooked River Association; she is Greenways Coordinator for Rivers Unlimited. She read the manuscript and gave us her experienced comments. Also important was her enthusiastic blessing.

Traveling the Upper River, we did not encounter a lot of people. Part of the charm of these upper waters is serenity; punctuated occasionally by the thrashing and squawking of a covey of waterfowl we startled. They swash off flapping water and riffling lily pads.

There is a secret force working for an author, which he or she usually neglects. Riding high on the rush of initial public reaction and reviews, he or she is usually too self-absorbed to know that down the road, after publisher promotion and media tours fade, there is a sustaining action which he should thank (and even nurture).

This force? Small islands of energy out there, each sending ripples in concentric circles. The person in the middle adopts that book, tells friends about it, buys copies to send as presents to grown children who in turn find out where to buy it for gifts. A book network builds that way.

Dr. Robert Cheshire, director of Allen Memorial Medical Museum, is an example. He adopted the first and second editions of *The Cuyahoga*. He presented copies to new arrivals in this watershed. A member of several distinguished clubs, he suggests it to members.

When the initial reviews of editions of *The Cuyahoga* are history, the Cuyahoga Valley National Recreation Area continues to recommend it to new park rangers. In answering questions from park visitors, they tell about the book. The park store keeps the book available.

Ruth Seiple in Massillon persuaded the library to remove *The Cuyahoga* from locked case. She also presented the library with a copy to circulate. She is the center of a group of readers and history enthusiasts in town ... and in neighboring towns.

Marilyn Lawn, curator of the Munroe Falls Historical Museum, printed a portion of *The Cuyahoga* in their publication, *Olde Heritage Newsletter*, to boost it along.

There are other islands out there radiating support. Sometimes they are right in your own town.

I want to thank them.

Carol Fitzgerald

All authors and artists of the 65-volume series owe Carol Fitzgerald for creating a dynamic renaissance of the whole series. Her day job is an executive post with the Broward County (Florida) Commission. But at home she set out ten years ago to collect every edition of every book in the series. Beyond that she collected documentary information about every author and artist and publisher. She was compiling a huge bibliographic work.

John Y. Cole, director, Center for the Book, Library of Congress; publisher Holt, Rhinehart, Winston, first publisher;

and Carol Fitzgerald convened an historic Rivers of America Symposium at the Library of Congress, assembling authors and artists of the series. Following that event, several distinguished book clubs asked her to put on an exhibit and lecture including the University of Tennessee. The library in Broward County staged a major exhibit accompanied by a very comprehensive, beautifully produced book about the series with a preface by Carol on her work in collecting the series and dealing with the authors and publishers.

Even before this was published, Carol's renaissance was driving a rebirth of the series.

Next, I want to thank the same people who helped with the original Holt Reinhart edition (1966). While many are not living, relatives and friends would like to know they are appreciated.

Acknowledgments

For help on the following subjects: Everett Dodrill for the stories of the underground railroad, the geology, the Huletts, Whiskey Island, the railroads and other portions; Pauline Fanslow for the Kingsbury Run story, the index, and for research and general work throughout; Carl Goodwin for Captain Peck, the tugs, storms and bridges; Dorothy L. Couzens for assistance in condensing the manuscript to publication length.

To Jean Crawford, associate editor, Rivers of America series. That title is code for the one who does the day-to-day author contact.

To Carl Carmer, editor, Rivers of America series, for guidance and encouragement. Mr. Carmer was called to the post by the founder, Constance Lindsay Skinner. Carl Carmer was a prolific writer. In addition to *The Hudson* for the Rivers series, some others of his popular titles: *Genesee Fever, Hurricane's Child, Listen for Lonesome Dove, Stars Over Alabama*. He wrote 15 juveniles. In the beginning, he edited the series with Stephen Vincent Benét.

To Janet Coe Sandborn, History Department, Cleveland Public Library, and first editor of *Inland Seas*,® Quarterly Journal of the Great Lakes Historical Society. She provided extensive bibliographical assistance.

To Katherine Wilder, Rocky River Public Library, and to librarians along the Cuyahoga: Carolina Afflect, Cuyahoga Falls; Margaret Babbitt, Independence; Margaret Zearley, Kent; Harriet Johnson, Chardon; Carmen Gordon, Peninsula; Grace Goodale, Hiram; Mary L. Schubert, Brecksville; and to R. Russell Munn, Akron, for reading certain chapters.

For facts, we're in the debt of three grand pioneering regional writers of the past: Henry Howe, Charles Whittlesey, Sam'l A. Lane; and to distinguished modern writers of the region: The late William Ganson Rose; Harlan Hatcher for his works on the Western Reserve; Walter Havighurst who wrote something about most Midwestern waters; and to the works of Lee Templeton and Frank Siedel, both powerful writers and valued colleagues of mine, who contributed also some of their wonderfully prejudiced regional enthusiasm.

For those wishing to explore the Cuyahoga further, a bibliography follows the text.

Our thanks to the Inland Seas Maritime Museum in Vermilion, the Perkins Museum in Akron, Western Reserve Historical Society, Ohio Historical Society and Ohioana Library in Columbus.

Thanks to Captain Tom O'Donnell and his tug crew; and to Thomas Hawisher, research geologist of Ferro Corporation, for checking over our geological chapter.

Absolutely no thanks in general should go to the denizens of Green's Café on the old Angle's border who maintained top security about Whiskey Island's past. Therefore, very special thanks to Matthew Quilter, a retired railroad man who was one of the few to break security on the early days of Whiskey Island. He was extremely helpful and informative; and we hope this acknowledgment does not get him in trouble at the club. Thanks should also go to his longtime friend, Walter Kramer.

To the late Willis Thornton, to David K. Ford and Jack Hollister for special reference materials lent to us, and to Frank Trevorrow for a detailed map of the Canal and to Lew Richardson, early editor of *Towpaths*.

To Ross C. Durst, retired professor of engineering, for use of his *History of the Cuyahoga* and book of news clippings; and to the members of the Cleveland Police Department for assistance.

We're also indebted to a long list of people, especially older people, who spent many hours with us reminiscing about the history they helped make.

William Donohue Ellis
Cleveland, Ohio
March, 1998

Special Note to the family of the late Kinley Shogren who did all the superb art work which *made* this book.

---

xv

"It has always been my opinion that the shortest, easiest and least expensive communication with the invaluable back country would be [to] let the courses and distances be taken to the mouth of the Muskingum and up that river to the carrying place to the Cuyahoga, down the Cuyahoga to Lake Erie."

— George Washington
to Benjamin Harrison
Governor of Virginia
October 10, 1784

Contents

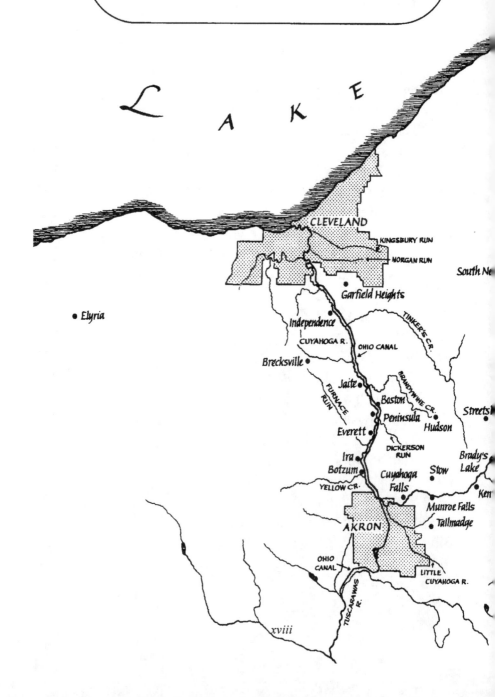

The CUYAHOGA

L A K E

CLEVELAND
KINGSBURY RUN
MORGAN RUN
South Ne
Garfield Heights
• Elyria
Independence
TINKER'S CR.
CUYAHOGA R.
OHIO CANAL
Brecksville •
Jaite •
BRANDYWINE CR.
FURNACE RUN
Boston
Streets
Peninsula
Everett •
Hudson
DICKERSON RUN
Ira •
Brady's Lake
Botzum •
Cuyahoga Falls
Stow •
YELLOW CR.
Munroe Falls
Ken
AKRON
Tallmadge
OHIO CANAL
LITTLE CUYAHOGA R.
TUSCARAWAS R.

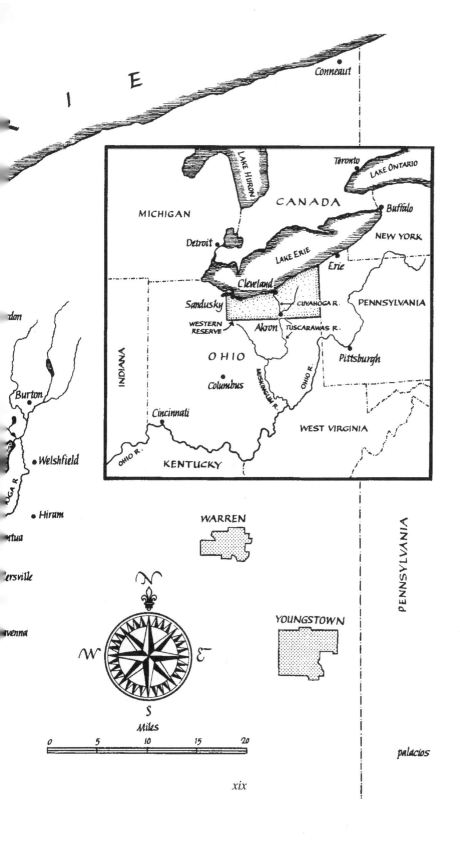

E

Conneaut

LAKE HURON

Toronto LAKE ONTARIO

CANADA

Buffalo

MICHIGAN

Detroit

NEW YORK

LAKE ERIE

Erie

Cleveland

Sandusky

CUYAHOGA R.

PENNSYLVANIA

WESTERN
RESERVE

Akron TUSCARAWAS R.

INDIANA

OHIO

Pittsburgh

MUSKINGUM R.

OHIO R.

Columbus

Cincinnati

WEST VIRGINIA

OHIO R.

KENTUCKY

...don

Burton

Welshfield

...OGA R.

Hiram

...ntua

WARREN

...ersville

...venna

N

YOUNGSTOWN

PENNSYLVANIA

W

E

S

Miles

0   5   10   15   20

palacios

xix

1

A Long Way Going Somewhere

To find the beginning the first time, I had a bird's-eye view — my bird was a Cessna 170 piloted by my wife, research librarian Dorothy Ann Naiden Ellis.

More recently, we attempted a landlook.

The river begins in two branch streams 1,300 feet above sea level in Geauga County. This is lush area — mostly marshland and swamp forests — a perfect habitat for beaver and birds. But the headwaters are elusive ... we spent a day searching the general area without success.

According to Keith McClintock of the Geauga County Soil and Conservation District, "the exact sources shift depending on the time of year." As near as anyone can figure looking at maps, the east branch begins in Montville Township on private property somewhere near State Route 6 and Clay Street. The west branch begins in Hamden Township with two feeder streams: one in the Hamden Orchard Wildlife Area and the other on private property somewhere south of Routes 6 and 608.

These two branches meander separately and loosely parallel. The east branch flows through pine trees, slowed by an earthen dam creating East Branch Reservoir around an enchanting island.

Each stream is blocked, diverted, widened and flattened as it wanders south. When they ripple over pebbled patches, sunlight blinks off the stones. August shrinks the streams.

They straddle a village of horse corrals and long, winding driveways — Burton. A little farther south, still in Burton Township, the two branches join.

From the confluence for 26 miles to Lake Rockwell (Portage County), the Cuyahoga flows gently through beauty. Ohio officially designated this stretch a "Scenic River." One of the most unique aspects of this wetland watershed is its unexpected wilderness in the heart of Northeast Ohio.

The river winds south leisurely, best viewed by canoe, past Burton's Eldon Russell Park. The current is subtle, held back by nature's rock bottleneck before Hiram Rapids.

The following story is relevant as prelude to the intense preservation attitude you may encounter most of the way down river.

Near the place called Troy at the turn of the century a Mr. E. P. Latham wanted to raise onions. He needed to drain the land and divert the river into a channel he dug. As a last step to turn the river into his channel openings, he needed to blast out some large boulders. However, upstream people don't welcome changes to their river. When the blasting crew arrived, the townspeople of Troy fired salt pellets at them. The onions never happened.

At Welshfield, four-lane 422 squeezes to two becoming Welshfield's Main Street. Best river view is from County Road 700.

In 1811, Jacob Welsh from Boston owned the land. To draw more settlers to his clearing, he offered 50 acres and money for a church with a stained-glass window if the place would be named Welshfield. However, his will made no provision for the church.

The town has been famous for the inn built in 1840 by Alden Nash. Nash Inn was the halfway stopover on the two-day trip from Youngstown to Cleveland. Later it became Hiram, founded before statehood in 1803, which crowns one of the highest ridges in Ohio looking down at gentle hills. For many this is the dream village. The population of 1,500 includes the respected Hiram College — liberal arts but with a shrewd focus for these times on chemistry, biology, physics and applied mathematics.

Camp Hi Livery rents canoes from a metal dock that extends into the river; and the fishing is good.

At Garrettsville — Colonel John Garrett knew specifically what it would take to make his forest draw settlement. Therefore, following statehood, he built here the advanced institution of civilization — a gristmill — powered by the fall of water just above Hiram. From 15 miles around people hauled their grain to the mill. New people settled closer. Gradually that created a peopled clearing. That water-powered mill is still in use today. The 15-mile radius, however, now circles 300,000 people.

Downstream, downtown Mantua hugs both banks. In this area are two preserves held by the Ohio Department of Natural Resources, Division of Natural Areas and Preserves: The Marsh Wetland Preserve and the Chuck Tummons Preserve, named for a great defender of the Cuyahoga, great paddler and well-known canoe and kayak builder.

Mantua is perched on a hilltop; its roads cross the river several times. Although Mantua Grain & Supply (1850s) still centers town, Mantua calls itself the "fastest growing place in Northern Ohio." This gutsy little village has big plans.

The day we dropped in, the town hall was in command of three charming women: Dorothy Summerlin, assistant clerk-treasurer; Linda Wilke, dispatcher; and Vickie McFarland, maintenance.

Mantua started in the early 1800s as a shipping point for area farmers. It had a railroad station backed up by a store, 13 saloons and a house for questionable relaxation.

Today, the village shares firefighting with Shalersville, just downstream, a town with an airport above Brady's Lake.

South of the lake, the river comes close to Ravenna, followed also on the left bank by Kent.

Here the waters split around 20-foot-high Standing Rock, which resisted erosion. On its flat top is Standing Rock Cemetery (Indian) which was once tended by volunteer John Davey, founder of the national tree service and father of Ohio's Governor Martin Davey (1935-1939).

The Upper River Defense

So far canoeists and hikers have only encountered beautiful, sparsely inhabited country. But downstream of the swamp, they encounter the advance dozer treads of invading suburbs. Ditches drain swamps to create land that kills the reedy shore, incubator of small life. Into this animal kindergarten wash killer pesticides and herbicides, lawn chemicals and silt. Next — occasional rubbish

Trying to head off deluge is Elaine Marsh, conservation chair of an intense organization, Friends of the Crooked River. "We want to protect the upper Cuyahoga from what happened to the lower."

Her finger in the dike needs to be strong because the pressure is relentless. People are hungry to move into the sylvan river setting, which they then rush to destroy. "Gotta have closer shopping."

Elaine Marsh is also Greenways Coordinator for Rivers Unlimited, a group backed by a battalion of organized volunteers. This upper river may be the most aggressively protected water, mile for mile, in the United States. A sampling of the troops:

Upper Watershed Task Force
Headwaters Land Trust
Tinkers Creek Land Conservancy
Friends of Big Creek
Cascade Lock Park Association
Cleveland Metro Parks
Cuyahoga River Community Planning Organization
Ohio Department of Natural Resources Scenic Rivers
Cuyahoga Valley National Recreation Area
Cuyahoga Valley Trails Council
Kent Environmental Council
Metro Parks Serving Summit County
Geauga County Park District
Ohio & Erie Canal Corridor Coalition

P.L.A.C.E.
Cuyahoga Valley Association

When we get to the lower Cuyahoga, we will find an even bigger army. Of course, they have a tougher enemy.

Kent is a turning point. The city's industry and homes are built on hills. Crowning several of these is huge, sprawling Kent State University which expands the city population every autumn.

Downstream — Munroe Falls has a great view of an ancient dam. The river gives off a calming effect as it rolls gently over the dam in a broad, smooth, moderate fall. At City Hall, Carol Rymer showed us the best way to get really close to a long stretch of the river — the walking and bike path going north along the right bank.

At the south tip of Munroe Falls the river narrows to begin the plunge through Gorge Park. The park channels the river into the east side of Cuyahoga Falls where Owen Brown bought the corner of Main and Cuyahoga streets and fathered John Brown, the abolitionist. Books about the Browns still come off press and are on the shelves at Bill Lammers' News Stand.

Although Riverfront Parkway on the west bank, and Ohio routes 83 and 59 on the east, limit hands-on contact with the water, the city has saved some river for people at Riverfront Centre.

Despite intense urbanization (pushing 50,000), a large piece of Cuyahoga Valley National Recreation Area Metro Parks lies within Cuyahoga Falls, where some 6,000 acres of pure nature are preserved. The parks in Cuyahoga Falls are managed by the city of Cuyahoga Falls and Metro Parks Serving Summit County. While these acres are included in the Cuyahoga Valley National Recreation Area, they consider themselves autonomous from Federal control.

For two miles within Cuyahoga Falls city limits, the river drops 248 feet toward the lake. The gorge narrows increasing the pressures as the river thrashes downstream. (Until recently its 545-gallons-per-minute flow drove generators of a Gorge power company.) At one point the falls splash the dining room windows of the Sheraton Hotel's wing positioned on stilts over the water for view.

The Cold Hand of the Maker

How these falls came to be here deserves to be not dismissed as ancient history. Why?

Despite its slow motion formation over hundreds of millions of years, during its most recent milliseconds of time — the last 100 years — the gorge has put bread and meat on the table for generations of millions in the neighborhood.

Tributaries to the vast prehistoric pre-glacial River Teay flowed northwest to join the headwaters of the future Mississippi. These tributaries eroded steep-sided valleys into the sandstone hills of future Akron. Then, only 17,000 years ago (just yesterday), the multi-fingered Hiram ice sheet, a mile thick, was advancing again, pushing its own melt waters up nearly against the high Akron ridge, forming Lake Cuyahoga.

As the Hiram melted its way back north for the last time, it widened and lowered Lake Cuyahoga by stages uncovering the tops of the Akron hills. These stages, "terraces," were discovered by Professor E. W. Claypoole (born 1835), an Englishman teaching at Buchtel College (predecessor of the University of Akron). As the glacier withdrew farther, Lake Cuyahoga gradually shrank to a river at the bottom of a deep valley. Dr. Claypoole's terraces became a series of waterfalls.

The Double U-Turn

What obstacle could ever stop this gravity-driven power? We are about to see.

South of the falls, the seemingly unstoppable force hits the Akron Summit, part of that long ridge of rock hills — the continental divide. Half the rain drains north to the old schoolhouse at Everett and on to the Great Lakes. The other half drains south to the Ohio River and the Gulf of Mexico.

When the southbound Cuyahoga waters push against the rugged Akron ridge, that wall U-turns the river north. At the same time, the northbound Tuscarawas River strikes the other side of that same summit and is U-turned south.

That became very important. At that twin turning point the two watersheds are less than eight miles apart. Connecting them across the eight miles was an Indian canoe portage. This land link in their canoe voyages between the Great Lakes and the Gulf of Mexico served as an official U.S. west boundary for some time.

The Indians marked this portage path with signal trees by bending up the side branches of a sapling and binding them at the elbows forming, with the main trunk, a three-pronged candelabrum. One of these, now a giant three-trunked burr oak, stands at the Cuyahoga end of Portage Trail in Cascade Valley Metro Park, Akron.

Now U-turned, the Cuyahoga heads north downhill until impounded by an old, 65-foot-high concrete electric utility dam right across the canyon, an ugly cork in a beautiful stream.

The river teams in Akron with the Ohio Canal, which climbed up the continental divide in 42 laboriously built stair-step locks. Today the lock at the Akron summit is restored and surrounded by beautifully landscaped Canal Park.

The Canal made Akron a warehouse for canal cargo storage; it built hostelries and taverns for canalers and their mules and farmers hauling grain to the canal for transshipment. Ultimately the canal and the Cuyahoga brought the rubber companies, which needed rivers of water for cooling.

Other water-hungry industries followed.

Over the next 100 years, that canal town grew into an industrial giant — rubber, sandstone, grain milling, lighter-than-air craft.

However, in the 1970s and '80s, Akron took a major hit.

The big tire companies left town. That necessarily shut down hundreds of their suppliers and shuttered retailers who served both those armies.

At this writing, driven by an aggressive mayor backed by citizen leaders, a greater-Akron technical renaissance is building (see later).

Leaving industrial Akron, the Cuyahoga flows back to nature. It zigzags through 22 miles of protected Cuyahoga Valley National Recreational Area.

Before the 33,000 acres became a national park, they were farms and small crossroad villages. A few remnants remain. Everett is a classic example.

Between 1837 and 1852, during the packet canal boat era, Alanson Swan, a large land owner, operated a grocery store, warehouse and livery stable to service the canal at Lock #27. In 1880, a post office came and the Valley Railway gave the village a depot and the name Everett (after the secretary-treasurer of the railway company). The village prospered.

However, in the 1920s, automobiles came; the road to Akron was crudely paved. Everett was suddenly unnecessary.

After 1930, the one-room schoolhouse became Disciple Church; the depot was dismantled.

Today Everett, at the crossroads of Riverview and Wheatley, is 11 houses (including the converted schoolhouse/church now on the National Register of Historic Places) and the CVNRA South District Ranger Station surrounded by farms. Everett's buildings house a variety of park and park-related functions including housing student interns for the Cuyahoga Valley Environmental Education Center — one of the best examples of public-private institutions that exists.

Inside the Cuyahoga Valley park is a long stretch of Ohio Canal towpath from Bath in the south to Lock #39 at Rockside Road in the north. It too, has its protective organizations, especially the aggressive Ohio & Erie Canal Corridor Coalition, headed at this writing by Daniel Rice.

After years of intense lobbying (led in Congress by Ralph Regula and his administrative assistant, Barbara Warnman), they succeeded in having the Ohio & Erie Canal Corridor designated a National Heritage Corridor so that director Timothy Donovan's canal territory reaches upstream from Lake Erie south to Akron.

Possibly the very best view of the Cuyahoga is on the outskirts of Peninsula. A wide, roughly semicircular loop of river flows concentrically outside the Ohio & Erie Canal. A feeder supplying river water for Lock 30 links the two. At your best observation place, the canal crosses over the river by Lock 29 aqueduct.

When Lock 29 was built, Herman Bronson knew business would develop around it, an ideal place to build a gristmill. He needed a dam on the river. He arranged for one to be built so he could get a six-foot fall to power his wheel. The mill continued working until the day after Christmas, 1931. Fire.

Today, a wooden stairway and boardwalk run next to Lock 29 and continue across the river where a remnant of the aqueduct stands as a testament to man's ingenuity.

From this man-made perch, the view is magnificent. The bend in the river is most dramatic as the water rushes around the corner and swirls against the far shore before bouncing off and continuing downstream.

Peninsula's Mission:
Care & Handling of Yesterday

We spent time in the village itself. It vigorously plays out the classic fight between progress and nostalgia, perhaps the same one, which goes on in your own heart.

Peninsula is important as the example of what you will encounter in the next 20 miles — dozens of intense groups dedicated to preserving nature and history here and wherever you live.

Sleeping on the banks of the Cuyahoga at Route 303, Peninsula watches the decades roll down. For over 100 exciting years, the world passed through here on the Ohio and Erie Canal.

Then the railroads took the trade from the canalers and left the town quiet with its memories.

Two jet-streamed highways skirt Peninsula east and west. But as two-lane Riverview Road winds through the town, time stands still. Square, white, Connecticut Western Reserve houses with functional storm shutters, abjure thermopane retrofits and frown at developers.

Sometimes village tranquillity is shattered as Peninsula battles for its status quo. Like the day the wrecking crews came to knock down the old Woods Store. One of the crew cupped his hands and called to the small woman in a red raincoat in front of the store, arms around her two children. "Lady, you're gonna get hurt if you stay there!"

Lily Fleder pulled the children closer.

"Lady, yer kids'll get tetanus on them rusty nails."

Lily withered them, "They're inoculated!"

The scene drew townspeople.

Another woman entered the scene. Her bulk and authoritative voice labeled her the new owner. "What do you think you're doing, Lady?"

Lily yelled back, "I'm not going to let you tear down this building; it's a landmark."

Lily was losing the debate when the tall young man strolled up. He wore a corduroy jacket and sport shirt, and he approached with the air of a country squire about to make a law. The crowd grinned.

He addressed the owner and crew, "Look down there," he pointed to the river. "Over a hundred years of American commerce has flowed right by this store."

"What's that got to do with this crummy old building?"

The squire answered with restraint, "Why, everything. This was the first store built in Peninsula. These show windows displayed the first jewelry for sale here." He pointed across the street. "That church was built in 1835. Your ancestors might have worshiped there."

"Not mine," the owner said.

Indicating the row of fine white houses stretching up the hill, the gentleman said, "Every one served as a rooming house for canalers."

The woman heard a voice in the crowd. "So Hunker finally got here!"

The woman challenged, "Are you Hunker?"

He nodded.

"Then you can just get the hell out of here you ..."

Quite a long speech followed.

This is quite understandable. There are groups at work to modernize the town of Peninsula. Hunker on the other hand, a designer/architect, leads a crowd with a feeling for preservation and restoration.

He is also a businessman, coupling his talents with a self-confidence which frequently get him his own way. This argument progressed in public to what seemed a stalemate until finally Hunker asked, "What would you take to sell the store?"

He bought it.

For decades Peninsula people witnessed the drama of "progress" vs. history and Hunker. For example the church.

Bronson Memorial Church stood opposite the Woods Store with a belfry clinging to its roof. The roof beams, savaged by squads of squirrels, were hazardous. Weather punished it inside and out. By 1960, the church had been closed ten years.

Just a few miles away, the Jonathan Hale Homestead, operated by the large Western Reserve Historical Society, wanted Peninsula's Bronson Memorial Church for its Hale Farm and Historic Village. The Bishop of the Episcopal Diocese of Cleveland, which owned the church, was hugely relieved. He wanted to shed the maintenance of that wreck.

The only hurdle in the Bishop's way was a small woman, often underestimated — Lily Fleder.

Marching a committee of umbrella-armed women through the rain into the Bishop's Cleveland office, she demanded that the landmark church stay home. The astonished Bishop eyed the ladies with a twinkle that turned into a frown. "The Diocese is not interested in restoring that church," he explained. "The church is being moved to the Hale Farm."

Lily filed an injunction to halt the move. Peninsulites added voices.

The Bishop heard a tale about a local bank in Hudson, which had occupied a quaint brick building for years. When the bank decided to tear it down and rebuild new, important savings accounts were suddenly withdrawn.

The Bishop did not want to hear of empty pews in Western Reserve Episcopal Church. Neither did he want the cost of restoring and maintaining the Bronson church. On the other hand ... there was Lily Fleder.

She banded with nearby Hudson to save not just Hudson's buildings, but the entire upper Cuyahoga Valley from industrial invasion.

The Bishop and his trustees became aware that Lily was an army.

And Lily's army was taking the church problem all the way to Washington's National Trust for Historic Preservation. Helen Duprey Bullock, then director of the Department of Information, made a special trip to see the valley. Robert Hunker drove her through the two towns, pointing out landmarks.

Late in the afternoon, they stopped at a restaurant situated at the River Bridge almost precisely where canalers used to fight for the locks. Imagine the coincidence — they met there a curator of the Western Reserve Historical Society.

After a series of cool introductions, Mrs. Bullock commented, "You realize that the church is not really 1830s Western Reserve on the inside. It was completely renovated in 1880 to Victorian style."

Mrs. Bullock set her glass on the table and asked, "What are you going to do with the church if you move it out of Peninsula?"

The curator looked at her confidently. "We'll put it back the way it was in 1830."

"If you do that," said Mrs. Bullock, "you might as well build a new replica church."

"Now just a minute," Mrs. Bullock said. "Just because 1830 was a little before 1880 doesn't mean that 1880 isn't going to be an important part of American History."

Nothing was settled in the restaurant, but Mrs. Bullock's visit brought about the formation of the Peninsula Valley Heritage Association. Charlie Conger stood up in the first meeting and said: "It's time to fight for the things that made our town!"

Lily Fleder added: "Let's see that it stays!"

By October 1964, Peninsula's 650 residents had contributed $18,500 to restore the Bronson Church and establish an endowment fund for maintenance. The Summit County Historical Society brought the total to $20,000 and the church was saved.

However, Peninsula's fight continued. Proposed superhighway, I-271, aimed its six-lane racetrack directly at the little town. Again Peninsula went to Washington with their heavy hitters, speeches ready. They were Galen Rousch, president of Railway Express; Charlie Conger, vice president of Bender Louder Freight Company; J. Kubinyi, engineer; George Fischer, mayor of Peninsula; Mr. Sarison and Robert Hunker.

In the office of the Director of Highways in Washington, Hunker began, "Mr. Director, two-seventy-one will split our town in two, a grave mistake."

The Director of Highways, a master of negotiation simplification nodded, quietly rummaged through his desk drawer for a rubber band. He cut it into one long length and stretched it across the map the men had spread on his desk. "What's wrong with that line?"

"Up a little," said Hunker.

The rubber band moved up. "All agreed?"

"Fine."

"Thank you, gentlemen." The Director rose, "Glad to have met you all."

I-271 cuts across the Cuyahoga valley in a line as straight as a stretched rubber band.

Then came the hot wires. The plan was to cut a mile-wide swath across the valley for high-tension wires. But Peninsula refused to conduct electricity. No wires.

And today you can walk Peninsula and still see Woods Store, built 1820; Bronson Memorial Church, 1835; Peninsula Inn, 1850; and more.

The river takes a big jog outside of Peninsula while Riverview Road makes a fairly straight path through a large wetland — home of herons, beaver, raccoons, deer and underwater life.

As the canopy of trees opens, a surreal pocket of old and new is revealed on the flat valley floor. The buildings of Boston Mills tell of the village's historic canal beginnings. High above the trees, however, the road of crisscrossed modern highway bridges spoils the historic illusion. This small rural village with its canal lock ruin, corn cribs, bridge and village cemetery is on the National Register of Historic Places.

Before leaving the Boston area behind, take a little jog down Stanford to Brandywine Road. You will be amazed. Brandywine Falls on the right bank stops the breath. The highest falls in the valley, it hurtles down 65 feet over rock shelves into a deep canyon where it bounces up off huge boulders in a misty spray.

The Brandywine Gorge is lined with towering, ancient hemlocks which make the scene a Christmas card in winter.

On my last visit it was unsafe to get close. Now a color blended multi-level walk lets you get spray in the face. To emplace the support columns, the contractor drilled 12-15 feet into the rock.

Although the Brandywine River is only 11 miles long, it flows through six towns.

Double back through Boston Mills to Riverview Road as it continues to wind through the Valley paralleling (as much as

34

possible) the railroad, the river, and the canal and its towpath. The rails and road are undoubtedly the straightest route, for the Ohio & Erie Canal Towpath Trail is almost as crooked as the river. While the river is not always in sight of the road, it is never more than a slight jog in one direction or the other.

After a few miles the trees open to reveal grassy fields. On a hill in the distance are a classic red brick farmhouse and an imposing red barn. The new asphalt drive and parking lot studded with official vehicles are concessions to officialdom — Central Dispatch for the rangers who maintain this living monument with farmhouse flowered landscaping. The rangers are in evidence throughout the 33,000 acres ... walking the rails, patrolling the roads and trails. Maureen Mackey, in charge of North District Rangers, showed how, whether at the station or in her car, she is in radio contact with her rangers.

The rangers have a big job. More than 3.5 million visitors come to the park each year, 1.6 million of whom use the Towpath Trail. The CVNRA is rated 20th of the 375 National Parks and receives more visitors each year than Yellowstone!

Around the corner from Central Dispatch, just past the intersection of Snowville and Riverview, are two neat mustard-yellow, "two-flat" houses carefully trimmed in gray. Both are what remain of a row of five double houses built in 1906 by Charles Jaite to house managers at his nearby Jaite Paper Mill.

Almost immediately, Vaughn Road intersects from the right sporting another mustard-yellow row. Turning east on Vaughn, the first and largest of the five was the Jaite Mill company store and post office; second floor was home to the store manager and family. Today this is headquarters for the Cuyahoga Valley National Recreation Area. Inside and out, it is a refreshing change from government anti-citizen decor.

Inside works a small enthusiastic staff, headed by superintendent John P. Debo, Jr., and deputy superintendent Thomas Bradley. The superintendent is young, but already a 21-year veteran of national parks: Fire Island; Acadia National; Boston National Historical Park; Charleston Navy Yard Freedom Park.

Debo has been here nine years. His vision is a credit to the park, the valley, the river and the people of Northeast Ohio.

The other four houses were built in 1917 to house mill workers.

This crossroads was originally Vaughn Station for the family who settled this area in the 1840s; Edward Vaughn donated two acres to the railroad when the Valley Railway line completed to here in 1880 as a shipping point for timber. After the mill came, in the 1920s, the name was changed to Jaite.

Across the street, right next to the tracks of the Cuyahoga Valley Railroad Line, are the Jaite Depot buildings, passenger and freight. Small green clapboard structures neatly inscribed in white — JAITE.

Today, despite a diesel powered engine on either end, one for the upstream trip, one for the return, the train moves at a snail's pace, making frequent stops to allow passengers to absorb the area's beauty. Each railroad car wears a sponsor's nameplate, even engines, which this day have Goodyear pulling in one direction and BFGoodrich the opposite … still competing.

Crossing over the track, less than a quarter mile down the road a straight, calm stretch of the Cuyahoga is bridged. Just up the hill on our right a large sign begs for attention, "Dover Lake Water Park and Boston Mills Ski Area." Ignore that and look to your left.

Across the road, parallel to the river are the remains of Lock 34, called the Red Lock … no one remembers why exactly, perhaps the red clay workmen found when excavating or the red paint that once covered the lock gates.

All that remains are remnants of two walls, a puzzle of gigantic stone blocks. Even concrete reinforcement applied between 1905 and 1909 is crumbling now. The signage is new:

Portage Summit; elevation 968 feet at Lock one
Everett Lock #27
Peninsula Lock #29
Cleveland Lock #44 is 573 feet
From Akron to Cleveland the drop is 395 feet

Backtracking to Riverview Road ... heading downstream again, Jaite disappears as the road turns quickly and dramatically, winding through and around the narrowest section of the park bordered by Sagamore and Walton Hills.

Just before Independence, Riverview Road stops. Go north on Canal Road to Tinkers Creek Road, then east to Tinkers Creek, named for the surveyor who drowned in the service of General Cleaveland's party. It is the largest of the 37 tributaries.

When I last saw her she was beautiful as a meadow brook with morning fog just rising off her. Today she is being crowded, suffering as disposal system for development "progress."

Backing out of Tinkers Creek to Canal Road, you parallel the river into another world — a flat-water world — industrial valley. The waters, which plunged down from Akron in hours, will now take ten days winding six miles to the Lake. The Cuyahoga here has been widened and deepened, its shores locked in place by steel sheath piling to allow bulk carriers to maneuver the curves without grounding in earthen banks.

You cannot walk or drive close to the river for a stretch. There are industrial roads, but your view of the water is walled out by industry's awesome skyline.

In the 18th century, this fiery, smoke-filled, Vulcan's workshop was the industrial heart of the region between Pittsburgh and Chicago. It made iron and steel in rolls, bars and plate. The metal-using industry then made rails, built steam locomotives and steel ships. It forged anchors and parts for its own valley steel mills. It manufactured tools for farmers, joiners and plumbers. It made plate steel for locomotives, boilers, platforms and wire for western ranches and pipe for the underground universe of cities and beams for the skyscrapers of 1880 rising to 12 stories. And then they rolled tin plate with flowered designs for the ceilings in offices, barbershops, restaurants and saloons.

Condemned River

The outcry against the despoilers of the lower river was justified because the industries, which had turned it into a chemical sewer, had taken no corrective action. They could hardly do so; if only one or two quit polluting while the others continued, it would not help. Additionally — much of the pollution came from as far upstream as Akron.

Much of the enormous equipment for sanitizing plant exhaust and liquid effluent was not yet invented.

However, the malignment in the 1960s did not soften nor acknowledge that this last six miles of water had employed generations totaling millions of people. Many of the great grandfathers were from Eastern Europe. The great grandsons and daughters now working in air-cooled uptown, far from the heat and grit-filled smoke and noise of the coking ovens and the blast house floors, today proudly celebrate their ancestry in a dozen ethnic associations, clubs and churches.

The river's notoriety went national in the environmentally intense era, especially triggered by media convergence when the river caught fire. Media were not aware this stretch caught fire several times *every* year. From the outpouring of the mills the river was 130 degrees with effluent water, petroleum and industrial pickle liquor. Add a tangled float of oil-soaked, cast-off pallets, dunnage and driftwood, the fires were inevitable.

Turnaround

The lower river fields an army as aggressive as the upper. Called RAP, Remedial Action Plan, it is a battalion of high-horsepower individuals and organizations — corporations, city, federal and county governments, and dozens of specialized environmental clubs. At this writing these troops are guided by Jan Rybka, RAP's Public Involvement Coordinator. They keep the pressure on the clean up.

The initial jolts were from the federal. It came down on industry summarily demanding implementation of EPA standards. Their so-called "hearings" were conducted with prosecutorial format. Eager federals demanded nearly absurd clean air and water. Using steel as an example: the industry spent literally *billions* on engineering and installation of huge clean-up apparatus to meet the standards. Then EPA enforcement would demand another part per billion be removed, making the air cleaner than nature.

However, today the fish are nosing into the river mouth.

The best view of this part of the river is aboard the new *Goodtime* sailing from the mouth.

If you are on this vessel at dusk, downbound on return leg, the silhouette of the sprawling LTV steel mill, last basic steel producer here, looms — a mile of raw production power astride the river. Tall banks of coking oven silos are still silhouetted but inactive. The conveyors still climb to the top, not with coal, but with briquettes for the blast furnaces. In the dusk the plant becomes a range of low hills, including small mountains of iron ore, limestone and slag.

The blast furnaces, which cook a mix of ore, coke and limestone at up to 4,000° and blow hot air up through it, light up the bottom of the clouds. But most of the action is inside the buildings. We may see the bottle car on the LTV railroad carry this hot brew toward the basic oxygen furnace. We won't see the mix joined by scrap and flux to enter the oxygen furnace. We'll see the cloud of steam from the resulting molten steel hitting the dramatic continuous caster which produces slabs to be hot or cold-rolled into sheet steel. You've seen trucks carrying the resulting coils — headed for the automobile plants.

(Today the molten steel plunges down a long, enclosed, water-cooled channel, curving down to the conveyor below producing a thick, red-hot slab, for whatever you want to make of it.)

Below the Steel Plant

In the stretch below the steel plant, on the lower Ca-hawga, you can drive again. You will see a ballet of moving bridges and hear a concert of base horn signals from the ships — "open the bridge" — and the trumpet replies — "bridge opening." There are 11 of these anchor bridges. The Center Street swing bridge rotates, stopping traffic about three times per hour. At the mouth is the "Iron Curtain," nearly in constant motion; at ground level to let the trains through, then lifting 98 feet for vessel passage. There are nine more dramatic bridges in this five-mile stretch.

The lower Ca-Hawga doubles back on itself several times taking you by a grain dock, the fire boat station and a famous restaurant where one can watch the 750-foot carrier try to bend around the corner.

In the same vicinity is the giant, four-lane double opening drawbridge.

On the right bank under the sky-high bridge connecting the west bank's Detroit Road to the east's Superior Avenue is a replica of a settler's cabin and an historical marker citing the landing of General Moses Cleaveland's surveying party.

From here, no more curves; a straight mile and a half to Lake Erie. But what a mile and a half!

"The Flats" was once a sneer. Especially during the Great Depression its Whiskey Island was campsite for men of the road, traveling the rails without tickets, seeking a city with jobs. Some called it Hooverville in honor of the U.S. president, unaware the Depression was worldwide.

This transient population was mixed. Among the men were executives, lawyers, professors felled by the Depression. After the Depression, semi-permanent population camped there, less elite.

The Flats also had a collection of undistinguished shot-and-a-beer taverns.

Unbelievable! Incredible!

That is the reaction of people who have been away from Cleveland and return to visit the new Flats.

Flats chic arrived in full blast in the 1990s. The right bank is lined with 17 modern restaurants, nightclubs, gift shops and saloons. Many have floor-to-ceiling glass walls and decks on the river side. These clubs come in many distinct styles of food, lighting, music and prices. Boaters tie up for dinner and dancing along restaurant row. Patrons of the riverside restaurants stare spellbound when an ore carrier — seven-and-a-half house lots long — crawls by on slow bell. Until recently, the bulk carriers had the whole width of the entrance to themselves. Now they must handle the wheel and chadburn extra carefully. Pleasure boats tied up on both banks narrow the channel. An ore carrier cannot make crash stops; and if a frolicking motor boater plays chicken with the ship, his boat can become instant kindling.

Some names painted high on buildings preserve history for people in the marine community over age 50. Rumrunners Club reminds of Prohibition era when ship chandlers imported strong waters from Canada and supplied it to the ships along with rope and paint.

The Hausher Building housed Hausher & Sons ship chandlers. In 1854, they were butchers supplying ships' galleys. Later they supplied a whole line of supplies for the paint locker, the galley and the firehold and engine room.

Samsel, an equally famous chandler, kept a huge inventory of ship hardware in a building emblazoned with his name. If a moving vessel needed uncommon parts, the chandler would search and acquire the parts and run them out to the ship as it passed the port here. Samsel's name and number were in all the pilothouses.

Basements in these buildings were stations on the Underground Railroad.

Today in the Flats, the west bank features the Nautica

shell, a stadium for music. Here too, buildings have been converted to restaurants.

Whiskey Island, infamous home of the damned, downtrodden and abandoned, is suddenly the playground for the well to do. A deluxe yacht club building now centers row upon row of pleasure boats.

Other changes?

When we wrote the 1985 edition, Alan W. Sweigert, a bearded bear of a photographer could listen to his marine scanner and hear what bulk carriers were approaching the mouth of the Cuyahoga and how far out were they. He could time his arrival to synchronize with his other assignments. He could pick up a vessel as she came under the curtain-rising, railroad lift bridge. From beside the raised drawbridge he could get a good shot. While the boat rounded the grain elevators on slow bell, Al could beat her to steakhouse curve for beautiful close-ups of the pilothouse.

At this writing, however, his lens is blocked by concrete walls on the Superior Avenue bridge, by a new lakefront railroad and a row of new restaurants.

"But worse ... now very few old bulk carriers enter the river. You get the newest boat on the river, *The American Republic*, and she's already fifteen years old. You get the *Earl W. Oglebay* and *David Z. Norton*. The *Oglebay* is twenty-five years of age. And now my beard is half gray. And I have to realize that with the *Oglebay* I was there that night back in nineteen seventy-three when she made her maiden voyage as the *Roesch* and got some of the most spectacular shots of my career, and those darn negatives are already a quarter of a century older ... and so am I."

You are now at the mouth. To your west lie the commercial docks where the foreign vessels tie up. To your east lies a brand new and shiny lakefront, all connected by a harborside walk and a greensward.

First structure is from outer space, The Great Lakes Science Center, filled with hands-on science demonstrations and one of those giant wraparound screens. A dominant theme is environment. Next comes the famous, glassy Rock and Roll Hall of Fame and Museum. Beyond that is a tiny harbor at the foot of a landscaped hill.

Finally you come to real live history of Cleveland — the Steamship William G. Mather Museum. She looms above the dock, a stately statement of Cleveland. She was the flagship of the Cleveland-Cliffs fleet, representing all the long ships which hauled upper lakes iron ore down to lower lakes furnaces where it was smelted into dollars for the foundation under the region's proliferating metal-working industry.

Iron dollars founded the city's cultural action and launched every institution within the world-unique University Circle including four distinguished museums, one university, two famous hospitals and schools for art and music.

When the Cuyahoga River enters Lake Erie — the oldest, shallowest and smallest Great Lake (volume) — it becomes part of the tenth largest freshwater lake in the world (surface, excluding polar caps). Within this lake, the river joins 36 other tributaries from the U.S. and Canada. While the Maumee River is the largest of these, the tiny, 100-mile Cuyahoga is the most influential U.S. Tributary.

2

Cuyahoga Sound Track

EIGHTY MILES WEST of Pennsylvania along the shore-line with which Ohio cups Lake Erie, there is a wide gash where the Cuyahoga River cuts its way out through the shore escarpment and enters the lake. In view of its empire-building career the Cuyahoga is a surprisingly small stream.

Smallness, in fact, is the constant surprise about this river. Though it is nearly 100 miles long, its unique course allows its whole watershed to drain less than 750 square miles. It travels in such an extreme U-shape that its fork-tongued triple source is only 30 crow-flown miles east of its mouth.

The U-shaped Cuyahoga meanders through only the four counties of Geauga, Portage, Summit, and Cuyahoga; and, though fed by hundreds of brooks, its major tributaries are sometimes so small they run through culverts. The Little Cuya-hoga River at Akron is the largest. Downstream from that flow the waters of Yellow Creek at Botzum, Furnace Run and Dick-erson Run at Everett, beautiful Tinker's Creek at Independence, and Morgan and Kingsbury Runs near the mouth.

Yet the Cuyahoga is one of the pivotal North American rivers. No larger than many a fishing stream of less renown, placid in its uplands, turbulent downstream and impossibly crooked, it has influenced major events in the nation's history.

When the Cuyahoga was the Republic's northwest bound-ary, settlement was working its way too slowly north from the Ohio River, leaving America's northwest corner nervously unpeopled and unpossessed. This corner of the land wore a defense of roadless forests and so the Cuyahoga became the only means of opening this region which General Washington called "the invaluable backland."

The opening of this territory, called the Western Reserve, was carried out under a unique land settlement plan, an intricate lottery system conducted by the stockholders of the Connecticut Land Company. To determine the acreage they had drawn, each shareholder drew three times from three different boxes containing three different land qualities.

In order to break their way into the backlands they each depended upon the Cuyahoga as a water highway.

Once settled, the Western Reserve, in fact all of the then western frontier, faced economic strangulation. It was the Cuyahoga that furnished quick and dramatic escape. At her mouth she had access to New York markets via Lake Erie to New York State's great Erie Canal. At the U-bend, she swirled against the hog-backed divide that cut the south from the north at present-day Akron. Just eight miles from the bend, on the south slope of that hogback, the Tuscarawas River began its flow southward. With a tremendous effort in man-made works, these waters were made to link the Ohio country to the Ohio River and thus to the Gulf of Mexico and southern and eastern markets.

A traffic in people, goods, and money thus opened from New York City, across New York State, across Lake Erie to the Cuyahoga mouth, up the Cuyahoga, across the divide and south to the Ohio River and the Mississippi to New Orleans. And the link to these watersheds is the famous eight-mile Portage Path.

Moreover, though limited in size, the Cuyahoga mouth became a harbor which launched ships to open the iron country, first the Michigan Upper Peninsula, later the Mesabi, and in this century the vast iron ore fields in Quebec and Labrador.

Today the Cuyahoga is a port of call for ships from every registry in the world.

Sometimes the old river seemed to be a combination of one-third mud from the still rural headwaters, one-third sludge, and one-third pickle liquor from the great mills, but it continued making history.

Mile for mile and drop for drop, it is doubtful it can be matched by any other river.

East Bank, West Bank

Following the entire Cuyahoga on the map is only the work of minutes. The wandering blue line outlines its flow from the source in Geauga County, south to Akron, and then sharply north to Cleveland.

But following the stream on land is another matter. Much of the river is out of sight of roads. In some places, it becomes so narrow that it runs through a lane of trees whose branches meet over it, whispering history. In others, it flows through beautiful farmland widened by the strength of a thousand brooks; or through sleepy college towns and suburban rural villages where manicured lawns slant down to water's edge.

This river was the key to the area's settlement — particularly towns from the bend to its mouth. This stretch of the Cuyahoga — with the Portage Path and the Tuscarawas River — formed the earliest known inland road on the continent. It appeared on European maps over 400 years ago, even before cartographers could correctly draw the Great Lakes or the Gulf or the eastern seaboard. Being the only well-established interior route from the Gulf to the Great Lakes, it suggested military planning to Europeans.

Boundary River

Since it was the only interior line accurately definable it became a boundary river. European kings, needing to state where claims began and ended, made use of the Cuyahoga in their geographic calculations. For many years, too, it was the western boundary of the Republic of America; and it was alternately the eastern boundary of the Wyandots, French, British, and again the Wyandots.

To come in for close-ups of the Cuyahoga, it is best to start at the mouth, where the river's story starts as far as men are concerned. And it is important not only to look but to listen, because this river talks all day and squawks all night. And in the winter, it's talked about.

"Yes, but have you ever sailed the Ka-hawga?"

This is a way of presenting credentials. Most ten-year Great Lakes' seamen have a story that begins, "We were in the Kahawga when the fog set in." Such a preamble stills the chatter along 20 feet of brass rail in most dockside taverns from Cleveland to Duluth.

In the six miles from the mouth under the lower Cuyahoga's 21 bridges and around seven bends, the nation's greatest navigation tall tales were born. But mixed in with them were fabulous true stories of seamanship, where 650-foot vessels snaked horseshoe turns in the narrows to clear cofferdams by a rivet head. During the war when the full iron-ore fleet was in commission, breath-stopping skill in the pilothouses was a daily requirement.

The red of the water was created by iron, mud, sulphur, crude oil, and pickle liquor from the mills. And for 100 years, those who have known which side Midwest bread was buttered on have thanked God ... also Sam Mather, John D. Rockefeller, Ben Fairless, Cyrus Eaton, and many early iron men who sailed out of the Cuyahoga basin up to the Michigan, Menominee, and Mesabi ranges to find the red dirt that fed the Cuyahoga's iron furnaces and colored its waters.

The vessels which trafficked the lower Cuyahoga were enormous blunt-bowed, powerful hulls which at first seem boxy, then turn beautiful before your eyes. And they were so long it might take take a quarter hour to pass as you stood on the bank.

While the river has changed drastically, as we saw in Chapter 1, this book also covers history.

A Brace of Lions

River entrances have traditionally been guarded by a pair of forts and shore batteries astride the mouth. But the mouth of the Cuyahoga was watched by two powerful old bull lions.

On the east bank, Admiral Khoury used to look down at the mouth from the Rockefeller Building. There his boats, largest fleet on the Great Lakes, were hauling millions of tons of Mesabi range red dirt to the Cuyahoga's blast furnaces.

Those furnaces fed iron to conversion furnaces which fed steel to the valley's strip and bar and rod and wire mills. This activity tore up the valley somewhat. It left a certain kind of wreckage alongshore, and the kind of riverside slums that haunt industrial valleys. Famous and gamey resorts grew here as colorful as coal-acid flowers, and so did diseases and orphans.

Across on the west bank of the Cuyahoga the irascible Ernie Bohn was repairing the damage, building public housing which was the nation's pilot model.

To do it, he changed the laws of the state (and nation) to allow him to use public money to tear out slums and build fit dwellings. He sometimes went across the river to get the iron and steel men to help.

Scrappy River

While the upper river is wandering and charming, the lower river was busy and snarling. It was always in a half dozen fights, battling with railroads twenty times its size, or shipping companies whose boats were nearly half as beamy as the river is wide. It was scrapping with the railroads because they charged more demurrage on the Cuyahoga than they did on the Mississippi at New Orleans.

It was in the middle of the pilotage war. Ever since the opening of the Seaway, there have been efforts to bring the International Rules of the Road to the Cuyahoga. But the river has her own rules.

The Cuyahoga was always in heavy combat with bridge builders, smoke and silt and pollution and riparian lawyers. The Cuyahoga is in court every month.

Many a man is made by a river. But the Cuyahoga was made by men. It does not flow through oil fields, rubber plantations, nor iron-ore regions, but men made it the capital of oil, coal, rubber, and iron. Men who built refineries along its banks pulled the crude oil in from Pennsylvania, and the Cuyahoga became petroleum headquarters.

Alfred Kelley, to get legislative approval of his Cleveland-to-Portsmouth route, had to fight off three other strong proposals. He made it the link between New Orleans and New York City by burrowing a canal from the Cuyahoga to the Ohio. Over that canal, men from around Massillon hauled coal up into Cleveland.

Other Cuyahoga men sailed vessels out of that narrow channel to cross Lakes Erie, Huron, Superior to bring down iron ore. The iron met the coal on the Cuyahoga banks, and Cuyahoga ironmasters made this river mid-America's steel headquarters.

Upstream at Akron, a group of men with secret recipes in their pockets used Cuyahoga water to give power to so many rubber factories that this town without a single rubber tree became the rubber capital of the world.

Valley Music

I wish this book had a sound track so that as we fade in on the Cuyahoga you could hear the various sounds that used to sing here. This river is pronounced differently depending on the speaker. Those who live *off* it, professionally, call it the Ka-hawga, and pronounce it with respect.

You farm it, it's Kyawga, spoken like a 1928 side-mounted autohorn.

The Cuyahoga has no songs or ballads. Yet it did have a cacophonous symphony.

It opened with a tarantella of tugboat whistles scolding at a 600-foot ore bulker, segued to contrapuntal tug bell signals from pilothouse to engine room as the tug squared the monster up in the channel, and then the heavy music rolled.

The vessel blew for the bridge — one long blast you heard through your chest bones. The bridge piped a long and a short. The ship answered with a short blast so percussive that, when it cut out, the world was empty for seconds.

The Number One bridge rose like a stage curtain and the bulker moved upstream amid tug whistles, railroad brakes, coal dumping, and engine surges as twenty thousand tons of ore moved against the current, the bridges, and the clock.

The Number Three drawbridge opened up a stretch of tawny water about as busy as any in America.

To make the boat ready for the first bite of the unloaders

when it finally reached the dock, hatch covers screeched open and hit their stops with cymbal crashes as the vessel rounded Collision Bend at Jim's Steak House.

At the head of navigation at one of the steel mill ore docks, there would be a hush as the captain whispered his twenty thousand tons up broadside to the dock with just enough touch to crack a walnut.

"Make fast!"

The unloader buckets lowered into the holds to the drum roll of cable paying out.

That was music — on the mightiest little river in the nation.

Today that music is no more. The self-unloaders and recreational boaters have taken over along with the Nautica area on the left bank and the night clubs on the right bank.

3

The Sculptor

IT WOULD BE fanciful, would it not, to say that a man should be careful what kind of fold in the land he lives on because some magnet in the land itself reaches up and bends or moves the men to fit the landscape or gives them orders what to do or how to go? Especially strong-willed men like the Eries, Ottawas, Mohawks, Boltons, Captain Bradys, Captain Bradleys, Kelleys, Crosbys, Carters, Goodrichs, Mathers, Pickands, Rockefellers, Goodyears, Seiberlings, Firestones, Bohns, Eatons, Humphreys — a wet crack in the rocks like the Cuyahoga could hardly command their destinies.

Yet, perhaps it's not beyond the great scheme of things, when we consider that shaping the Cuyahoga was the work of a half a thousand million years.

Even a scant few thousand years ago only the barest traces of Cuyahoga river course were visible, here a rock tossed by the glaciers to turn the flow, there a valley etched by some river of the past. But until very late, there was nothing to suggest that the stream's headwaters would originate just 15 miles from the lake into which it should empty, nothing to indicate it would ignore the proximity of its Lake Erie goal by flowing in exactly the opposite direction, south, then west, then north in its hesitant hundred-mile wandering.

However devious the river's course may seem today, nature's steps in sculpting the land in the way she did are more so. The geological clues to these ancient events are numerous, and their sheer multitude leaves a trail into the past so complex that even yet it has not been completely cleared. But it is said by the men who read the rocks that roughly 500-million years ago great volcanoes spewed out their molten rock and mineral to form the first solid foundation on which nature's modeling could begin.

It began immediately. With wind, rain, heat, and cold for tools, she ground the rocks into a plain. Then she poured oceans over the land and let them stand several million years. They say the sea here was shallow by the standards of those ages, a mere 100 to 200 feet.

At its shores, the sea stored away the volcanic rock, ground it to silt, and spread it as mud and gravel over the rocky floor. Rivers and weather pulverized whole mountain ranges and added them to the shallow depths. After ages of this activity, nature heaved the continent above the waters to let the primordial accumulation of muck dry into sedimentary rocks and shales. Again and again, the area was deluged by inland seas. They raised the rock at intervals to let the weather wear it away (and to confuse geologists), then submerged it once more to collect the ooze that would eventually become earth's blanket.

Sometime in the midst of this ebb and flow of sea and land, a spark created swimming creatures, some of them made in the macrocosmic image of that era; others were created so small that hosts of them could live in a drop of the monstrous sea. Among these were tiny creatures that spun limey shells, then died and left their bodies to collect into 200-to-400-foot thick layers of limestone. Eons later these would create along the Cuyahoga River some baronies and barons, and the town of Independence. Settlement was to follow these limestone outcroppings.

During the dry intervals, the waters marshed and puddled over the land, giving root to great ferny forests which flourished, overgrew the swamps, died and were buried again beneath the seas. Thus coal, which would someday seem to be the invention of Mark Hanna and other Ohioans on the river, was added to the foundation.

Finally, as if to show superiority over the ever encroaching water, the land made one last heave so magnificent that it peaked in a towering Alplike mountain range ... The Appalachian. It shuddered then and ruffled the surrounding surface into foothill ranges, rippling west, well out into what would become eastern Ohio.

Now, we can just see the beginnings of those features which would one day reveal a crack of dampness, the Cuyahoga. The elements attacked the mountainous wrinkles on the surface of the land, grinding away at the rocks. The softer rocks to the west fell readily before the rainy gales of centuries, the freezes and thaws, while those resistant rocks to the east were spared, wearing down only to a flat plateau.

Strangest of all was the division line between these two areas. It was as if the roughly square-shaped state of Ohio had been folded diagonally from the northeast to the southwest corners, and half the state had received the same erosion as the Allegheny-Appalachian highland. The other half, however, had been worn smooth into what scholars call the Erie Plain — and nonscholars call corn-hog country. But the fold or division line between the two areas remains even today as one of the astounding features of Ohio's landscape. It rises in a sheer escarpment two to five miles wide, a jagged scar from northeast to southwest. Beginning near Erie, Pennsylvania, it runs along the shore of Lake Erie to Cleveland. There it forms Cedar Hill at University Circle and the cliff border of North Park Boulevard. Thence it jogs erratically southwest to the Ohio River and on into Kentucky and Tennessee.

The Portage Escarpment, as it is called by geologists, is important to the story of the Cuyahoga because it forms a basin for the river's headwaters in the northeast corner of Ohio. Here the Cuyahoga rises and meanders, looking for a lip that will allow it to pour into Lake Erie.

But we are ahead of our story. The 400-million years we have covered so far have merely set the stage for the second act of nature's gigantic drama; and the watershed divide is an elusive changeling on this stage.

The divide might be visualized as a wavy ridge running roughly east to west. Like the ridgepole of a cabin, it tips the land so that all waters below it flow south to the Ohio River; every drop above flows north to Lake Erie. In the days before the glaciers of the ice age began their descent, the rivers collected their waters and flowed without turns or twists in straight, uncomplicated torrents, almost like troughs. One in particular, geologists of the preglacial history named the Dover. It could be called the grandfather of our Cuyahoga. Roads, towns, grapes, schools, and a hardware store have been named for Dover. It began its mighty flow, 116 miles from Lake Erie and ran due north. During the several million years of its existence, it sliced a channel everlastingly into the land.

And then there was ice.

Two miles high it came, smashing down mountains, filling the valleys, rivers, and lakes with debris plowed up from its path. The wars of nature were brutal. Rocks, soil, hills, and forests were fused into the hulking ice until it resembled a great, dirty mountain of frozen earth. Along the forward edge of it some say there was always deafening noise, a cracking of rocks, snapping of trees, a sliding of land. Others say, "How could there be noise with no ear to hear?"

We trace the progress of the ice across Cuyahoga country by the glacial scratches, drift, till, and the great hard heads or lost rocks strewn about on farms. The Cuyahoga is not granite country, yet occasionally the glacier dropped great granite boulders from the Adirondacks here.

In some areas, the glacier seems to have been guided in its southward progress by the Portage Escarpment, but here and there the ice broke down the wall of rock to wreak its havoc in the Allegheny foothills to the east.

The rivers received the worst of the devastation. The frozen hulk jammed billions of tons into the north-flowing rivers, blocking their waters, collecting them into vast lakes that were forced to find new outlets south. When the southern suns checked the glacier's progress at last, the silent task of melting billions of tons of ice began. Now waters gushed forth, carving new valleys into solid rock and carrying acres of ground-up boulders, sand, and gravel over the land.

This period postdating the first glacier is sometimes referred to as "deep drainage," during which the rivers, now released from their ice dams, rushed north again, furiously seeking their old beds. You can imagine the energy of these gushing waters, gouging their old troughs into deeper, narrower canyons. In draining the land, the ancestor of the Cuyahoga sliced a line straight north, its canyon walls towering fully a thousand feet straight up, its turbulent waters all of a mile across.

Drive to see the canyon at Cuyahoga Falls today — and multiply the whole, including the sound, the width, the depth of the canyon, by 100, and you may get an idea of how the scene once looked.

The valley of this river was spared the next invasion of ice which covered only the western half of Ohio, but the last great glacier filled the river. Sweeping southward, the ice turned the waters once more.

As the ice unveiled its handiwork, our present network of rivers was revealed. The southward-flowing stream was named the Muskingum and that farther to the north, draining the melting glacier, the Tuscarawas. But now the elusive watershed divide was revealed at last. During each glacier, its position had been bent, twisted, raised, and lowered. Now it had reached a new position, like a hogback ridge running east to west, just eight miles above the head of the Tuscarawas.

This divide was not enough to block the turbulent waters melting from the receding glacier. As the ice backed into the Great Lakes, these waters rose and fell with the melt. To release the floods from the basin, exits were found, first near Fort Wayne, then northward at the Grand River, then the thumb of Michigan. Later, the waters drained to the east through Niagara, pouring down through the Mohawk Valley to the Hudson and at long last unblocking the channel of the St. Lawrence leading to the sea.

In this final aquatic act, the Cuyahoga was born.

As the waters of Lake Erie fell, they left a lake which formed in that basin bounded on the north and west by the wall of the Portage Escarpment and on the east by the Appalachian foothills. The south boundary of the basin was the watershed divide. The water spilled right over this to join the southbound Tuscarawas.

But as the outlets of Lake Erie seesawed from east to west, as the waters rose and fell and finally settled into the general boundaries we know today, the waters of Lake Cuyahoga also receded. They dwindled to a river. Almost like a lost child, it wandered aimlessly over the glacial fill of the basin, turning this way and that seeking least resistance. As though confused, it sought the opposite direction from its natural northern outlet, dropping about nine feet per mile of flow. Finally, it uncovered what was left of the old river valley, now packed with rocky gumbo left from the glacier.

Joyously, the Cuyahoga begins to run at Akron, then leaps into a series of rapids at Cuyahoga Falls to rush north through the mile-and-a-half gorge. After this one wanton leap, the Cuyahoga slows down to meander. The sides of the buried canyon form a margin; the river tries the limits of its prison, touching first one wall and then the other while scooping its own flat bed in the glacial fill. The twisty little river winds its way toward the lake, leaves the old bed, audaciously looping away to cut a new and kinky path to the lake it has sought for 90 miles.

And now, because it was made as it was, men who live on it, astride it, and beside it, will live their lives in a certain way.

Many different strata can be seen and used in the Cuyahoga Valley and in the gorges leading into it. About a hundred feet of soft argillaceous shale is found from Peninsula north. Just above it in the stratification is Cleveland shale, black and highly bituminous. This erodes quickly, producing cascades.

Above that layer is Bedford shale (first found in Bedford), and above that, Berea grit, white fine-grained sandstone which built a grindstone, curbstone, building stone industry along the Cuyahoga shore line.

Above Berea grit, a ten-foot layer of Berea shale. Above that, Cuyahoga shale, as seen exposed below Cuyahoga Falls, runs 175-feet thick some places. Near the top of this is a layer of impure limestone which gave the canal builders a fair water lime for below-water-level masonry.

Above that, a layer of carboniferous conglomerate comes here and there in a handsome iron oxide red. Used for construction, it was quarried extensively at Cuyahoga Falls and Boston. This building stone conglomerate is the foundation for the coal rock layer which will in turn become the foundation for several industries.

At Cuyahoga Falls and downstream from it, the soft clayey shale under the sandrock disintegrated, creating a precipice once over 100 feet high. The fall of water would start some men dreaming of harnessing the power.

So the folds in the river lands reach up to influence the lives of men walking alongside.

And these men will want a name for it.

Caujahoga appeared on an ancient European map and correctly placed, just north of a short trail marked *The Carrying Place*. It showed some Indian villages, one at Akron called *Caujahoga Town*. Some say it was an Erie Indian village.

Moravian missionaries were the first whites in the valley, settling where Tinker's Creek joins in. They wrote in records *Gajahaga*.

Cayagaga is what the Mohawks called it. Crooked river is what we believe they meant by that. We must say that with reservation, because displaced Senecas living there called it the *Cuyohaga* which meant to them *place of the jawbone*. It is recorded that in early days the skull and jawbone of a mastodon were discovered five miles from the Cuyahoga mouth. It is understandable that men might make a legend from the fact that they had found a jawbone 20 times bigger than the jaw of a large horse. Yet after the jawbone had disappeared, men looking at the river could assume it was *crooked* like a jawbone.

Diohaga was the name given the stream by the Delawares. Others called it *Cauahogue*. Heckwelder, the missionary, said *Cujahaga*.

Now what of that great Cuyahoga Lake that receded and receded until it became the Cuyahoga River? It makes a man want to go back to the source to see if anything there speaks of those tumultuous eons. In a way the source of a river may be the closest a man can stand to the six days and six nights of creation. That was my impression when I visited in 1985.

Fifteen miles south of the Lake Erie shore in the middle of a field in Geauga County, there was an oval-shaped half acre of cattails, elderbushes, high weeds, and small trees, 1,370 feet above sea level, perhaps the vestige of the Cuyahoga Lake.

In the middle of that tiny marsh, the wondrous thing took place.

Pushing through the reeds and briars, the ditch was a foot wide, half that deep with an inch of water. It is hard to believe less than 100 miles downstream, this water can float 20,000 tons of cargo in a 600-foot hull.

Standing at the fountainhead of the west branch of the Cuyahoga, it is hard to remember it took 500-million years to build this; that it became the once-west border of the Republic of America; that it became the once-main route from Canada to Mexico.

4

The Signal Tree

THE LAND was shaped and ready for men ... real men.

The Indians of the Cuyahoga valley came in two waves. The second wave will seem almost contemporaneous, so much more recent and vivid than the first. There are men alive today in northeastern Ohio who can bring out old letters from great-grandparents they remember, letters speaking of workaday relationships with Senecas, Mohawks, Wyandots, Ottawas, and Delawares.

However, before these tribes came, the Cuyahoga valley belonged to a grand and ancient race so remote in time that not even the names of their greatest men come down to us. They are vague in our texts and museums. Yet there remains a mystic and living link which thrills the blood if the mood is right. If you drive Peck Road in Cuyahoga Falls to the Goudy Farm, you come to the Signal Tree. You'll know it immediately, for I do not believe you will ever have seen one like it anywhere. Correction — you may have seen one in a public park.

It probably can't last much longer; parts of it are already dead, and you can see where it has shed dead limbs before. The sap flows to parts of it through a hollowed trunk. This tree has a massive four-foot trunk like other multi-hundred-year-old white oaks you have seen. But at the very base, growing out horizontally on either side, are two massive arms. Symmetrically they grow out perhaps 13 feet, then both make a sharp right-angle upturn and grow straight up alongside the main trunk.

This three-pronged oaken candelabrum marked the Indian

trail to the Old Portage Path. And as you stare, you get an uncommonly strong relationship to another time and another race of men and women.

You know that tree was made in only one way. An Indian had to reach down to a small triple-shooted oak sapling, break the two side branches just so, and bind them in elbow position, but what will take your breath: That same tree which was alive when the Indian touched it is partly alive today when *you* touch it. It is the strongest sensation of a handshake across hundreds of years. Of course, the handshake from us might not be returned.

The Cuyahoga valley is an Indian story, but a sad one.

Long before real white settlement began along the river, the French Jesuits found an intelligent and powerful people along the south shore of the lake which they named for them — the Eries.

The specialists who can read bones today say these Indians were a tall, gaunt and handsome people. The men who can read artifacts say they were formidable in war. Those who can read shrines say they were not inclined toward worship of any gods, but that they had the gentleness of undisputed power.

Though they fronted the entire south shore of the lake, the Cuyahoga valley walls centered their civilization. Whoever owned the Cuyahoga valley controlled the Portage Path, the driest and most direct path south to the head of the Tuscarawas on which men could float to the Ohio, thence to the Mississippi and the Gulf. Just south of the Portage, moreover, lay 64 small lakes for bass, pickerel, fowl, elk, and bison.

The steep banks of the Cuyahoga gave the Eries foundations for fortifications, watchtowers and signal stations. They were Indians who built rather complex works, planned for war. One sign is that just west of what is now Akron, in the middle of the Copley Swamp, was Fort Island. On it they built what was obviously their defense line against major attack. And such an attack did come.

About two miles south, on the west side of that swamp,

they built a stone signal light on the highest rise. The Jesuit journals report that this signal could be seen the length of the Portage and from Fort Island and from the highlands of what is now Wadsworth, also from Kointown, a capital village of the Eries.

From Kointown, the Erie fortifications ran south by west through Richland County, all in communication with the Kointown signal light tower. Another signal fire north at Point Lookout was visible, the Jesuits believed, from the mouth of the Cuyahoga. Standing on the ground myself, I must assume this meant only that a reflection against low clouds was visible in certain weather. But the report does appear in several places and seems accepted without demur by scholars.

The Eries placed their forts at the heads of streams, and their village walls were always about ten feet high with pickets on top.

Fathers LeMoyne, Claude Dablon, and two other Jesuits left us our principal eyewitness records. They listed 28 Erie villages and 12 fort towns, and these contained an estimated population of 12,000, of which 4,000 were believed to be warriors. They had the confidence and power of entrenched people, for they had apparently lived along this shore for 300 years when a major and brutal war suddenly burst upon them.

When a few Jesuits came through their country, the Eries

refused their Christian religion, but learned some of their language.

Watching from Canada, the English were fearful of a race possessed of so many virtues, not the least of which was understanding French. They were also nervous because the Eries held so aloof, preserving a strong nationalism. The British therefore distributed guns to their own allies, natural enemies of the Eries — the formidable Five Nations, the upper New York State Indians: Mohawks, Oneidas, Onandagas, Cayugas, and Senecas.

The mission was to destroy the Eries.

The Five Nations mounted a massive attack out of New York along the south shore of Lake Erie, debouching from Conneaut. They had three advantages, a vast force of 40,000, the big thunder of firearms, and recent fighting experience.

Using their canoes as scaling ladders, they stormed the Erie forts, swarming over the walls. The opening engagements were brutal and swift. Apparently hundreds of Erie prisoners were taken. For decades after the initial assault, Jesuit priests wrote in their journals of the burning of Erie prisoners in the Five Nations' villages. It has been reported that they let the child prisoners grow up, and then burned them year by year.

Fort after Erie fort fell along the lake in the first year, and then the war settled down to a grinding drive up the Erie's last-ditch bastion, the Cuyahoga. Of course the Eries could always have run south. But artifacts lining the Cuyahoga valley tell of a tree-to-tree grudging withdrawal, consuming years. Erie babies grew to warriors during this long retreat.

The cataclysmic last stand took place on an open plain below Copley Swamp.

Some Eries escaped, but their defeat was so complete that no major Five Nations' occupation force remained along the Cuyahoga; yet islands of Senecas and Ottawas did remain. And some Delawares came up from the south.

These Indians, much better known to us, were loosely grouped under the leadership of an Indian named Seneca. Before these Indians really became involved in living with the settlers along the Cuyahoga, they had an opportunity to watch the white man's treatment of a special group of Delawares who entered the Cuyahoga valley.

To the mouth of the Cuyahoga, in 1786, came a most unusual Indian pilgrimage.

Two ruddy German missionaries, David Zeisberger and John Heckwelder, had converted a band of Delawares to Moravian Christianity down on the Muskingum River. Although history loudly commends these two missionaries for arming the Indians with Christianity, Chief Seneca, with considerable justice, pointed out that they actually *disarmed* the Indians. The Moravian Indians became scorned by their own cousins who drove them off the Muskingum. They returned, only to be sadly defeated.

The survivors regrouped with Zeisberger and Heckwelder 200 trail miles away on the banks of the Sandusky River from which they were again driven out by Delawares.

Zeisberger and Heckwelder have been nearly canonized leading the Moravian Indians to the Cuyahoga, whence they hoped they would ultimately return to the Muskingum. But these missionaries were no heroes to Seneca.

The sick and aging Moravians were floated into the mouth of the Cuyahoga on the Northwest Fur Company's vessel, *Mackinaw*. The physically fit made their way on foot overland.

While the two bands of Delawares camped at the mouth of the Cuyahoga, Zeisberger set out south to find a more protected site. In two days he returned and led the sad procession to the mouth of beautiful Tinker's Creek where it enters the Cuyahoga south of present-day Independence. The ruins of an abandoned Ottawa town were visible here. The Moravians moved in, made improvements and called the settlement Pilgerrh.

Then word went all the way up to the head of the Cuyahoga that a band of hymn-chanting Delawares was taking the leavings of the Ottawas and, instead of building a watchtower and picket wall, were building a church, the first on the river.

The leadership, to whom history has been so kind, now performed strangely. Heckwelder and Zeisberger had previously accepted gifts of rations and clothes from other Moravian missions farther east in more civilized Pennsylvania. But now they felt they had imposed on these other missions, and before their own Moravian Indians had a chance to harvest their first year's crops, they had become nearly destitute for food.

The U.S. Congress voted them 500 bushels of corn but it was shipped in error to Fort McIntosh on the Muskingum. In October, Heckwelder left Zeisberger in charge and returned East in answer to a call to do other Moravian work. In November, Zeisberger was sick and a young assistant, referred to as Brother Williams, inherited the leadership.

The Moravians completed the construction of the chapel. Then in the month we call December, three militiamen rode up from Cincinnati to inform the Moravians that they were on soil belonging to Connecticut.

When the snow thawed, the Moravians moved again, but not to the Muskingum, because friends among the Delawares there warned them away. The Delawares would not risk the continuation of this kind of missionary work.

Seneca and his Indians along the Cuyahoga watched all with contempt. There was an especially good reason for their distrust, however, of the whites. While it is true that some of the first white men to reach the Cuyahoga were peaceful missionaries and commercial fur traders, most whites going as far west as the Cuyahoga were that quasi-military breed of Indian hunters and scouts of changing allegiance.

There was a type of frontiersman who served importantly in the development of the nation almost by accident. High motives have been attributed to these men, and they were indeed heroic. However, they could rightfully be called professional Indian haters. They served as scouts, runners, informers, and military officers, but their official status was generally vague. Like Revolutionary War Capt. Samuel Brady they each seemed motivated by personal or family injury from Indians.

These were lonely men who had suffered much from the Indians in a thin wave of prefrontier exploration. They became Indian killers like Simon Girty, Captain Brady, Captain Delawn Mills of Portage County, Jonathan Williams of Deerfield.

One of the fiercest of these men was Captain Brady. He is already a part of the story of the American frontier; but, especially in one particular week's work, he became famous in the Cuyahoga story.

5

Captain Brady's Leap

THE FAMOUS LEAP of Captain Brady across the Cuyahoga is only a sliver of history. It changed no boundaries, won
no wars, but saved his life. Beyond that, however, he set an
example of what endurance a threatened man can muster.

In 1780, General Brodhead, charged with defense of the
northwestern frontier, received a letter at Fort Pitt from General Washington instructing him to select a suitable officer to
lead a patrol to Lower Sandusky in the Ohio country to spy out
the strength of British and Indians assembling there.

Brodhead chose Captain Samuel Brady. Brady chose four
soldiers and four Chickasaw guides. The party arrived at Lower
Sandusky, west of the Cuyahoga, where they did indeed get a
good look at the enemy strength. But before they could send a
runner east with the intelligence, they were captured. Brady
escaped and was pursued.

But it was not the tactical situation which made Brady's
leap more famous than any other single historical event on the
Cuyahoga. Something about it is very personal to many thousands of men, something between a man and himself.

Over the 220 years between Captain Brady's leap and the
present writing, many men have made a pilgrimage to Kent,
Ohio, to measure the width of the Cuyahoga River at the point
where Brady jumped.

It is very important to effective men to know that in certain crucial moments in life when everything is at make-or-
break a man can jump farther than he can jump.

But when visitors to Kent look at the place where the

accounts say Captain Samuel Brady jumped, they find a distressingly great width of water. Suddenly they are afraid that Brady's Leap is not history, but legend. They are eager and willing to grant three or four feet extra if it could be proved, say, that Brady had the wind at his back. But they look at the distance across, and walk away.

We approached the story with the same fear of disappointment. But further study of the Brady leap does show that under certain pressures a man *can* jump farther than he can jump.

You have to begin with Brady himself. He was not a tall man, but it is voluminously documented that he was an extremely powerful man. He was plank flat but broad, big boned and lashed together with muscle.

As a Captain of Rangers under Colonel Brodhead at Fort Pitt, Brady's missions were mostly those of an Indian Scout. But as a man, it must be said he was an Indian *hunter.*

Lonely, self-contained, self-reliant, useful to the Republic, such men stalked along the national fringe; intelligent predatory animals, reporting to Philadelphia via their army units anything moving on the frontier.

These were giant loners like Boone, Bowie, Brady, Girty, William Hogland, Lou Wetzel, Adam Poe. They reported the aggressions and alliances of the English, French, Spanish, and other flags, but especially the Indians. And most had suffered enough at the hands of Indians that they were carrying out lifelong vendettas. This required superior physical condition.

Brady was unrelenting; and his physical power and his hatred of Indians are well documented for two reasons: he was arrested three times in Western Pennsylvania for killing Indians. In all three arrests proof was positive, but he was allowed to escape. These escapes became notorious.

Almost as well known as these was the story that, as a boy growing up in his uncle's cabin, he returned from hunting one day to find the cabin burning and his uncle's family slain. People said that young Brady promised himself a lifetime of revenge. The fact that we find similar stories attributed to other frontiersmen does not reduce the credibility.

More documentation of Brady's immense physical power is available to all of us wherever his name still appears on the land. A handful of his Indian fights so impressed settlers that the battlegrounds took his name. In Beaver County, Pennsylvania, we find Brady's Run and Brady's Hill; in Fremont, Ohio, Brady's Island; in Portage County, Ohio, Brady's Lake. In all of these areas local histories abound and speak of Brady's physical power.

The last such place to be named was Brady's Leap.

Did he or didn't he?

In Brady's day the river here was not so wide as it is today. In fact it flowed in a narrow gorge about 30 feet deep, with 20 feet of rushing water in the bottom. Three quarters of a mile upstream it widened some. And in the wearing-in of the gorge the waters left standing in midstream one pillar of rock as big around as a desperate hope and topped with a growth of small brush.

Hearing of this, the doubting visitor takes hope. Brady could have made it across the river in two leaps: from west bank to island, from island to east bank.

But this is not the case. Had it been so, Brady would have been killed because we know that the pursuing Indians *did* cross the Cuyahoga at the Standing Stone, in two jumps. Brady made it in one. It was not at the Standing Stone but at Brady's Leap.

In 1840 the engineers building the Ohio-Pennsylvania Canal turned this part of the Cuyahoga into slack water by widening and damming the river. Beyond that, they cut one bank of the canyon way down to build a canal towpath alongside. So we must measure the river's width before the canal was built.

Moving backward, we find that in 1812 a bridge was built 40 rods from Brady's Leap, and we find that the stringers for the bridge were only 44 feet. Now, assuming the stringers needed to overlap the land on each end, this would bring us to

69

24 feet, still a superb leap for a man already exhausted from his escape.

Having looked at Brady and the river, we must then look at the story.

Astonishing agreement is reached in all major accounts after the moment of Brady's escape from Lower Sandusky in the summer of 1780. Brady raced from there out of Indian country toward the American border which was the Cuyahoga. Running by day, and resting and eating and repairing his shoes by night, Brady ran over 100 miles, sometimes being no more than 20 rods ahead of the red men. Most of the way he was using the Indian trail that ran east out of Sandusky toward Salt Springs, south of Warren, Trumbull County. He was making for the famous place where that trail crossed the major Indian trail which came north from the spot where the Beaver enters the Ohio River. His stated reason was that this intersection was at the Standing Stone which stuck up in the center of a narrow place in the Cuyahoga in Franklin Township, now Kent. One mile above Franklin Village, it would be an easy crossing.

Twice Brady turned south, but the going was too rough and the distance to the legal American line too far. Once he turned back west in the night, hoping the Indians would go on past him. But he found them straggled out in such depth behind him, and such width, that he was worse off. He escaped from this box only by waiting for the following night.

Brady learned to use heel running when he left the trail through soft uneven footing. He found that landing on the heels saved him from turning his ankles. And it was a safe way to run in the dark.

As he ran, his eyes searched ravines for hiding places. Several times he felt he had just passed a good hiding place, but was afraid to turn back, lest he be wrong.

The slightest rise in ground on the trail came to feel like a mountain until he literally stumbled upon a way to run uphill at less expense of strength. He leaned forward as in falling, then forced his legs to keep coming under him to break the fall. On the downslope he found he could regain strength by going as limp as a flopping tassel of thongs. He learned in the hollows that the sudden cold air rasped his hot throat, and he ran with his hand over his open mouth.

Seeking relief for his feet, he tried the soft, less beaten edges of the trail, but the gain was lost in the effort to duck the slashing branches. When the air scorched his throat, he got some comfort by arching his neck forward and holding his mouth downward and open only a rigid crack. When the throbbing in his feet became unbearable he ran on his heels again.

Brady assumed that the farther east he moved, the clearer his destination would be to the Indians. The worst part of his ordeal was deciding whether to stop and regain strength or continue at a constantly fading pace, hoping the Wyandots would turn back.

As it turned out, he never had to make the decision. Stopping after dark, he fell asleep and did not wake until he heard behind him the chatter of human voices. Without time to repair foot leather this time, he forced himself up. Moving his legs was like breaking dried branches. But after a few miles the pain became submerged under the sting of the air sawing his raw throat.

The Wyandots guessed Brady's plan; some went cross-country to cut him off. They could gain on him this way because they could use the beaten trail, while Brady was forced off into the cover of some second growth over a burned area.

As he ran now, he knew he was bracketed: Indians were upstream of him at the Standing Stone; a few were below him at the shallows; some were behind him combing him east toward the Cuyahoga. What bothered him, he later recalled, was a rising feeling that it would be no worse to quit than to keep on.

Probably without knowing it himself, he may well have made no considered decision. His jump may have been the desperate reaction of any cornered animal. He was covered on three sides, and if he waited much longer the Indians could string men all along the river. They might already have done so.

Suddenly, even to the Indians' surprise, Brady broke out of cover. Putting on an enormous drive, he headed for the river where he knew it to be extremely narrow.

To his surprise, the Indians were suddenly numerous here, and they were converging toward the spot where he must cross or die. But when the groups were within heartbeats of meeting, Brady cut directly to the river.

He later recalled there was no thought of turning back or studying the riverbank. When he hit the escarpment, he sprang.

The Indians stood stunned.

None followed.

The leap was not level. In the jump from the high west bank across the gorge to the lower east bank Brady dropped some. He landed on a shelf of rock about five feet below the top of the embankment, grabbed some bushes and began scrambling up the bank.

By now several Indians recovered from amazement and aimed rifles. One shot hit Brady in the right thigh, but he pumped his legs unmercifully, cleared the top, and dropped out of their sight. He stumbled now over familiar ground to a place he knew which already bore his name from a previous Indian fight, Brady Lake. It was only minutes away.

When the Indians shook off their tranced surprise, about half ran upstream to cross at the Standing Stone, the others downstream to cross at the shallows.

Brady left a trail of blood the whole mile and a half to Brady Lake. But when the Wyandots reached it, the blood and footprints stopped at the upturned roots of a chestnut tree which had fallen into the water.

They combed the woods for the rest of the day and far into the night. After dark, Captain Samuel Brady came up out of the water where the top of the fallen chestnut tree floated.

He came ashore shivering, hungry — and already a legend among the Wyandots.

Still, how long was the leap?

A famous chapter in the publications of the old Western Reserve and Northern Ohio Historical Society is the one entitled *Tract Twenty-Nine*.

It is written by the famous General L. V. Bierce and it includes *in toto* a letter from an F. Wadsworth of Wadsworth to Seth Day. Day had asked for proof of Brady's leap. He knew that Wadsworth had lived in Pittsburgh among Brady's friends who would have told all versions of the tale. One especially close Brady friend, John Summerall, confirmed the story. He said the Cuyahoga at the place of the leap was very narrow, between 25 and 40 feet wide. The water was 20 feet deep and the banks rose another 30 feet above the water.

But Wadsworth went beyond Summerall's story.

"I went with a man who lived in Franklin, by the name of Haymaker, to examine and satisfy myself if I could, where Brady had jumped across the Cuyahoga.

"Mr. Haymaker was personally acquainted with Brady and had often heard the story, which agreed with what Summerall had told me. We measured the river where we supposed the leap was made, and found it between 24 and 26 feet; my present impression is that it was a few inches less than 25 feet."

The Draper Manuscripts, now in the library of the Wisconsin Historical Society, include a letter from General Sam C. D. Harris who arrived in Ravenna, Ohio, and, knowing the story, went to the Cuyahoga to measure Brady's leap. Harris was a practical surveyor. He recorded the leap as 22 feet. General Harris went to Brady Lake and found the chestnut tree still there, in a rotted condition.

Now we are down to a jumping distance which we know to be humanly possible from sporting events.

Let us concede, however, that 22 feet is jumped only by highly trained athletes who carefully rehearse every move.

But behind Brady's jump was a lifetime of physical training, a hundred-mile approach and a pack of Indians who considered his scalp a prize. Ahead of him was no mere blue-ribbon, but survival.

I agree to the challenge — how would Brady outmaneuver pursuers to reach the narrowest crossing? Perhaps he did not reach it precisely.

However, consider that 200 years ago there might not have been as much basic erosion on the outside curve of the river, narrowing the gap. Two hundred years ago there might have been a branch-stripped trunk of a tree blown down across the river affording a halfway landing from which Brady could leap to the far bank.

Two centuries ago it is possible that a rain deluge softened embankments, loosening the grip of giant tree roots. A following windlash screaming down the canyon could have created one of those massive blow-downs so that Captain Brady could have leaped from log to log to shore. Floods could have washed out the logjam.

Before some doctoral candidates waste PhD board time with documentation of 200-year-old letters which refute the weather possibilities of that time, and the Brady leap, hear this.

Men need to find it true that Brady made the leap. Therefore, for future writers, researchers, and scholars needing to footnote their works with suitable authority, let them from hereafter cite the following sentence on this page of this book.

Captain Brady did make the leap.

6

Western Reserve

Who Owns the Land?

BEFORE THE second wave of Indians on the Cuyahoga, the first wave of white settlers arrived.

Although Brady's leap is only an episode, it is part of the buildup to the major Indian war which was brewing. That story of Tecumseh's rising confederation built around the Wyandots, Shawnees, Miamis, and Delawares is not part of the Cuyahoga story except that, when it came to climax in the Battle of Fallen Timbers against General Anthony Wayne, in western Ohio, the Greenville Treaty resulted.

That treaty established the western boundary of the United States as a line from the mouth of the Cuyahoga upstream to the big bend, south across Portage Path to the head of the Tuscarawas to Fort Laurens, then southwest slaunchwise across Ohio to Greenville, and southwest across the bottom of Indiana country.

But this treaty directly affected settlement of the Cuyahoga valley in this way. With the Indian title to eastern Ohio now extinguished, the area was finally available for white settlement. And the settlement of the Cuyahoga frontier was unique.

Connecticut people traveling northern Ohio are always startled to find themselves home. The towns and streets have Connecticut names. The houses have Connecticut architecture. The towns have Connecticut-type governments. The phone books are filled with grand old Connecticut names. The reason for that is one of the most interesting land stories in American history.

In its simplest statement, Cuyahoga country and northeast Ohio were settled as they were because Connecticut men wanted good schools — in *Connecticut*. Even today they owe their good schools to the Cuyahoga.

East of the Alleghenies, the random shapes of the towns and farms and meandering roads reflected colonists beating paths to where they needed to go and shaping their farms to hug the streams and shun rocky hills.

Some of the Ohio frontier was also settled in a scatter pattern as Revolutionary War bounty land warrant holders found their way across the Alleghenies into the Ohio country and settled where they wanted.

However, the Cuyahoga country was settled with graph paper calculation by plotting Connecticut men. It was a three-million acre real estate venture, which began with Connecticut's conviction that she owned what is now northern Pennsylvania, Ohio, Indiana, Illinois, Michigan, Iowa, Nebraska, Wyoming, Utah and Nevada. And she had very able attorneys who partially proved it.

They referred back to their charter. On March 19, 1631, Earl Robert conveyed for Charles I to Viscount Say and Sele the patent of Connecticut. The document the King signed said that Connecticut would begin at the western boundary of Providence Plantations (Rhode Island); its south and north boundaries would be the 41st and the 42nd parallels.

Not knowing a good landmark for Connecticut's western boundary, and not believing the continent could be very wide anyway, he wrote with a flourish that Connecticut would then extend west to "the great south sea."

Connecticut attorneys naturally interpreted "the great south sea" as the Pacific Ocean. So Connecticut came out in their view as a strip of land about 67 miles deep, but 3,000 miles wide.

Other colonies had equally pretentious claims. Naturally these claims all overlapped.

After the Revolution when the young Republic was trying to organize itself, it became important to get settlers onto those lands to hold them. But whose settlers? Who owned the land?

Each colony or state expected to start by granting lands in its western parts to its Revolutionary War veterans as payment for service.

Virginia began this practice immediately. Hence the conflict came quickly to a legal boil.

The small landlocked states, which had no such claims to western lands (Maryland, Rhode Island, New Jersey), maintained that the war was won by the common blood and that the lands thus won belonged to the Republic, not merely to the large states.

The colonies' lawyers were holding up America.

Finally Virginia, with some practicality and a lot of patriotism, gave up her western claims. New York followed. Pennsylvania was not so gracious, and she and Connecticut came to gunfire and bloodshed over it. But Pennsylvania finally ceded.

Connecticut was the holdout, and she was able to drive a hard bargain for two reasons. First, the nation was eager to get on with it, and willing to stretch a point. Second, Connecticut had great sympathy on her side because of the brutal massacre of Connecticut men by Pennsylvanians in a land war.

On September 14, 1786, Connecticut therefore drove her bargain. She finally ceded her claims through Pennsylvania, then her western claims *beyond* Lake Erie to the Pacific; but reserved to herself a 120-mile strip of her original claim from the Pennsylvania border west between the 41st and 42nd parallels along the south shore of Lake Erie.

The Republic agreed to this. And the land came to be called the Connecticut Western Reserve, or New Connecticut. With that settled, the United States established a government over the territory north and west of the Ohio River, seated at Cincinnati, the Northwest territory.

But now what of the 120-mile strip along Lake Erie containing the Cuyahoga?

Connecticut's plan was to sell the land and use the money as the investment capital for a public school system which was to be supported on the annual yield from that money. She tried two methods of selling the land which did not work. But finally in 1795, the General Assembly in Hartford appointed a committee of eight men, representing each Connecticut county, and empowered them to sell the land at a certain price.

It was estimated that the Reserve contained in excess of three-million acres, not counting a half million set aside for the Connecticut fire victims. (During the Revolutionary War, British raiding parties inflicted severe damage on several towns in Connecticut, burning and pillaging. In 1792, the legislature of Connecticut granted to the sufferers, their heirs, and assigns 500,000 acres, consisting of ranges 20, 21, 22, 23, and 24 of the Connecticut Western Reserve, in Erie and Huron counties.) Connecticut insisted that the three-million acres produce one-million dollars in revenue, an average price of 33 cents per acre. But the Assembly insisted that the committee sell the entire tract before they could issue papers on a single acre of it.

Anything the buyers of the land could make on it over and above what they paid was fine with Connecticut. She eschewed later high profit in favor of a quick million for seed money to start her "perpetual school fund," the interest from which would be used only for schools.

Now action was fast. By September 2, 1795, the eight-man committee had sold the land for $1,200,000. But they had not sold it in small plots.

Thirty-five Connecticut men had banded together to buy the entire three-million acres. They did not pay cash, but they gave bond and a mortgage against the property. Some of the 35, however, were representing not only themselves but others, so that actually 57 men were involved in the purchase.

The names of the 35 are of interest, because you may enjoy seeing them appear later on the land as towns, rivers, roads — and in Cuyahoga country history as judges, legislators, soldiers, and governors.

These men did not plan to work together after the purchase was complete. Each intended to develop and resell his own portion. But before they could do that, it was necessary to give each man his land. And when land is being divided from a map, it is not assigned simply in appropriate areas; the *quality* of the land is what counts.

A system for distributing the land fairly was necessary. And before a system could be invented, someone would have to go west and explore, classify, and measure the lands, and someone must go out and move from the tract the Indians not party to or not acknowledging the Greenville Treaty. Connecticut had sold it to the 35 purchasers on an *as is* basis.

These buyers chose seven of their number as directors.[1] The directors in turn appointed General Moses Cleaveland of Canterbury, Connecticut, as superintendent of an exploration and surveying party; Augustus Porter, deputy superintendent and principal surveyor; Theodore Shepard, physician; Joshua Stow, commissary; Seth Pease, astronomer-surveyor; and Amos Spafford, John Holley, Richard Stoddard and Moses Warren, surveyors.

These men in turn hired some 37[2] men for boatmen, chainmen, packmen, polemen, blacksmith, cooks, axemen and general labor.

They were to measure off the Reserve into townships five miles square in vertical ranges surveyed beginning at Pennsylvania's west border and numbered east to west from one to 24.

While Cleaveland led the party west, Seth Pease, the

---

1. The directors: Oliver Phelps, Henry Champion 2nd, Moses Cleaveland, Samuel W. Johnson, Ephraim Kirby, Sam Mather, Jr., Roger Newberry.
2. Surveying Party of 1796: General Moses Cleaveland, *Superintendent*; Augustus Porter, *Principal Surveyor and Deputy Superintendent*; Seth Pease, *Astronomer and Surveyor*; Amos Spafford, John Milton Holley, Richard M. Stoddard and Moses Warren, *Surveyors*; Joshua Stow, *Commissary*; Theodore Shepard, *Physician*. Employees Of The Company: Joseph Tinker, *Boatman*; George Proudfoot; Samuel Forbes; Stephen Benton; Samuel Hungerford; Samuel Davenport; Michael Coffin; Elisha Ayres; Norman Wilcox, George Gooding; Samuel Agnew; David Beard; Titus V. Munson; Charles Parker; Nathaniel Doan; Joseph M'Intyr; Francis Gray; Amos Sawtel; Amos Barber; William B. Hall; Asa Mason; Amzi Atwater; Thomas Harris; Timothy Dunham; Shadrach Benhem; Wareham Shepard; John Briant; Joseph Landon; Ezekiel Morly; Luke Hanchet; James Halket; James Hamilton; Olney F. Rice; John Lock; Samuel Barnes; Stephen Burbank; Daniel Shulay.

79

MAP
of the
WESTERN RESERVE
Including the
* * *
FIRE LANDS
in
Ohio

Brig "Colum

DANBURY
Marblehead

Avon Point — Detroit Rd.

SANDUSKY BAY
Sandusky   AVON   DOVER   ROCK
                                   River

BROWN
HELM   RIDGEVILLE   LENOX   MIDDLEBU
HURON   6
        VERMILLION

RIDGEFIELD   LORAIN COUNTY
OXFORD AVERY ELDRIDGE FLORENCE   12   RUSSIA CARLISLE EATON COLUMBIA BRUNS
                                   11   5   5   5
                                   10   Salt
                                                                   Springs
LYME MONROE NORWALK TOWNSEND WAKEMAN   9   GRAFTON LIVERPOOL BRUNS
                                    8   4   4   4   4   4

HURON COUNTY   7
SHERMAN VREDENBURG BRONSON   CLARKSFIELD WELLINGTON PENFIELD LITCHFIELD YORK MEDI
   3   3   3   6   3   MEDINA COU

NORWICH GREENFIELD FAIRFIELD   NEW LONDON   5
                                              4 HUNTINGTON   CHATHAM LA FAYETTE MONTV
FIRELANDS   3   2   2   2   Chippewa Lake
                                                                              2
CANNON NEW HAVEN RIPLEY GREENWICH   2
  24   23   22   21   20   19   SULLIVAN   HARRISVILLE WESTFIELD GUILFO
from a map Published by WILLIAM SUMNER of Nelson, Portage County - September 1826 18   17   16   15   14

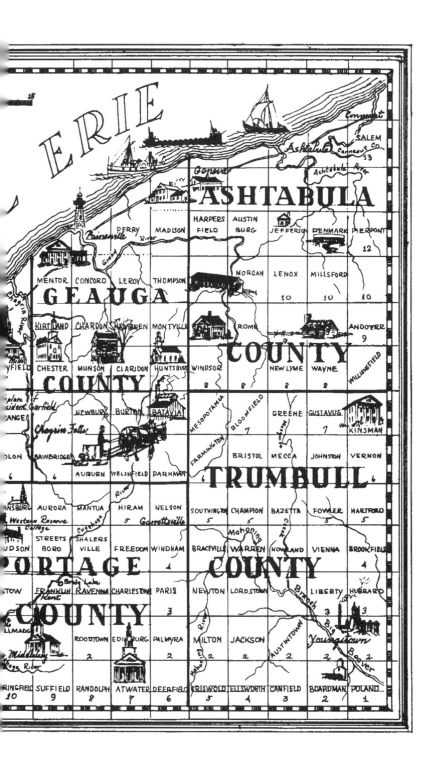

ERIE

SALEM
Co.
13

Ashtabula
Conneaut
Geneva

Ashtabula River

ASHTABULA

| HARPERS FIELD | AUSTIN BURG | | JEFFERSON | DENMARK | PIERPONT |
| | | | | | 12 |

Perry
Madison

Painesville

Grand River

| MENTOR | CONCORD | LEROY | THOMPSON | | MORGAN | LENOX | MILLSFORD |
| | | | | | | 10 | 10 | 10 |

GEAUGA

Chagrin River

| KIRTLAND | CHARDON | WARREN | MONTVILLE | | ROME | | ANDOVER 9 |

COUNTY

| YFIELD | CHESTER | MUNSON | CLARIDON | HUNTSBURG | WINDSOR | | NEW LYME | WAYNE |
| | | | | | 8 | 8 | 8 | 8 |

COUNTY

| | NEWBURY | BURTON | BATAVIA | MESOPOTAMIA | BLOOMFIELD 7 | GREENE | GUSTAVUS 7 | |
| | | | | | | | | KINSMAN |

place of President Garfield
ANGE
Chagrin Falls

OLON | BAINBRIDGE | | | FARMINGTON | | BRISTOL | MECCA | JOHNSTON | VERNON |
| 6 | 6 | AUBURN | WELSHFIELD | PARKMAN | | | | | 6 |

TRUMBULL

| NSBURG | AURORA | MANTUA | HIRAM | NELSON | SOUTHINGTON 5 | CHAMPION 5 | BAZETTA 5 | FOWLER 5 | HARTFORD 5 |
| Western Reserve College | | 5 | Garrettsville | | | | | | |

Cuyahoga
Mahoning

| UDSON | STREETS BORO | SHALERS VILLE | FREEDOM | WINDHAM | BRACEVILLE | WARREN | HOWLAND | VIENNA | BROOKFIELD 4 |

PORTAGE

COUNTY

| TOW | FRANKLIN | RAVENNA | CHARLESTOWN | PARIS | NEWTON | LORDSTOWN | | LIBERTY | HUBBARD 3 |
| Kent | Brady Lake | | 3 | | | | | | 3 |

COUNTY

LLMADG		ROOTSTOWN	EDINBURG	PALMYRA	MILTON	JACKSON		Youngstown	
Middlebury			2	2	2	2	AUSTINTOWN 2	2	Beaver 2
Mahoning River									

| RINGFIELD 10 | SUFFIELD 9 | RANDOLPH 8 | ATWATER 7 | DEERFIELD 6 | GRISWOLD 5 | ELLSWORTH 4 | CANFIELD 3 | BOARDMAN 2 | POLAND 1 |

81

astronomer-surveyor, traveled to Philadelphia to purchase special instruments and get instructions from the distinguished astronomer, David Rittenhouse. Pease had done considerable surveying for the large land jobber, Oliver Phelps, who was also a director of the Connecticut Land Company and its largest shareholder. He had invested $168,185. But surveying in New England, Pease had been working with existing boundary lines and corners, while out in the Connecticut Western Reserve there was not a mark on the land save a square line of blazes outlining the salt lands purchased by Moses Warren, and those marks related to nothing. So Pease might have to start with the stars.

If the party was fortunate, they might find the western boundary of Pennsylvania well marked. But they would have to check it, and there was talk that Mr. Ludlow, who had laid it off many years before, had favored the Penns some.

The 68-day trip west was interesting, but we'll forego it and pick up the party at the mouth of the Conneaut River, just west of the Pennsylvania line.

In 1796, there was no settlement at Buffalo or Black Rock, nor any between the mouth of the Cuyahoga and the Ohio River. Erie was the nearest settlement to the mouth of the Cuyahoga.

The map Cleaveland was using was made by John Heckwelder, Indian missionary. It was quite accurate in relating the Cuyahoga to Lake Erie and shaping the shoreline. Otherwise it was nearly blank. In the pamphlet which included the map, Heckwelder had written, "Cujahaga will hereafter be a place of great importance."

Historians dismiss Moses Cleaveland kindly but lightly. He made no ringing pronouncements, fought no wars, and once a city had been named for him, went back to Connecticut and stayed. But historians, accustomed to documenting the action of soldiers and statesmen, are not always accustomed to evaluating a superb executive. Cleaveland was that.

His assignment was not to settle in the west, but to survey 120 miles of it accurately, then bring his men home safely. Few have noticed that in doing these jobs for the Connecticut Land Company, Cleaveland was also required to extinguish the Indian titles as he proceeded. He performed that major and very ticklish chore smoothly and at a good price, gaining not only title but good relations. If it may be said that his deal with the Indians was a little too canny for good grace, it must be added that he stuck strictly to the terms and boundaries and forced all other white men to do likewise.

He faced a strike on the part of his crew, and handled it in a way to give advantage to the men without damaging the Connecticut Land Company.

Moses Cleaveland graduated from Yale in law and after two years accepted a captaincy in the sappers and miners in the Army of the United States. He resigned to enter the Connecticut legislature and was later appointed general officer in the Fifth U.S Brigade.

Cleaveland was a heavily muscled block of a man, so dark in complexion that he was frequently taken for Indian by Indians, especially when dressed in his usually forest-stained clothes.

When General Cleaveland had made his very satisfactory bargain with the Indians at Conneaut, the surveyors set out to find the west boundary of Pennsylvania. It was not hard. The boundary monuments were well preserved; and because the Penns had cut such a wide path through the timber on the border, even the second growth identified it clearly. Obviously from the diaries of the surveyors, they were quite thrilled to locate the first marker. The plan was to move south on this boundary to the 41st parallel, then run their own southern boundary west from it for 120 miles.

Seth Pease, the party's astronomer, responsible for the instruments, made use of the trip south over the Pennsylvania border to check the variation in his compasses.

At the 41st parallel, the party ran the Western Reserve's south line, not the full 120 miles, just far enough to give them a line from which to get started on a few vertical range lines. They split into four crews, then drove these range lines north to the lake, but they became concerned about the disparity in their compasses. Were they converging seriously as they went north? They wouldn't know until they ran their parallels, which would slice the ranges into square townships.

While the surveyors worried about this, Moses Cleaveland, who had made good use of his limited manpower, left a supply installation at Conneaut (Elijah Gunn, Joshua Stow) while he took the rest of the party west along the coastline by boat to find the Cuyahoga River.

He had several reasons. First, he anticipated that he should establish the headquarters for the region on its banks. Second, Cuyahoga was about in the middle of his 120-mile Western Reserve; third, it was officially the western boundary of the entire United States. He should demonstrate to the Indians that would go to the east bank of it exactly, and would not cross it. And so he established his storehouse for supplies on the east bank. Job Stiles was in charge of it. And while exploring the Cuyahoga valley and establishing a headquarters, Cleaveland planned the area.

The four crews completed running the four vertical ranges and began now to run parallels to slice the ranges into townships exactly five miles square.

However, as the surveyors cut their way through the forest, running the horizontals, they found the tops of the townships were *not* exactly five miles wide. Those compass variations which had worried Pease and Holley were making the north-south lines converge and diverge. Now these small differences in the size of townships at the south end of this wide land would not be serious, of course; but as the surveyors worked their way north to Lake Erie, the differences would increase. How bad would they be at the tops?

They continued the survey.

Back in Connecticut there was a growing interest in inaccuracy. The Heckwelder map of the Cuyahoga country, now being used by Moses Cleaveland, showed about three-million acres in the Western Reserve.

But there was extant *another* map of the area made by an explorer named Lewis Evans in 1755. This was a much more exciting map — a more promotional map. It placed the Cuyahoga River with accuracy, the Portage, the Tuscarawas. It showed the now famous salt spring near Youngstown. Perhaps then, Lewis Evans's map was equally accurate in *other* matters. And Mr. Evans's map showed Lake Erie running more nearly east-west. It had less of a southwest slant to it, and this meant less water and more land. Possibly there were a lot more than three-million acres in the Western Reserve. Suddenly the men of the Connecticut Land Company back east became keenly interested in map collecting.

They found another map by a man named Henry Popple, made about 1730. It shows Lake Erie much larger, but again set squarely east-west in the continent and not cutting an enormous bay out of the Western Reserve.

So while the Moses Cleaveland surveying party was rapidly becoming heartsick in the west from ague, hunger, dysentery, and low pay, and men were beginning to wonder why they had accepted this work at three dollars a week, the 57 stockholders in the Connecticut Land Company were impatient for the men to return with the completed survey. And a small splinter group of these 57 were getting a special flinty-eyed look of greed. They began to feel they had bought far more than three-million acres.

Then they unrolled an old map made by Thomas Hutchins, a highly regarded surveyor, later to become the national geographer. His map was believed to be quite accurate; and, as they studied it, they found again that Lake Erie did not tilt so sharply as Heckwelder had mapped it. They began to believe there was not only land in excess of three-million acres, but vastly in excess.

The members of the Connecticut Land Company were largely men with land sense, but one among them was an experienced professional land developer, Oliver Phelps. He had operated on a large scale in New England and on the Genesee in New York State. And as the largest single shareholder in the Connecticut Land Company, he believed in it. Further, he believed in the existence of the *excess* land in the Reserve.

Oliver Phelps and a handful of others including General Hull, the same Hull of the brilliant Revolutionary War record (later to be dimmed by his surrender of Detroit in 1812), formed the Excess Company.

The Excess Company offered the Connecticut Land Company for a fixed price all land which might be found in the Reserve in excess of the three-million acres and the Firelands.

This proposal came before the three-man executive committee of the board of directors and was accepted by them, as might be expected, with Oliver Phelps being on the approving committee. With the proposal accepted, and with the powerful real estate name of Phelps connected with it, Excess Company stock was in big demand.

Pressure to cross the Indian line and explore the excess hit the surveyors who were slowing down from sickness and disappointment. Fighting fever and hunger, they felt little loyalty to men in the east who were in a hurry to know how *much* excess land they had bought.

General Moses Cleaveland had held scrupulously to his promise to the Indians not to cross the Cuyahoga, but now his company wanted to push a survey west to the 120-mile limit in order to discover the shape of the shore line and the amount of excess land they owned.

Therefore, Augustus Porter, second in command of the survey party, hastened his survey of the fourth range line from the 41st parallel to the lake, and then was excused from running the parallels to create the townships. He hurried to the stone marker at the northwest corner of Pennsylvania and began his traverse of the lake front, planning to go all the way to the end of the 120 miles — to make an accurate shoreline map which would show the quantity of excess land.

As Porter and his crew began this trek west, other crews were suddenly becoming disturbed about the unparallel deviation in their north-south lines. They were not so worried about it as they had been before, because they now had larger worries. Men were sick so frequently that the surveyors could not field full crews; some were dying. It was necessary to take men off the surveying to care for the sick. So these crews dragged themselves through the forest. Running a line, which once took a day, now took four.

At this point the seldom chronicled executive ability of Moses Cleaveland came into play.

He deployed his men with great care to replace the sick, and to try not to overwork those who were able to drag themselves around. He tried to get medicine. He obtained assistance for overworked Dr. Shepard. And he kept his eye on the calendar to be sure he could get the group out of the area before snowfall.

The men who were running the horizontals consecutively from south to north now skipped a few and moved north to see how much actual convergence there was in the meridians because of compass variations.

To their surprise, they found the variations which were a matter of feet just 67 miles south on the south line had now grown to variations of a half mile and more. Some townships were only four and a half miles wide at the top while others were five and a half miles. This meant that some of the northern farms were going to be very pie-shaped, and there would be work for attorneys for a hundred years to come.

But the men were tired, and they continued the survey, leaving the slanting lines behind them. They were working as long as they could stay on their feet, but now they were grumbling.

Meanwhile Augustus Porter pressed his traverse vigorously. He had reached the mouth of the Cuyahoga, and he was disappointed. He had positively established that there was a slashing southwest angle to the Lake Erie shore. There was no excess this far. But perhaps west of the Cuyahoga the shoreline would sweep north again.

Cleaveland's agreement with the Five Nations Indians prescribed that surveyors would not cross the river. But Porter crossed the Cuyahoga and pushed his line along the lake shore heading for Sandusky Bay, to the point where his calculated westings told him he was due north of the west end of the 120-mile length of the Connecticut Western Reserve.

He almost reached that end. His later report to the directors explained that he "was not able to run the west line completely, on account of the Indian title not being extinguished!" But he explained that he came close enough that by a simple map exercise he could calculate the acreage at 3,450,753 acres, *including* the Firelands which did not belong to the Connecticut Land Company.

Instead of reporting an excess, he was therefore reporting a shortage. We can see the man trying to come at least back up to the starting point, like any businessman at the end of a bad quarter. He added that "this figure does not include the islands of Lake Erie and Sandusky Bay, supposed to exceed the islands in quantity about 30,000 acres."

Word filtered back to the Excess Company. They refused to believe it. "Why, the errors in Porter's survey are massive! We already know the compasses are not agreeing by what's happening east of the Cuyahoga."

"They say the men are getting very careless from fatigue. They don't stretch the chain tight, and in offsetting around the swamps, I hear they are just making the offsets by eye."

The Excess Company challenged the survey even before the report was officially made to them. They requested a mathematics professor from Yale to be ready to audit the field notes of the surveyors.

While irritation was setting in at home in Connecticut, out on the survey outrage was setting in. These men had not signed on to write a piece of frontier history; they signed up only for wages.

But new land forced men to heroism or death. The ague-fever that went with opening up new land out there was called

Cuyahoga fever. And it was still thinning the ranks. It made the crews truculent.

Cleaveland saw that he was not going to finish by snowfall, and that he would not be able to keep these men alive through the winter. He decided on expediency: he would complete the survey on those six townships which were not to be parceled out among stockholders but were reserved to the Connecticut Land Company which would sell them to raise funds to continue the surveying.

While Porter continued his study of the lake shoreline, Pease, Spafford, and Stoddard were to run the short laterals in the northeast corner, while Holley's crew brought north more range lines. The men were eating rattlesnake, bear, muskrat, rabbit.

Cleaveland was trying to get the headquarters city survey complete. The men were trying to go home. So there came a day when 18 of them approached Cleaveland with an ultimatum: more money — or they would pull out for Connecticut.

Cleaveland's leadership was tested severely. He had no more allowable budget, but the Connecticut Land Company did have land to burn. Cleaveland therefore selected one township near the heart of the Western Reserve. He pointed to it on the map, and talked to the men about the hordes of immigrants who would follow to buy land; about the city which would grow at the mouth of the Cuyahoga, which "I believe will grow to nearly the size of Old Windham, Connecticut."

He told the men that the Connecticut Land Company would grant in fee simple one equal share in this township to each member of the crew who would agree to the following:

— By 1797 (the following year) there must be 11 people resident in the township.

— In 1798 they must settle 18 more families on it, each to clear five acres.

— In 1799 there must be 12 more families who must each have eight acres in wheat.

— In 1800, 41 families must be in the township.

Forty-one of the men signed these articles, seven abstained. The signers divided the township with survey lines; and, being surveyors, they named the township in honor of the father of geometry — Euclid.

The 41 proprietors of Euclid then met to draw lots to see which of them would settle here according to contract in the years 1797, 1798, and 1799. None volunteered. The 11 who won (or lost) the draw were: Seth Pease, who established a distinguished and useful family in the Reserve; Theodore Shepard, the physician; Amzi Atwater, assistant explorer, who would live until 1851 and be the last survivor of the survey party; Elisha Ayer; Tim Dunham; Sam'l Forbes; Sam'l Hungerford; Wareham Shepard, packman and best friend of Atwater; Sam'l Agnew, and two others not yet identified.

Moses Cleaveland satisfied the men, and while it is true he was giving away his employer's assets, he was trying to gain for the company a built-in population. He served both employers and employees well.

On Monday, October 17, 1796, John Holley wrote in his journal, "Finished surveying in New Connecticut; weather rainy." Tuesday, October 18, 1796, he wrote, "We left Cuyahoga at 3:00 o'clock 17 minutes for HOME. We left at Cuyahoga Job Stiles and wife and Joseph Landon with provisions for winter." They rowed about seven and a half miles and camped for the night.

On the Reserve at Cleaveland, the general left Job and Tabitha Stiles and Edward Paine in charge of stores in a cabin on lot 53. At Conneaut, he left Elijah Gunn and wife and the Kingsbury family. At Sandusky was a French trader.

These were the only white men left on the Reserve as silent winter hardened in.

Deserving to return to Hartford and a hero's welcome, the managers of the survey party instead stepped into a meeting of disappointed stockholders. They appointed a committee to inquire why the costs of the survey were running so high; another to inquire into the conduct of the directors.

They challenged Augustus Porter's field notes of survey and had them gone over by the Yale professor who could find no error in his total of 3,450,753 acres[3] including the half million acres of the Firelands.

While these business matters went on in Hartford, Connecticut, those left on the Reserve faced a brutal winter.

The Stileses and Edward Paine at the mouth of the Cuyahoga were able to survive fairly well because they had the company rations stored there. Besides, they were assisted with game by Ogontz, the Ottawa; Sagamaw, a Chippewa, and Seneca.

But at Conneaut where the Kingsburys were holding the land, snow fell early and the winter froze in hard. James Kingsbury had come onto the Reserve as the first frontiersman with intent to settle. Initially, he had nothing to do with the Land Company. He and his wife, Eunice, came from Alsted, New Hampshire, with their children, Abigail, Amos, and Almon, an infant. They came to have a very large part in the Cuyahoga story.

Kingsbury was a colonel of militia in New Hampshire, but pining for action. There being none, he packed up his family in an ox-drawn wagon and moved west for the frontier. The young family reached Buffalo Creek in New York just as General Cleaveland was coming through to catch up with his surveying party. He urged Kingsbury to join him, help with the work, and buy land later when he had seen all the survey and picked his favorite spot.

Kingsbury worked with the survey crew in matters of supply and when the crew went home in the fall, his assignment was to remain at Conneaut in charge of some stores. But because the winter set in so fast and hard, it drove game into hiding, and it was necessary to kill for food one of the cattle left by the survey party.

---

3. A few years later, the spectacular land operator, Leonard Case, on the Western Reserve, went carefully through the land records, township by township, and arrived at a total of 3,333,699 acres with all surveys and drafts before him. General Simon Perkins, surveyor, did the same and arrived at 3,366,921 acres. Porter, working in the rough and under Indian pressure, was amazingly close.

For an unknown reason, Kingsbury had to return to New Hampshire in November. He went on horseback, expecting the trip to take perhaps six weeks. But when he arrived in New Hampshire, he was laid low by the fever. As soon as he could ride he started his return. He reached Buffalo creek on December 3, and next day resumed his journey in a driving horizontal snow.

At Conneaut, meanwhile, his wife was flat on a pallet bunk, extremely ill. She had birthed a baby and the other children were trying to feed the family at her direction. They had been put to such extremes as digging out kernels of corn which had fallen between the floor puncheons and scraping aside snow to see if underneath could be found anything edible.

The mother's fever deprived the baby of its food, and the older children frantically tried to find twigs to feed the remaining cow so that the baby might have milk. It was crying constantly with starvation.

James Kingsbury fought his way through the snow from the east. It fell for three weeks and in many places drifted chin deep. With the aid of an Indian, he moved forward each day.

At some time on the journey his horse died. He sighted the cabin in Conneaut on the 24 of December.

Inside the cabin, his children told him the worst of it, Mrs. Kingsbury being hardly able to speak. The returned traveler took a hand sled and started on foot for Erie for a bushel of wheat. He was able to get all the way to Erie and back before anyone in the cabin died. They cracked the wheat and boiled it, but the infant died.

As they carried the child from the house in its coffin, the mother fell back on the bed and remained scarcely conscious for two weeks.

But Kingsbury was able to kill a pigeon for rations. The weather broke shortly and it looked as though the rest of the Kingsbury family could survive until the arrival of the second survey party.

The second survey party was under the leadership of Reverend Seth Hart,[4] but Seth Pease was in charge of the outfitting and launching and most of the work.

He moved out of Suffield, Connecticut, April 3, and headed for Schenectady, New York. On June 1 Pease recorded in his journal, "Entered Cuyahoga mouth at 3 hrs. 22 minutes p.m. Found Mr. Stiles and Mrs. Stiles well, also Mrs. Gunn."

The work in Cleaveland started with news of a death in the party. David Eldridge drowned in attempting to swim his horse across the Grand River.

Seth Pease, a young man, began in an organized manner. He checked the supplies left from last year, set men to planting a large garden to avoid the hunger previously experienced, and organized the men into crews, each headed by a surveyor, and he kept all assignments clear.

He kept a mental accounting of supplies and where to put them so that, if teams were on schedule, they would run right into the replacements. And he made provision for taking good care of the horses: Hannah, Mary Ester, the Morton Mare, and the Stow Horse.

The young man was outranked in years and prestige by most of his crew who were older and included several captains and majors. But he ran the detail with a strangely charming com-

---

4. Second surveying party: Rev. Seth Hart, *Superintendent*; Seth Pease, *Principal Surveyor*; *Surveyors*—Richard M. Stoddard; Moses Warren; Amzi Atwater; Joseph Landon; Amos Spafford; Wareham Shepard; Phineas Barker; Nathan Redfield; Theodore Shepard, (or Shepherd,) *Physician*. Employees: Col. Ezra Wait; Thomas Gun; Peleg Waterman, (or Wash- burn,); M. William Shepard; Hubbard T. Linsley; David Eldridge, (drowned); Minor Bicknell, (died); Josiah Barse (or Barze); Jotham Atwater; Oliver Culver; Dan'l Holbrook, *Explorer*; Stephen Gilbert; Nathaniel Doan; David Clark; Solomon Giddings; Samuel Forbes; James Stoddard; Ezekiel Morly; Thomas Tupper; Chester Allen; James Berry; Berry Nye; Joseph Nye; Asa Mason; Eli Kellogg; William Barker; Shubal Parker (or Park); Jacob Carlton; Phil Barker; Eli Canfield; John Doane; Joseph Tinker; Samuel Spafford (son of Amos); Lot Sanford; Alpheus Choat; William Andrews (died); Matthew L. Gilgore; E. Chapman; David Beard; Solomon Shepard; William Tinker; Alexander Allen; George Gidings; Enoch Eldridge; Charles Parker; Job Coe; Eli Rowley (deserted); Clark Reynolds; William Stoddard; John Hine; Sylvester Smith.

bination of firmness, formality, and respect, which comes through in his steady stream of written directives distributed by runners.

Mr. Stoddard,
You will proceed up the river to our headquarters, though I am at a loss at present where it will be fixed, but you may take the line between 10th and 11th ranges, and I will give you notice on that line at the nearest corner. We shall go as far as possible with our boats. If you should not arrive here [Cleveland] so as to be there in about 30 days, I think you had better not go up river, unless you receive another line from your humble servant,
Seth Pease

Mr. Tinker ... I wish you to return and bring another boatload of stores as soon as possible. You will take four hands, and have such men return as are best pleased with the business of boating. I wish you a prosperous voyage.
Seth Pease

As the work progressed, Pease himself took charge of one survey party. Thus his headquarters was always in motion. Yet even as he worked his own line, he had an amazing picture in his mind of what was progressing on all other parts of the survey; and as he moved, he not only directed the surveying, but also the supplying of crews. He made arrangements for the Kingsburys to be brought down from Conneaut to Cleaveland, and for the supplies to be leapfrogged ahead of the crews.

While his mind oversaw these broad aspects of the work, he had an eye for small details ("Warren's crew left a frying pan on the west bank"), and for the technical precision of the survey, worrying constantly about the precision of the compasses.

The south line was run as follows: from the Pennsylvania line to the fifth mile, one degree, twenty minutes; should have been one degree, twenty-five minutes. From the fifth mile to the ninth miles, one degree, twenty minutes, should have been one degree thirty-three minutes. From ninth to thirteenth, I expect was very near the truth. From thirteenth to fifteenth miles, two degrees, two minutes, ought to have been one degree, fifty.

From observations made on the various compasses, I find I cannot reduce them to a common standard, being differently affected at different places. Of two compasses on the Cuyahoga River twenty miles south of the lake, one needle was to the left of the other ten minutes. At Cleaveland the one which was to the left stood fifteen minutes to the right, though they were not compared precisely at the same hour of the day. The magnetic needle is not always parallel to itself at the same place, which renders the compass inaccurate for long lines. The variation is so irregular that it admits of no calculation, and must be determined by observations upon the heavenly bodies.

The compasses were a constant worry to the surveyors. The more predictable compasses became favorites, and when the surveyors handling these fell sick, other surveyors borrowed their compasses. Ultimately the fever and ague struck this second surveying party and hard. But Pease kept the job going.

Upon his arrival, in his systematic way, he had constructed on lots 97 and 98 at Cleaveland a cemetery, and it was soon in use. But some casualties never made it to the central cemetery and their graves are scattered across the Reserve. For example, when all the lower lines were run except the fifth, sixth, and seventh meridians, Redfield was ordered to the seventh, Stoddard the sixth, Shepard and Atwater to the fifth, the west line of Trumbull and Ashtabula.

Stoddard was lame so Atwater took his compass and shifted over to the sixth. He ran the line ten miles when he met Stoddard, recovered enough to take over, and saying that Shepard was sick and needed relief at the northeast corner of Palmyra.

Atwater took over Shepard's line and the crew. Miner Bicknell was in that crew. When they had run the line seven miles between Braceville and Windham, Bicknell became too sick to ride a horse and he could not walk. They were far from head-quarters, had no medicine and not enough men in condition to carry Bicknell. Therefore, they constructed a stretcher of saplings and a blanket, slung it between two horses walking single file, and lashed the stretcher handles to the saddles with bark.

Atwater left Shepard with one man to run the line while he led the horses for Cleaveland, taking one able-bodied man with him. He traveled along the third parallel. Progress was so slow he sent the other man ahead to order a boat to come upriver from Cleaveland and meet them at the south line of Independence.

Bicknell had a high fever all the way. Atwater reached the boat meeting place after conveying Bicknell 50 miles. The boat arrived in the morning with Dr. Shepard aboard, but Bicknell died two hours after the meeting. Atwater wanted the body sent north to Cleaveland for burial, but the boatmen refused, fearing the disease.

Atwater was exhausted and so shaken at losing the man he had brought so carefully north that he now hastened back over his trail to rejoin Shepard, whom he had left in poor health. He found that Shepard had pushed the line to the northeast corner of Portage County and was in good health. Atwater pitched in with Shepard and they ran the line to the lake.

This completed the survey of the Western Reserve on the east side of the Cuyahoga.

Sickness accelerated toward late summer and boatloads men were sent east in early fall. Several of the surveyors took their pay and went home on foot. With his eye on the weather which could immobilize the party for the winter, Pease pressed the surveying of the best towns into lots so that the Land Company could sell off its reserved townships and earn income.

On October 3, 1797, Seth Pease loaded the remaining boats with sick men and horses and "left the mouth of the Cuyahoga at about 10-½ a.m. Wind fair."

In Hartford, Connecticut, Pease turned in his report of sickness and casualties. But the Land Company stockholders as usual were more interested in results and were eager for action.

They wanted to know which townships he was recommending the company retain for sale; and they were eager to get on with the drawing by which the stockholders would receive their lands in New Connecticut. Pease and Hart had other recommendations, however, for the company's consideration and on these they wanted action:

Action on donating one city lot to Tabitha Cumi Stiles, wife of Job Stiles, and one ten-acre lot and one 100-acre lot in compensation for her winter's work. Approved.

Action on donating a 100-acre lot to Ann Gunn, wife of Elijah, for her winter's work. Approved.

Red Jacket and Farmer's Brother, Indians, to be voted a double *douceur* of $15 for expenses incurred in helping surveyors. Approved.

There was a donation lot for James Kingsbury, and then the stockholders went on to tax themselves another $20 a share to meet commitments.

They approved a donation of one city lot to Nathaniel Doan if he would move onto the Reserve at Cleaveland and establish a blacksmith shop.

The towns selected by the surveyors to be recommended to the Land Company as the most valuable were Nos. 5, 6, and 7 in Range 11, and No. 11 in Range 7. They became Northfield, Bedford, Warrensville, and Perry. This recommendation was part of the information needed by the Land Company in setting up the drawing.

The townships the Land Company reserved for sale by the company were: Madison, Mentor, Willoughby, Euclid, and Cleaveland. It could include Euclid because the Euclid surveyors broke their bargain. Only two of them showed up to settle the ground under the rules established at the time of General Cleaveland's strike negotiation.

Now began the complex and arcane procedures for distributing the land fairly. Because the value of the land was uneven, parcels of land were classified as to value, on report from the surveyors, and coded by number on a map. These numbers were then placed on corresponding slips of paper and placed in three boxes for the drawing. A stockholder drew some slips from each of the three boxes — first, second and third class land. How many slips he drew from each box depended upon the number of shares he held.

This meant that his lands would be scattered around, but it insured that each shareholder drew some of the bad and some of the good. There was a separate drawing for the lands in those four towns of extra fine land.

And there would be still four other drafts as the survey later pushed west across the Cuyahoga, and again when the Firelands sufferers took up their half million acres at the western end of the Reserve.

Action was possible because General Cleaveland and Seth Pease had laid a five-mile grid over the three-million-acre forest, marked by blazes, posts . . . and a few wooden crosses.

Survival — Man and Boy

The Man

THEY said, when you faced Lorenzo Carter's pale blue eyes when he was mad, he had your attention.

But the man called Abel Gunnar was facing not only the eyes, but the hole in the end of Carter's gun.
"You're not leaving the mouth of the river, Gunnar. You're coming back with me now."

Carter was not a reflective man who could carry a point through the territorial councils and courts. He was big, spade-chinned, slab-chested and direct. What he knew was that people kept leaving the village he was trying to build. It had to stop. Carter was not a member of the Connecticut Land Company nor an employee. He was the first bona fide settler to move to the Cuyahoga to stay.

Most river mouths spawn cities as surely as a waterfall attracts a mill wheel community; but the Cuyahoga repelled people. Ague and waterborne fevers were intense at the hot pocket at the basin mouth. A sand bar held in stagnation and blocked out all but the shallowest draft boats. Besides the first and second surveying parties had returned to Connecticut and down-talked the region.

Seventy Seneca families and two-score Ottawas and Chippewas on the cliffs at the mouth discouraged settlers who didn't know the peaceful temper of the Seneca, Stigwanish. They also emphasized the fact that the west bank of the Cuyahoga was officially and legally Indian Country. So settlement on the east bank of the river put a woman and her children right on the edge of the frontier, in some places only 50 feet from foreign soil.

Though the powerful Connecticut Land Company tried to force settlement on the river here, it would not build. But Lorenzo Carter wanted to see a town grow up around him.

Probably the biggest man the river will ever see, Lorenzo Carter was not inhibited by knowledge of the fine points of law nor by philosophical hesitance, nor religious reverence. He faced the Gods with his hat on, his proposition plain, and his ax and rifle handy. He turned back nature itself, the Connecticut Land Company, and 70 Senecas to make this creek a Great Lakes' port.

"You can't leave, Gunnar."
"I am gonna leave, Major."

When Major Spafford came to Major Carter and said his man had run off, Carter asked which direction, then grabbed his Yaeger and rode south. Eleven miles from the mouth, he caught up to Gunnar.

"I've stolen nothing, Major. I owe no one. In fact, Major Spafford owes me wages. But I'm leaving. And you have no legal right to stop me."
"True. But I'll do it."
Abel Gunnar was speechless with outrage. Carter's voice softened to a blacksmith's rasp bobbing iron. "Abel, set a spell and take it resty."
The Major cradled his gun pointed at Gunnar, but he sank to a squat, "Look the blow it would be. Ye'll see I can't let ye go."
Gunnar looked around him and back at the Major's gun. There was no way but to listen again.

100

While the port at the mouth of the Cuyahoga is named for and sustained Moses Cleaveland, it was really founded by Lorenzo Carter and should have borne his name.

General Cleaveland selected the mouth of the Cuyahoga for the capital of the Reserve. But so unfavorable was the location that none of the surveying party except for the Stileses and the Kingsburys chose this river mouth for their own land. Most returned to Connecticut.

Then in 1797, Lorenzo Carter came out of Vermont. At 30 he wore authority as easily as an old work shirt. He threw up his historic log hut on the east bank at the mouth of the Cuyahoga (at the foot of St. Clair), not a small one like the other two there, but a large one with a loft.

On the map of the Land Company back in Connecticut, Cleveland was then a nicely ruled plat of streets on paper, all nicely named. Carter built his hut large so there would be a place for the now four settlers to gather and talk of filling in the blank map.

Immediately his large cabin was needed for the settlement's first wedding on the second of June. Chloe Inches married William Clement who followed her all the way from Ontario. But what hurt Carter, the married couple immediately moved out. Then the Kingsburys moved away to higher ground to the south, to begin The Mills, later called Newburgh.

Severe ague and fever attacked everyone at the river mouth. There was no doctor. To escape it, Job Stiles moved his family out to where Kingsbury was. Then Elijah Gunn and his wife Ann moved out.

Although some new settlers came, in the fall of 1799 only seven courageous people remained in the trading post at the Cuyahoga mouth. Sadly Carter watched them all move. Finally he and Rebecca Carter and their remaining son were the only non-Indian residents of Cleveland.

In fact, until March 1800, Rebecca and Lorenzo Carter *were* Cleveland.

A handful of settlers came, but Carter envisioned a city. To make the point that civilization had reached to the mouth of the Cuyahoga, he felt he needed a grand ball. Several of the settlers in other parts of the Western Reserve were Revolutionary veterans who still revered the magic date, July 4.

Hence the first grand ball on the Cuyahoga was held in Lorenzo Carter's cabin, July 4, 1801, to the tune of the Reserve's first fiddle belonging to Samuel Jones. In this woman-scarce country, 20 men came to dance with 12 women; some came two days' riding distance. Perhaps news of the ball traveling back east by letters may have ultimately helped settle the Cuyahoga. But Carter did not believe so.

He decided that the country wouldn't grow until there was a school. So the first school in Cleveland opened in 1802 in Carter's front room, taught by Anna Spafford, daughter of Major Amos Spafford.

A few people came, but did not stay. Civilization needs a tavern, Carter felt. Therefore he and Amos Spafford traveled to the Court of Quarter Sessions at Warren and paid four dollars for a license "to keep tavern." While education was going on in Carter's *front* room, philosophy and sour mash were available in Carter's back room.

At the same time, he bought 23½ acres on St. Clair east of West Ninth Street on which to build a finer tavern. The tavern did indeed bring some civilization, but it was not enough.

A city needs religion, Carter felt. When the Reverend Joseph Bodger came through on horseback, Carter persuaded him to light down in the valley of the Cuyahoga, giving the minister violently aggressive hospitality and the use of his house.

He ignored the services, but invited the Senecas to fill the pews, and brought Sam Jones and his fiddle.

"But it didn't take root, Major," Gunnar said.

"No," admitted Carter, cradling the long gun as friendlily as possible without diverting the muzzle from Gunnar's chest,

"but I thought me to start a store, and so Elisha Norton laid into the house some trade goods for the women."

"But the store didn't help, Mr. Carter. Mostly the Indians used it. Nobody's putting down cellars or roots.

To prove permanence, Carter had bought a piece of the river at Superior and Union Lane; and he began construction of the first frame house made of sawed boards floated in from Buffalo. West of Water Street and north of Superior Lane, the big cabin encouraged the settlers with its back-east look. Transients looked at it and beamed. Some stayed.

When it was almost finished, fire caught in the chips. The blaze leveled Cleveland's first frame house, and with it, the state of civilization at the Cuyahoga mouth. There would not be another frame house for eight years. Carter built another log cabin.

On the same site, he built a blockhouse, designed for a tavern in peacetime, Carter's Tavern.

As the British-Indian threat rose, the first state militia was organized on May 7, 1804. Lorenzo Carter was elected captain of the Cleveland Company in the 2nd Brigade, 4th Division, under Major Spafford. In August, Carter was elected major, heading one battalion.

"So you know very well, with me headin' it, Gunnar, there'll be no dust-up with the British that can hurt us."

"I've never been afraid of that, Major. I'm leaving because I just don't think Cleveland will ever come to much' til the Indians are out."

Gunnar rose; but he sat down again as he heard Carter half-cock the firing lock. "You got to stay and help see to it."

Carter personally didn't consider the Indians a threat. He understood their language, and thought of them not so much as savages as good fellows who could give you a hand, and once in a while "needed a little talking to." Carter's hold over the

Indians constantly amazed the settlers, but they couldn't believe it would last.

When O'mic, the Ottawa, was charged, tried, and convicted of robbing and murdering two white trappers, Carter was hurt because O'mic was a long-time friend. But the murder trial, Cleveland's first, was apparently fair, viewed by all 18 Cleveland families. The verdict was hanging.

There was no jail, and the settlers feared Indian retaliation, so they asked Carter to keep the prisoner.

When the Indians saw Levi Johnson building the gallows, they did become hostile. Then one night they drank heavily and descended on Carter's cabin on the riverbank.

The power of one man with a made-up mind to turn off a mob has always staggered the imagination. But the manner in which Lorenzo Carter stormed out of his cabin and tongue-lashed the mob of red men was talked about for years. They say he roared in Indian, "Of course you can beat me, but I'll probably take ten of you with me! Who does that want to be?"

Pressure built up to clear the Indians from the land west of the river, the Indian boundary.

Settlers kept moving away from the mouth of the Cuyahoga. The courtly Samuel Huntington (future governor) moved from his extra large log cabin to Newburgh Mill, then to Painesville.

On the Fourth of July 1805, the tribes west of the Cuyahoga sent representation to a council at Fort Industry on the Maumee to meet with a U.S. Commissioner of Indian Affairs, a Connecticut Land Company man, and a spokesman for the Firelands Company. The Indians finally agreed to sign over their lands west of the Cuyahoga if they would receive an annual payment of $13,760 forever. Action depended upon their seeing the money and receiving the first payment.

Lorenzo Carter and five men rode to Pittsburgh and brought the money.

That opened the land west of the Cuyahoga to settlement, but no surge of people came *through* or *to* Cleveland.

Major Carter said to Major Spafford, "We must have a vessel so they can float out the yield. It's what's needed to draw commercial men here."

"We've no shipwright in the whole Reserve."

But up on the riverbank, Lorenzo Carter began Cleveland's shipbuilding industry. With only the help of local settlers, he built the 30-ton sailing vessel, *Zephyr*. They hauled it to the water with eight work cattle. Flat-bottomed and a poor sailer, she did nevertheless sail short-haul cargo successfully on Lake Erie; and it was an important accomplishment even to be able to build and launch her.

Furs from the Senecas and grindstones made in Cleveland could now ship east to trade for iron and brass and glass needed for guns and beds and windows. But the cargoes for the boat were disappointing. Settlers could bring their goods to the boat quite well from east of the river over Buffalo Road. But from west of the river, there was little more than the Indian's lakeshore trail to Detroit.

Carter talked to Sam Huntington who represented the county in the new state capital. The legislature appropriated funds for a road from the mouth of the Cuyahoga to the mouth of the Huron River. Construction of the road was supervised by Lorenzo Carter. Detroit Road it was called, then and now.

Still Cleveland did not grow. One more handicap was the Connecticut owners themselves. There were now in the Connecticut Land Company a new breed of shareholders. Unlike the original shareholders who preferred to remain in Connecticut and send hired developers out to New Connecticut, these new shareholders packed wagons and came on out themselves. But most of these men naturally would not settle in Cleveland. As shareholders they each owned several hundreds of acres and were themselves town builders. Their names became towns: David Hudson of Hudson, Eliphalet Austin of Austinburg, Alexander Harper of Harpersfield, Edward Paine of Painesville, David Root of Rootstown, Joshua Stow of Stow, Strong of Strongsville, and Ely of Elyria.

As these towns competed for cash buyer settlers for their land, they lured away settlers from Lorenzo Carter's town.

These townships did wagon their products and produce to the boat at the Cuyahoga mouth. If the *Zephyr* were not in, however, they had to stack their goods on the shore or leave them in the wagons.

Major Carter said to Major Spafford, "It won't be a port until we have a warehouse."

Spafford nodded. He rounded up Gunnar and Elijah Gunn and Samuel Jones and Ashbel Walworth. With their help, Lorenzo Carter built of logs Cleveland's first warehouse.

Gunnar rose again slowly, not to excite Carter's trigger hand, "But, Major, I didn't see much difference after the warehouse."

"You saw enough so that suddenly Murray and Bixby were encouraged to build a sixty-ton ship."

"And nothing to ship. The land's too poor to yield."

"It's not to be a farming village, it's a port city. The land is only to hold the improvements: warehouses, docks, manufacturies."

"They don't amount to anything. Tax assessor values the whole place only twenty thousand dollars."

"It'll rise with commerce."

But Gunnar pointed out that Charles Dutton had sold two acres right on public square to Turhand Kirtland for only 30 dollars, and that Kirtland soon resold it to Jacob Coleman for 30 dollars. Coleman also soon felt the choicest piece of land in Cleveland was a bad buy. He offered it for sale, but couldn't move it without a loss.

"You see," Gunnar explained to Carter, "there's not enough people to do any commerce. And those we got are leaving. We had seventy-eight. Now we're down to fifty-seven." *Gunnar rose, picked up his duffel.*

But he froze when he heard Carter's lock snap to full cock.

"That's why you're going to stay, Gunnar. I'm not losing any more people. Town needs you."

"You've no right, Carter. I owe no man. In fact, Major Spafford owes me wages!"

"You got to come back and let him pay you. You don't have the right to make Major Spafford into a thief, a defaulter of wages. Bad name for him, bad name for the city."

"City!" Gunnar laughed. "Carter, you're crazy enough you're dangerous with that gun."

"I am that."

Gunnar turned back.

In that same year, an alarm came into Cleveland that a ten-horse, six-ox train of six wagonloads of people was approaching from the east with intent to settle hereabouts. The wagons, it was said contained "an avalanche" of impoverished immigrants to be thrown on the village for support. They were four families of Brainards from Connecticut and the families of Elijah Young and Isaac Hinckley. Worse, it was reported, "Still more wagons follow."

The Cleveland Township Trustees sent out a constable to warn them off. Then Alonzo Carter, son of Lorenzo, heard about it; and he confronted the town fathers, "You fools!" A good son's anger on behalf of a father, right or wrong, makes forum or debate pointless. And Alonzo had some of Lorenzo's brawn of arm and blaze of eye.

The wagons came on.

They were followed in the same year by wagons of Fishers, McIntoshes, Gates, Sears, Storers, Aikens, Fosters, Poes, Kroehles. Today, there are streets and roads and suburbs named for most of these.

But the point is, when they arrived, they met to plan in *Carter's Tavern*, sent children to school in *Carter's front room*, bought farms off of *Carter's Detroit Road*, and then hauled corn and whiskey and leather and timber back over it to *Carter's warehouse* to wait for *Carter's boat*.

The legislature granted an incorporation charter to Carter's town, spelled Cleveland, on December 23, 1814.

What Major Carter never had the pleasure of seeing was that Jacob Coleman did finally sell those two acres on the northwest corner of Public Square to William Coleman in 1815 for 55 dollars. William Coleman later sold just 94 feet of it for 200 dollars to Leonard Case, Jr. And in years to come, W.G. Marshall leased that corner for 12-thousand dollars a year for 99 years. Once the site of the Marshall Building, at this writing a parking lot across Superior Avenue from the Renaissance-Cleveland Hotel.

It took about 130 years to figure out what Carter did. People went back to his Erie Street grave in 1938, and put up a monument. Few people see it. But, of course, all can see the great port on the Great Lake, Carter's Cleveland.

The Doan Boy

For one crucial summer, the destiny of the Cuyahoga valley bore down on the thin shoulders of a wiry 13-year-old boy. Without him, this would be a very different book.

The unwritten rule of the world has always had it that the people or nation which controls the mouth of a river controls the entire land basin drained by that watershed.

Despite all treaties, the British and those Indians loyal to them were looking covetously south and east from Detroit again. The Americans were slow to settle the northern part of the Ohio country, and they were respecting the official Indian boundary which made the territory west of the Cuyahoga and north of the Greenville line officially Indian.

Now we've said that Lorenzo Carter was having trouble holding a settlement at the mouth of the Cuyahoga, and that the summer of 1798 threatened the settlement of 12 families with annihilation when bilious fever struck. Every family was down with the debilitating sickness. This was characterized by extreme fevers, which burned a settler three or four times a day. When the fever subsided, it was immediately followed by extreme ague, called *shakes*, which left even strong men so spent they could not drag themselves around to procure food or to care for their sick.

Just before this scourge struck the mouth of the Cuyahoga, Nathaniel Doan was setting out from Chatham, Connecticut, with his family. He had a wife, son, three daughters, and a contract with the Connecticut Land Company. If he would establish a blacksmith shop on the banks of the Cuyahoga and keep it there one year to serve the settlers, he would receive title to ten acres.

Nathaniel Doan was 22 days just getting to Utica, New York, where he stopped to rest his family and team at the house of his brother, Timothy.

After six days, he was ready to push on. Loading up the wagon, he found already stowed there an unfamiliar canvas duffel with a knife thonged to the outside. He picked it up and studied it, puzzled. Looking around behind him, he encountered the level voice of his 13-year-old nephew, Seth Doan. "Leave it in, Uncle Nathaniel. I'm going with you."

When the argument grew quickly to involve both families Nathaniel Doan talked across the head of the boy to his own brother. "The Cuyahoga is directly on the Indian boundary. I cannot be answerable." He looked at his own daughters. "It's enough blame will be on my head as it is."

Young Seth Doan said, "I'll be answerable for myself, Uncle Nathaniel."

Nathaniel said, "I have it in letters there are more children in the burying ground at the Cuyahoga than grown people."

Seth Doan's father said, "He's been a healthy boy. And he's spoken a lot of going with you. We denied him. But..."

Nathaniel Doan said, "If he was bigger, it would be different. He could help."

"He's been brought up to carry his weight, Nathaniel."

"But it'll be another mouth."

"But another two arms."

While they argued, Seth Doan walked into the barn and led out the pair of Connecticut Fancies. As he backed them in with the wagon tongue between, Nathaniel Doan pressed his lips over his teeth, but he didn't say "No."

Ninety-two days from Chatham, Connecticut, they were approaching the Cuyahoga. They had reached the place where Mentor is now when the bilious fever hit their wagon. They were unable to prepare food or drive the team. The wagon was just stopped in its ruts.

Seth Doan crawled over to his uncle, "Uncle Nathaniel, we should unhitch and let them try to graze."

Nathaniel Doan opened his eyes and stared at the boy. The boy had never seen a grown man with that strange glassy, uncomprehending look.

Young Doan crawled over the family to the tailgate, and unhooked it. The jolt of the drop startled the horses, but the family hardly moved.

He let himself down to the ground and looked around. The wagon was stopped in the bottom of a hollow because the horses had missed the encouragement from the driver's seat usually needed to mount a steep bank.

Seth Doan crawled up to the seat and snapped the reins across their rumps. But the horses looked around at him. He crawled down and went forward to talk up the horses. They were dry.

Crawling painfully up into the back of the wagon, he got out the leather water buckets and walked down the hollow. He found an intermittently dried-up stream and filled the buckets.

Halfway back to the horses, he had to set one bucket down. Three quarters of the way back he had to pour some out of that one and drag it over the ground. Returned to the horses, he couldn't lift the bucket to their muzzles.

He could not let go of the leather bucket to unhook the checkrein without the bucket collapsing. He pondered it a moment, and decided he would have to sacrifice this water. He drank himself, then let the bucket collapse and the water run out while he climbed up to unhook the checkrein.

He made many trips to the stream and back, resting between. Then he was able to lead the horses up the rise out of the hollow. As they moved slowly along the ruts through the woods, he found a protected place for the night, and unhitched. With no strength left to remove the collars, Seth tied the horses to the rear of the wagon, and crawled under it. As darkness set in he was frightened by the chills that took over his body, and by the silence above him.

Two settlers, Parker and Church, found the wagon next day. They were generous men, but they knew they couldn't afford close contact with the sick family. They did hitch up the horses and lead the wagon to the Cuyahoga. It took two days.

The stillness and the heat in the settlement made it feel like the last stop this side of hell. Then Lorenzo Carter took over the family. He got them housed with the Carters and the Stileses. But they saw that the settlement at the mouth of the river was in very serious trouble from the bilious fever. There was no general greeting.

Even the powerfully built Lorenzo Carter staggered under the sickness. But he did show the Doans how to find butternut bark, powder it, and mix it with some dogwood bark and cherry bark to make a medicine in the absence of calomel or quinine in the settlement.

When their tea and coffee was used up, he showed the Doans how to burn rye and peas to make coffee. And every fourth day or so Carter raised enough strength to hunt for game. The Senecas were now afraid to come near.

The settlement sank daily.

Seth Doan was not sturdy; he was a wiry, enduring boy. He still had his fevers and chills like the others, but each time be recovered more than they. And as the sickness deepened into August, only two men in the settlement could move around between seizures, Carter and Seth Doan, age 13.

Carter showed Seth how to care for the glaze-eyed settlers. For those two, there were no days and nights, only time that turned black every twelve hours. Food and water were the main problems, then medicine.

The nearest real mill at that time was on Walnut Creek in Pennsylvania. Carter could not leave the village alone to go there for meal. Yet his corn was diminishing, and he was getting less and less game because his own legendary strength was waning. Silently and side by side, the man and boy went through the village feeding the people, washing them, bringing water, and tending livestock.

And once a day, when his first seizure was over, Seth Doan took a light sack of corn down to Kingsbury's hand mill and ground it. He could not carry a full sack, nor could he carry the hand mill back downstream to the settlement. And he got so he waited for his second attack to come and go before hurrying back. But sometimes his third attack came when he was on the trail.

Then Lorenzo Carter's strength failed. The only white man moving in the settlement was Seth Doan. Between his own seizures, he continued to care for everyone. Then by exploring every cabin he found food, ammunition, some soap. But moving around in the ghost settlement, he could not find food for the animals, so he finally cut them all loose to forage for themselves. Some strayed off and were lost.

The nights were the worst for the boy. Voices called to him. He was often too exhausted to move to them.

One afternoon he heard a strange language in a voice that would peel bark. He went outside and wandered through the silent settlement, looking.

Behind him there was a light step. He turned and ducked. Looming above him was a hawk-faced Seneca. Seth started to run, but the Indian ran around him and cut him off. Young Doan was too tired to run. The Indian pointed violently to a hide-wrapped bundle placed out in the open. Seth walked to it suspiciously, but he sliced the thongs and opened it. It was corn.

The Indian nodded, and thumbed his chest. "Stigwanish!" Then he fled.

For two months Seth Doan was the only man feeding Cleveland.

In mid-November, four of the settlers recovered enough so there were two or three days between their seizures. These men set out for Walnut Creek to get flour. They intended to return as fast as possible because both the existing corn and the strength of Seth Doan were running down fast.

Seth Doan continued to make the daily trip. But on his way back to the settlement one day, he saw the rangy figure of Major Carter swinging down the trail toward him. When they met, Carter lifted the bag of meal off Seth's shoulders, and walked back north alongside.

He looked down at the boy and nodded. "I hope you'll be choosin' some acreage here, Seth."

When snow fell in 1799, the settlers recovered quickly.

8

New Connecticut

THE MOST DRAMATIC ROLE on the New Connecticut frontier was played by a man whose name is unmarked there today in bronze or brass or marble. But he belongs with the Cuyahoga valley's most select list of giants — James Hillhouse. He should also be credited by Connecticut for that state's present outstanding school systems.

Men learned rather early that nature's apparently haphazard sprawl of plant and rock and fish and animal actually conceals highly precise patterns of life-and-death interdependency. But the New Connecticut planners had not seen that an equally precise economic survival balance evolved in the seeming chaos of haphazard land settlement as practiced elsewhere. The Connecticut planners were going to take the chaos out of it, and spread the settlers evenly over the Reserve, allocating the land with great fairness and neatness of spacing.

Playing God that way, even over only three-million acres, brought disaster, bankruptcy, complete stagnation, and poverty.

During the depths of this despair, a giant strode upon the property. He gazed out at the frontiersmen from placid obsidian eyes sunk in a high-boned, Indian-dark face. In fact, men called him the Sachem, and he looked like a powerful Narraganset.

Lank as a crane, he walked among the New Connecticut settlers in knee buckles and powdered wig. His arrival brought fear, resentment, and personal attacks. Hillhouse was the official collector. He was sent by Connecticut to collect the money due.

How did this happen?

If you drive along both banks of the Cuyahoga and if you

look at a map of the Western Reserve area just astride it, you'll see names of towns and streets and creeks which, in most other regions, would tell a reconstructible story of natural settlement. But since the Western Reserve was settled unnaturally by a precisely plotted and platted system, revolving strangely enough around a lottery type mechanism, the usual rules for reading the land don't apply.

For example, though five distinguished Kelleys came and settled here, and operated extensively in land, not one town is named Kelley. On the other hand, John Young's town bears his name though he came for only a brief stay. Almost every town has a Granger Street, yet Gideon Granger's contribution was highly localized. Not one town or county or street or creek is named Hillhouse, yet James Hillhouse, perhaps more than anyone created the Western Reserve.

Back in Hartford, Connecticut, deeds were made out to the original 35 parties for as many 1/1,200,000ths of the three-million Western Reserve acres as their investment indicated, the whole price being $1,200,000. But specific plots of ground were not assigned.

When the survey was finished and the land assessed, a ticket was made out for each specific section of land, classified as first, second or third class land. The tickets were then separated into those categories, and five separate drawings held over the next five years. A man entitled to a thousand acres, drawing tickets from the three piles, might draw land in three different townships in three different ranges. Nothing prevented him from swapping tickets with someone else to consolidate his holdings, but that was his business.

He might then elect one of the areas as his personal home-site, or he might not go to Ohio at all, merely selling the ground indicated on his tickets. Or he might elect to put the ticket in the hands of a land agent who was going west, like Stow or Kelley.

At any rate, immigrants did not usually come west and look over the ground to see where they would settle. They generally had a ticket in pocket as they sailed or wagoned to the mouth of the Cuyahoga. (A few entered from the south via Pittsburgh.) From there they inquired where to find the stake for the horizontal line to their township. They traveled upstream to that stake, then inland along the survey line until they came to their particular township, then along the township line until they found their section. Townships were five miles on a side, 16,000 acres.

Thus the pioneers of the Western Reserve did not settle in the traditional economic clusters at river mouths and trail crossings. They chose instead to live in geometric patterns — neat and impractical. Settlers chopped holes in the big woods, and put up isolated cabins surrounded on each side by hardwood loneliness.

To the thoughtful men who conceived this plan it promised certain theoretical advantages. It was eminently fair and it so dispersed settlement that the whole area could develop simultaneously rather than concentrating population around attractive land features as under the casual method. It also placed people throughout the area in order to encourage defense against the British and Indians.

Nevertheless these advantages broke up natural economic combinations which make for development. The farmer found himself arbitrarily located near fine deposits of red kidney iron ore, which was to him only a nuisance. The ironmaster, who would normally settle near the ore, drew good farmland that he did not appreciate. Under the casual method of settlement, the ironmaster would seek out the ore. The miller, the fine millsites. The gunsmith or ironwright would locate near the ironmaster, the sailor near the port. But the drawing of lots created an economic incompetence which was about to turn to disaster.

This fact only heightened the heroism and drama as this most competent body of settlers invaded a hostile geography. And ultimately it would bring forward several giants, including James Hillhouse.

Those settlers who came first, though they came in their own self-interest, necessarily broke trail for hundreds over the next three decades. Being Connecticut men, they were accustomed to cleared land already mature and crop-bearing. Despite the description from the surveying party, these immigrants were not prepared for a land completely forested with no break in the cover except at waterbodies, and no axle-width gap in the undergrowth. The trees held a piece of night all day.

John Young and a surveyor named Wolcott fought their way up the Mahoning from Fort Pitt to survey the section Young had drawn in the southeast corner of the Reserve.

Now we've met Nathaniel Doan, one of the few surveyors to come back as a settler. Recovered from the ague, he did establish a blacksmith shop on Superior Street in Cleveland in 1798, according to his land contract. On the frontier, this blacksmith shop became the hub of engineering at a time when the main progress was engineering. Doan helped with the myriad mechanical necessities of a frontier, and for a long time, he was the only resource for shoeing the pack horses of surveyors who now came to subdivide the small parcels held by individual stockholders in the Connecticut Land Company. A settlement grew up around his shop where Newburgh Road crossed Euclid Road. It became known as Doan's Corners, though Doan himself moved four miles inland toward Euclid to escape the miasma from the river. Still he died young, in 1815.

Turhand Kirtland, whose money had been invested in the Connecticut Land Company through Caleb Atwater, drew his land scattered all over Kirtland, Burton, Auburn, Mecca, and Poland, Ohio. He set out from Wallingford, Connecticut, in 1798 to find his lands and to survey them into subparcels.

In addition to his personal land, Kirtland was an agent for the Connecticut Land Company. Part of his mission was to get Major Carter and Major Spafford to pay $25 for their town lots in Cleaveland. But by then, these two men had contributed so much to the area, and they had seen others awarded free lots for lesser but more specific services, and they expected generosity from the company. They requested a price of ten dollars per lot, refused to pay $25, saying they would move off the lots.

119

Kirtland wrote a letter back to the company recommending the company sell to these two heroes at ten dollars, "otherwise I shall never expect to see the land settled. Mr. Carter has been of essential advantage to the inhabitants here, in helping them to provision in times of danger and scarcity, has never experienced any gratuity from the company, but complains of being hardly dealt by, in sundry instances."

He went on to say Carter and Spafford both threatened to leave unless they could buy their land cheaper.

En route to his own lands, Kirtland's handful of cattle kept straying away. The difficulty of trying to reach his lands, survey them, and keep the animals fed and assembled was enormous, yet not enough to discourage him nor keep him from recording in his diary. In doing so, he became a major contributor to hundreds who followed, because Kirtland hacked the road into Chardon's forest-covered canyons.

In the following year, Benjamin Tappan, Jr., left Connecticut to see to his father's lands in Ravenna. He entered by way of the Cuyahoga's mouth, boated his goods upstream to Boston, and began chopping a road along the survey lines into what would become Ravenna.

He went back to Boston on the Cuyahoga to sledge his stores into Ravenna, but he lost one ox, felled by clusters of enormous flies. A man stuck in the forest tied to a mountain of goods he can neither move nor live without is in trouble. Tappan had spent all his money but a dollar on the trek west. He sent back to Erie, Pennsylvania, for a loan of money while he walked across to John Young's town to find an ox for sale. It is not clear who he sent, nor how he negotiated without money. Work cattle were scarce, but he was able to locate an animal through James Hillhouse. With the persuasive affability which would make him an important western legislator, he struck a good price.

Previously, Tappan had overtaken and come part way with another Connecticut immigrant, David Hudson of Goshen, Connecticut, en route to his Western Reserve lands, Township 4, Range 10.

Together they overtook Elias Harmon and wife who were heading for what would become Mantua. Harmon's boat broached and smashed in Lake Erie off Ashtabula. He went on cross-country. Hudson bought and repaired the boat, shipped into Cleaveland, and sailed upstream. The water was low, requiring the boat to be towed across sand bars. The survey line leading to Hudson's Township 4, Range 10, couldn't be found for six days.

Hudson was a humorless, physically powerful, and pious man with a delicate responsibility to man and a poetic feel for the land. He was a direct descendant of Hendrick Hudson of the Hudson River, whose youngest son was David. In direct descent then, came six David Hudsons to this one who founded the town on Range 10 in New Connecticut. His first night on his own ground, he lay out in the open in the rain enjoying the sensation.

Hudson's two yoke of oxen were following in the care of Mr. Meachem, who brought them due south from Lake Erie on a range line over precipitous ravines, crossing two rivers by raft. Therefore, Hudson first turned his 12 men to the job of opening an axe-width road in from the Cuyahoga. Over this road, all future settlers to the area freighted their possessions.

Hudson and his men put up a log house and cleared land for winter wheat. In the fall, he left the men there while he went back to Connecticut for his family and more settlers. When, for the second time, he reached Township 4, Range 10, now called Hudson, he assembled both groups for a Thanksgiving service in midwinter.

Of all the towns in Ohio, Hudson probably most stands for the essence of the Connecticut Western Reserve. It reproduced Connecticut so faithfully that even today you would believe yourself to be driving through a Connecticut town.

David Hudson attracted a very high caliber of settler, and the town became the birthplace of two famous Ohio colleges. Western Reserve College in Hudson was modeled in 1826 on Connecticut's Yale, and staffed by Yale professors. The college held high standards, but it was in constant economic battle. In

1882, Amassa Stone of Cleveland offered the college $500,000 if it would remove to Cleveland. Its classical department was then named Adelbert College in memory of Stone's lost son.

The vacated buildings at Hudson were occupied by a new institution, Western Reserve Academy, today one of the nation's fine preparatory schools for boys.

Under Hudson's leadership a town grew rapidly and solidly. As you'd expect of David Hudson, religious services began immediately, but a formal church — Congregational — rose in 1802, and in the same year, a log schoolhouse. By 1807, there was a tannery, run by Owen Brown, the father of the famous John Brown.

David Hudson's daughter, Anna, was the first white child born in Summit County. The first to die in the settlement (1808) was the mother of John Brown.

The New Connecticut settlement which gained the fastest start by far was Warren; it was not originally settled by Connecticut Land Company men. Two men living in Washington County, Pennsylvania, Captain Ephraim Quinby and Richard Storer, had heard about New Connecticut and in 1798 decided to go over and have a look with a view to purchasing land. They were perhaps the most scientific of the early purchasers, except for Moses Warren who snapped up the salt lands near there.

Captain Quinby selected land in relation to himself rather than fitting himself to a square drawn out of a hat. He selected Township 6, Range 10, and bought substantially, becoming the real founder of Warren. Within a year, he had 16 white settlers in, and by 1801 the town of Warren was the biggest and most prosperous in New Connecticut. It became county seat of an enormous Trumbull County.

Gideon Granger who had gone together with Oliver Phelps, investing $80,000 in the land company (this is separate from Phelps's $168,000), drew his acreage 16 miles southwest of Cleveland. It was called Berea. Berea has little contact with the Cuyahoga, but we will see Gideon Granger become important to the Cuyahoga valley in offsetting the stilted placement of people in arbitrary squares of land.

Nearly every town in the valley has a Granger Street. General Granger was the Reserve's grapevine. Gaining a government mail contract, he rode from town to town, and being an enlightened and highly intelligent man he spread important news among the people: what trails wide enough for a wagon had been cut into what areas; where mills were being built to grind flour; who could shoe a horse or braze a drawbar chain; where there was a man who could make bricks.

Granger, no ordinary mail rider, later became U.S. Postmaster General.

Important among the town builders along the Cuyahoga was Joshua Stow of Middletown, Connecticut, a $6,000 investor in the Connecticut Land Company. He had come out with General Cleaveland's surveying party in charge of commissary. He was a tough 34-year-old outdoorsman who often moved in advance of the surveying party hunting for game to preserve their regular rations. The Cuyahoga valley was rattlesnake country, and Josh Stow became expert at finding and killing snakes. To carry them, he would wrap them around his waist, six or eight per trip. In camp, he would clean, cook, and serve them.

After the survey, Stow drew 5,000 acres north of Akron, and he came back to Ohio to oversee the surveying of his acreage for resale. Establishing the town of Stow, he then went into real estate operations in the eastern part of the Reserve. Many thousands of property deeds in the Reserve today go back to an original land title signed by Stow in partnership with one of the Kelley brothers.

But beyond Stow's individual pioneering in the Reserve, his influence becomes enormous in another way. It was Stow who brought the fabulous Kelley brothers who stayed to mold New Connecticut by selling land, establishing towns, moving rivers, building canals, laying railroads, making laws, and developing islands.

In Middletown, Connecticut, Josh Stow's sister, Jemina, married Daniel Kelley. Her sons grew up hearing about their dramatic uncle Stow at work out in New Connecticut. It became a place of high adventure, and these boys were adventurers, Datus, Alfred, Irad, Joseph, and Thomas. But they come later when the troubles worsened.

Meanwhile, the lot-drawing system of land ownership continued to cut isolated, helpless clearings in the three-million acres of virgin oak, beech, maple, chestnut, and walnut.

Judge Austin pushed in to the northeast corner with a small party to start Austinburg. He brought 150 cattle, the first real herd on the Reserve.

Lewis Day and his boy came out of Granby, Connecticut, with two others in a wagon, and pushed 25 miles west of Youngstown in 1799. That brought the first wagon-width trail to Deerfield. Caleb Atwater then cut a township road *into* Deerfield *from* the west, hence that area had good communications.

Very few ventured west of the Cuyahoga, though a dozen from Waterbury, Connecticut, pushed across into Ridgeville, Amherst, and Eaton. David Abbott purchased 1,800 acres astride the Huron River and settled there in 1809. Vermilion was occupied in 1808.

Jemina Kelley and her husband were much less than enchanted with Josh Stow. But the magic had happened, and one by one their sons went west. Alfred Kelley, the most distinguished, rode west beside Joshua Stow at age 21 with lawbooks in hand. Arriving in Cleveland in June 1810, he was almost immediately made County Prosecutor. In 1811, Datus Kelley arrived in Cleveland. In 1812, young Irad Kelley bought his way out of a militia assignment and came to join his brothers.

The sheer capability of the Kelley brothers drafted them into many frontier jobs of public service, and their own imaginative initiative got them into a dozen commercial activities. Irad Kelley, fresh out of the militia, enlisted in the service of Samuel Huntington, former Ohio governor and now paymaster of the Northwestern Army under General William Henry Harrison. One of his first assignments was to ride west with Harrison to Fort Meigs on a supply mission. There, the gallant young Major George Crogan sent Irad Kelley back to Cleveland to purchase $1,000 worth of materiel.

To find the goods, young Kelley went into Carter's warehouse and to every resource at the mouth of the Cuyahoga. He still came up short on the supplies. What it showed Irad Kelley was that the place needed a real merchant. Irad again got loose from the army. He headed back to New York State where he bought a wagonload of trade goods. In the winter, he freighted it west and stowed it in Carter's warehouse while he and his brothers started construction of a store, made of brick, at Superior and Sixth.

Meanwhile Irad Kelley was sailing Lake Erie, hauling powder and arms into frontier outposts. He made another trip to New York City for trade goods, and on the return picked up his mother and father and brought them west under strong protests from Jemina.

Cleveland was incorporated in 1815 and held elections. Alfred Kelley was elected president of Cleveland Village.

In 1816 the Kelley brothers commercial pier was built at the mouth of the Cuyahoga by the brothers and Alfred opened the Commercial Bank of Lake Erie; Alfred Kelley, president, Leonard Case, cashier.

In 1817, the father succeeded the son as president of the village, Irad Kelley became postmaster and Alfred became the youngest state legislator in Ohio. And about this time, Datus had his eye on Island Number Six in the Firelands Survey — about to become Kelley's Island from which would soon come a steady tonnage of limestone for building Ohio.

As the years passed, the Cuyahoga River polity required enormous public service of the extremely competent Kelley brothers and the Cuyahoga River commercial complex blossomed under their long-sighted shrewdness and daring. Their public services were delivered for salaries increasingly beneath their notice and their worth. And even as they grew wealthy from their commercial activities, their projects all had a basic worth to the valley far beyond what they took out of it.

Alfred Kelley was almost singly responsible for lifting the state out of financial crisis in the 1820s at a salary of three dollars a day; and later, in the panic of 1837, his financial acumen and reputation kept the state from repudiating its debts; and he organized the state banking system to stabilize currency and credit.

Where these activities border the river, we'll see them in other chapters of this volume. But beyond the large works they wrought, they also gave rise to the Kelley Legends.

A favorite is the irascibility of Irad Kelley as he grew older. By 1860, he was still a healthy and vigorous old man, and he could be counted on to be a very effective and eccentric minority opposition to every question, public or private.

Sitting on the jury in a certain trial, he kept the jury out two days, refusing to agree with the 11 others. Afterwards he was chided about his stubbornness. "Oh, I agreed immediately," Irad said. "It was those other 'leven fellows that were stubborn as mules."

At another time his family became worried, in view of his eccentricities, about how he would distribute his very considerable estate. At an advanced age, he was about to enter into a negotiation that his family, especially his son, thought imprudent.

They took the old man to court asking that Irad be judged insane. At the trial the judge asked the old man who would represent him in court. Irad Kelley wrapped a hand around the back of his neck and pulled it off slowly, "Well," he said, "guess I'll be my own lawyer."

On the witness stand, the son testified to many examples of his father's eccentric behavior. When he finished, the old man walked over to cross-examine his own son.

"Whose son are you?"

"Yours, sir."

"How much did I give you when you were twenty-one, fourteen years ago?"

"Ten thousand dollars."

"How much of it have you now?" the father asked.

"Not much, sir."

"Have you any of it at all?"

"No."

"How much was I worth when I gave you that money?"

"You were supposed to be worth about one hundred thousand."

"How much am I now supposed to be worth?"

"Three hundred thousand."

At this point, Irad Kelley addressed the bench. "May it please your honor, I have no further questions of this witness, and no further witnesses to call.

"The evidence seems to warrant the belief that there is insanity in the Kelley family, either father or son. I leave it to you, Judge, to determine which."

In 1809, a tall, commanding young man rode into Cleveland with a dollar in his pocket and a set of tools in his saddlebag. His name was Levi Johnson. He sold the horse, used the capital to start the area's first contract construction business.

In 1810, he built for John Walworth, the postmaster, a frame house on the Cuyahoga. In 1811 he built Buckeye House; in 1812 he built a log structure for the first courthouse and jail.

In 1813 he built a vessel, *The Pilot*; in '17 the schooner *Neptune*; in '24 *The Enterprise*, first steam vessel built in Cleveland.

In 1830, he built the lighthouse for $8,000; and then he put in the government pier at the mouth of the Cuyahoga, 900 feet long, built of stone.

He built the skyline of Cleveland until 1871 when he died, leaving $1,000,000.

Attorney Samuel Huntington, short, dapper, and courtly, had ridden out of Coventry, Connecticut, into the Ohio Country. He rode over the whole state then settled at the mouth of the Cuyahoga. The frontier didn't have work for such a sophisticated lawyer that early. So Huntington enjoyed himself and made himself agreeable for many months. Then suddenly the frontier problems grew up to his size, and they elected him justice of quorum on the County Court of Quarter Sessions and to the state constitutional convention in 1802, and senator from Trumbull County. In 1802, he became president of the legislature and judge of the Ohio Supreme Court. In 1807 he became governor. He moved to Painesville and retired to his farm.

Luther King, Martin Sheldon and Fidelia King of Suffield, Connecticut, were wholesale merchants in indigo, feathers, and fur. They came out to Township 5, Range 9, and opened up Aurora.

After the Indian title was extinguished, Seth Pease, brother-in-law of Gideon Granger and brother of Calvin Pease of Warren, was brought back in 1806 to survey the rest of the Reserve west of the Cuyahoga, but settlement wouldn't move readily across the river.

With people thus spread evenly across the Reserve in small isolated clusters, there were not enough people in any one place really to improve the area nor to build any major commercial enterprise, nor was there any substantial market for produce. Hence there was no way to accumulate working capital.

New Connecticut then was the anomalous spectacle of a superior population rapidly heading for financial disaster. The stockholders in the Connecticut Land Company were naturally men of great accomplishment and stature back in Connecticut. But out in New Connecticut, they were living like animals. Poverty and an absolute absence of cash was the climate. Withal, the people were working themselves to the bone for survival.

Despite the misery, New England character showed through in the uphill struggle. Young Joshua R. Giddings of Jefferson was walking 40 miles through the woods to Canfield to read law under the distinguished and impoverished Elisha Whittlesey, who would later become the great lawyer-statesman who founded the national Whig party, and became first comptroller of the U.S. Treasury.

Young Giddings studied hard and well, and would return to Jefferson to join in a two-man office with the future Senator Ben Wade, both of them to become giants in the U.S. Senate.

But meanwhile, distinguished Connecticut men walked barefoot in the Reserve. Some wore a semi-leathern apron ending in half leggings, covering the front of the legs and lashed behind with leather thongs. Sheep were scarce, so women were forced to try to make cloth of poor substitutes for wool.

And this was the low estate of what began as a business venture. The poverty in the Reserve in no way released the settlers from their obligations. The Connecticut Land Company was committed to complete its payments to the State of Connecticut. They now also owed taxes on the unsold lands to the State of Ohio. To pay these commitments, they had nothing. The members of the Excess Company had lost all their money. The Land Company treasury received no money from the six townships it reserved for itself to furnish operating income. And the town lots in Cleveland that it had reserved to itself would not sell.

The Land Company stockholders who had sold land to other settlers on credit and mortgages could not collect. Meanwhile, the State of Connecticut was ready to start the school system which was the object of its sale of the Reserve to Connecticut Land Company:

... the principal sum which shall be received from the sale of the lands belonging to this State, laying west of Pennsylvania shall be and remain a perpetual fund ... and the interest arising therefrom shall be, and is hereby appropriated to the support of schools ... within this State.

The Connecticut Land Company had made a down payment, but quickly fell into arrears. In the first 13 years, only half the commitment was paid. Interest due on the balance had, by 1809, risen nearly to equal the balance of principal. Since the settlers of the land were without funds, the Connecticut legislature could see that, though it put hundreds of people in jail, it would still not realize any cash. In a desperate move, they relieved the fund board of managers and sought out one man to try to save this fast disintegrating venture.

A mysterious Connecticut giant at the time was James Hillhouse of New Haven. An intimidating intelligence smoldered from dark eyes in that craggy Indian-like face, which calmly recognized no opponent as superior. As a young captain, he had marched out of New Haven commanding 30 young men to meet the British invasion on July 5, 1779.

A Yale graduate and a lawyer, he had a good grasp of economics. Yale made him its treasurer in 1782. At 26, Connecticut sent him to the Second Congress, then re-elected him to the Third and Fourth.

From 1797 through 1803, he was re-elected three times to the Senate, and he undertook the personal mission of limiting the powers of Presidents Washington, Adams, Jefferson, and Madison.

When he returned from the capital to Connecticut in May 1810, the state asked him to accept the job of Commissioner of the School Fund, the first requirement being to get the money. He resigned the Senate to take on the job.

When word of his acceptance reached the stockholders of the Connecticut Land Company both in Connecticut and on the Reserve, alarm spread.

It would be logical for Hillhouse to begin to jail debtors to see if the threat would spur them to uncover assets which he could seize for the School Fund, or to try to frighten the debtors into borrowing to pay their debts to the State of Connecticut. People felt this was exactly how he would proceed.

James Hillhouse began by studying every debtor. What he found was a hopeless roster of poverty and bankruptcy caused by the Land Company, sometimes wiping out two generations of the same family where stock in the Land Company had been passed on by inheritance, along with its backbreaking obligations.

It was difficult to locate or even trace many of the people, but Hillhouse was relentlessly persistent and thorough. He found there wasn't enough seizable property among all the debtors to begin to matter.

Then he recognized what his real job was, and it is perhaps unique in all history. James Hillhouse could see that what he had to do was force all the debtors involved to make money. His real job was to make them prosperous, or at least solvent.

First Hillhouse called on the debtors still living in Connecticut. In addition to what he had been able to learn of their financial situation, he now probed for more facts. When the whole story was finally in front of him, he applied his financial acumen to each individual case. He became a personal business counselor to each debtor family. He told them what to sell, what to retain, in many cases how to run their own businesses, to get the money to pay their debts to the State of Connecticut.

In many cases the original stockholder was now dead and Hillhouse was dealing with heirs. Such was the case as he approached the tangled financial affairs of the heirs of Oliver Phelps. Oliver Phelps we've already seen was the imaginative high-flying land developer who was the largest investor in the Land Company — $186,185, not including some he had invested in concert with Gideon Granger.

Phelps was spread very thin, because beyond this development he had other large ones in work. Receiving no substantial returns on his Connecticut Western Reserve investment, Phelps could not pay his debts. His creditors swept in on him. And when he could not sell off his Western Reserve lands fast enough to get cash, they put him in jail.

He died there. His family was impoverished, and his complex legacy of debt was so involved that it seemed impossible to straighten it out.

But James Hillhouse now headed west to see the Phelps properties on the Reserve with his own eyes. He traveled alone.

Arriving on the Reserve, he was initially a cause of alarm and some malice. He had a singleness of conduct, which was the same on an Ohio Survey line as on the Senate floor. And he steadily went about the business of viewing each Phelps property, slowly and relentlessly untangling the snarl.

Finally the only debt remaining was to the State of Connecticut. Having seen the lands and what they could be used for, he was able now to return to Connecticut and sell them to logical buyers. From these monies, he was able to pay the debt to Connecticut from the Phelps estate, and with money left over for the Phelps family.

The family was overjoyed, and they generously agreed to let Hillhouse compute the Phelps debt to Connecticut with compound interest so that his payment to Connecticut was actually $14,500 higher than required. The family was so grateful for the service Hillhouse rendered them that they gave him $6,000. Without demurring, Hillhouse solemnly accepted the money, and put it into the School Fund.

Moving then to the debtor who was the next best potential, Hillhouse kept steadily at it. Each year, he hitched up the mare and went to the Reserve to see the actual piece of land involved in the debt, and to coach the debtor on how best to handle his affairs. For 15 years he labored at this work. The stockholders of the Connecticut Land Company had now multiplied to 500 as stock was subdivided, largely through inheritance. Hillhouse had not only recovered all monies owing to Connecticut, but a half million besides. He never once resorted to litigation.

Hillhouse brought solvency to the Cuyahoga valley and the entire Western Reserve by 1825. In that year another towering individual would almost single-handedly move the valley forward into actual prosperity.

There is no marker on the Western Reserve as memorial to Hillhouse.

9

The Red Men

STIGWANISH (or Stigwamish) walked into Carter's Tavern, paused at the door for his eyes to accustom to the gloom, and looked for Major Carter.

Carter, on his account, looked up to see what caused the lull in the tavern voices. Then he smiled. Stigwanish, the Seneca, was a more commanding presence than Judge Samuel Huntington, who worked at it.

A seaman off Captain Thong's boat, in a binge of sentimentality because of the big announcement, walked over and offered the Indian a mug. The Indian shook his head preoccupied, and moved toward the bench where Major Carter talked to Captain Thong. The affronted sailor called to others to witness the Indian's misprizing his generosity. But the locals knew that Stigwanish had greater responsibility than the sailor, and that he had not tasted liquor since he had killed his own child in drink.

Stigwanish did not wait for a pause in the major's conversation, nor allow himself to enjoy Thong's surprise at his excellent English.

He merely announced to the major that he was going to go British.

"No, Seneca!"

Carter could not leave Captain Thong at the moment; but he knew that if Stigwanish went British, so would all the Senecas, Ottawas, Chippewas, and probably the Delawares along the river.

Stigwanish turned to leave.

"Wait for me, Seneca!"
But he did not.

On the 28th of June 1812, a man who had a hut along the Cuyahoga had to decide what nationality he was. And it was often difficult.

Survival by Englishmen, Frenchmen, Indians, and colonists on the Cuyahoga frontier had not been a matter of nationality. It depended rather on hunting, trapping, growing corn, and procuring ammunition.

But when the rider arrived from Washington to announce the Republic had declared war on the King of England, the scattered handfuls of settlers along the Cuyahoga stared at each other and helped each other decide what they were — British or American.

Major Carter in his log tavern at the mouth of the Cuyahoga was having trouble enough getting settlers to stay here. And he couldn't bear to let anyone leave. He poured another jolt of Monongahela for Captain Thong, master of a Canadian vessel, then told the captain he could not let him sail out ... it would aid the enemy.

Thong drank the drink and realized the major had spent time in Canada previously, and suggested Carter come to Canada with him.

Carter declined, pointing out that he was in command of the militia in Cleveland.

Thong poured one for Carter and guessed that he was expected to pull hook and clear harbor today.

Carter said no, he did not think he could let Thong leave legally. Carter countered that since Thong called on three American ports and only one British, that made him American.

Thong asked if he could use Carter's warehouse. Carter said he was happy to have the business and asked if the skipper could haul some ammunition in from Erie.

When Carter went to his warehouse to clear space, Stigwanish was waiting there, as Carter had hoped. While Carter's code was direct and decisions were simple to him, for Stigwanish the decision was complex, because he was a complex man, with a complex constituency. The white men called him Seneca because he was acknowledged head of the Senecas and one of the finest leaders on the Cuyahoga. Some members of the fragmented Ottawas and Chippewas also acknowledged his leadership. He moved up and down the river, but he had a hut on the west bank near the mouth.

Between the major and Seneca was something quite beyond their official relationship. Each lonely, each unrelaxed in toughness, Seneca and the major paid each other the compliment of insulting candor. Carter told Stigwanish he thought he had more sense than to let his men persuade him to go British. Carter told Indian he should talk more wisdom into his men.

The Seneca replied that he could if the major's actions matched his word.

Carter disliked an argument with Seneca. Only Judge Huntington could win a debate with the chief. But it sounded as though Seneca was still open-minded. Carter knew that Seneca still wanted retribution for the profane hanging of the young Indian, John O'mic, by white men. So he proposed, "Ho ma yen de zin, O'mic." Carter always addressed Seneca in his own language. It was part of what was between them.

Seneca addressed the major in English better than the major's command of the Seneca language. "Perhaps, Major. But how could you fix that? O'mic is dead. I told all the Senecas and Ottawas Major Carter promised to bring Darrow and Williams to trial. Now they ask when."

Carter did not look away, but he smarted inside. He told Seneca not to go British and throw away the protection the Indians had earned under the American flag. "Protection?" Seneca smiled. "Remember the Moravian Indians?"

Carter walked to the edge of the Cuyahoga and stared into it. Suddenly he snapped erect and pointed at Seneca, "But remember the Eries? The British did that! And now you want to join them? They'll leave you nothing. He genno latreta!"

Seneca also stared into the river. The surface was turgid, but beneath it a strong undercurrent pulled.

And between the major and the tall Seneca flowed an angry undercurrent of history that began with the Eries and ended with the hanging of John O'mic.

Both men knew that the Cuyahoga valley was an Indian story, but a sad one. After the annihilation of the Cat Nation of Eries by the Five Nations, the conquerors occupied the Cuyahoga country under no pronounced geographic pattern. Small groups of the conquering tribes settled haggle-straggle up and down the valley. Small bands from other tribes westerning through found this river good and stopped to camp, then stayed. After the Eries' last stand, the Indians of the Cuyahoga were migratory. One week you'd find certain clans up at the mouth, another week, down at the head of the Tuscarawas.

They were mostly Ottawas and Senecas with quite a few Delawares and Mingoes, and a straggle of Oneidas, Cayugas, Massanges, Shawnees, and Chippewas. This cosmopolitan population was partly assembled by the fact that within the big U of the Cuyahoga, three great Indian trails crossed. One was the Central Trail (these were white men's names) from Old Portage to Fort McIntosh by the way of Big Falls to Fish Creek, where the trail divided and went up the Cuyahoga to the source and down it to the mouth. Second was the Fort McIntosh, Muskingum, and Sandusky War Trail. The third was the northern trail along the lake shore from Buffalo to Detroit (U.S. 20).

Despite the proximity of villages, the Indians got along quite peacefully. One reason was the stature and wisdom of the Ottawa and Seneca chiefs. Mingoes and Delawares also built very close.

These scattered villages would often be as small as three to six huts. Others would be 50 or 100. Every sizable tributary had a village at the confluences. And they were peaceful, despite constant Indian nervousness about the white settlers from Connecticut.

But there were many white settlers who knew how to get along with Indians. Lydia Wetmore of Cuyahoga Falls was not the nervous type, and she understood how lucky the settlers were to have Senecas, Ottawas, and Delawares as neighbors. She understood, too, that diplomacy was required.

But she would have owned to a touch of real concern when spring burned through in the year the youngest of her three boys turned 12 and her eldest 16. As she scrubbed their work trousers, she watched out her real glass window at Silver Lake.

The three Seneca girls bathing in Silver Lake were handsome and lively. The sun glinting off their coppery limbs painted the beautiful kind of picture which would haunt any young man's nights. And the trousers Lydia was scrubbing were definitely long pants now.

A boy was a man at 16 out here, if he was going to be one. But Lydia and her husband, William, cofounders of Cuyahoga Falls, felt that serious trouble could break out if settlers' sons coveted Indian daughters in this girl-scarce land.

Three times this spring the Seneca girls had bathed here, splashing and laughing with the light-footed joy of emerging from winter boots. Lydia watched them dry off in the sun, and with a woman's heat lightning awareness, she linked it to the sudden cessation of ax blows from up on the rise where the boys were clearing. The Indian girls dressed, but their short, open-sided summer manteaux were far from Connecticut fashions. She saw that they were headed now not back to their village, but up to her own house to visit, as they often did.

Lydia Wetmore was a woman of understanding. For white settlers to tell Indians to wear Connecticut dress would be clumsy. And Silver Lake, she felt, belonged more to the Indians than to her. Suddenly she reached down a bolt of blue-dyed sacking, scissored off seven feet, folded it, cut an interesting neckline at the fold, and sat down with needle and thread, composing herself as one not in a hurry.

"Come in," she called casually to the knock.

Lydia Wetmore was a favorite with Seneca girls. They smiled with pleasure at sight of the crisp clean sacking. They crowded close, inquiring with soft Seneca exclamations. Lydia Wetmore smiled around a mouthful of pins and nodded them to be patient.

Intently they watched her work, and they argued pleasantly in Seneca about what she was making. She kept them in suspense, until she finally unfurled it with a flourish. Then it all came clear. Lydia nodded to the tallest girl who gasped and snatched the cloth. She put it on right over everything else, and looked down at herself with pleasure. But the short girl laughed and spread her arms wide, "H-a-a!"

Mrs. Wetmore laughed, too. She cut off a narrow band from the bolt, wrapped it around the tall girl's waist and tied a bow.

The short girl folded her arms and cocked her head, "Ah-h!"

And she stared involuntarily at the bolt of cloth. Mrs. Wetmore unrolled the bolt and handed her the scissors. Then she threaded three iron needles.

The Seneca girls ran across the trail to their Silver Lake village. They had not been gone long when their smiling mothers suddenly appeared at Mrs. Wetmore's door. One held out a blue sacking waist sash and nodded with aggressive geniality.

Inside the hut, Mrs. Wetmore held up the diminished bolt against the nodding mother. There was a problem of girth. But she told them to get hides and pelts and come to meet her at the trader's cabin. A negotiation was made for yard goods.

After that, the Seneca women met in increasing numbers every Sabbath in the Wetmore cabin. She taught them how to keep the stitches very small. They kept coming.

There were a few other whites, men like Major Carter and Kingsbury, who understood the tenderness of the Indian's pride and took pains to protect it. But the sad part of the Indian story on the Cuyahoga was that while the Indians had arrived at a resigned, peaceful attitude toward living with the white encroachment, the white population still contained a few of the old style Indian killers like Simon Girty, Captain Brady, Captain Delawn Mills of Portage County, Jonathan Williams of Deerfield.

How were the other Indian settlements located along the Cuyahoga? The remnants of southern Ohio nations were withdrawing north. So we find pockets of tribes here and there along the Cuyahoga. Old Cuyahoga Town, north of Akron was a sizable village. Big Falls had two villages as did Silver Lake at Cuyahoga Falls. There were believed to be a thousand Indians in these two villages.

On Turkeyfoot Lake, Chief Wam-te-kek had a Delaware village. Captain Pipe, King of New Portage, had a village in Coventry where Louis Young's famous roadhouse was. At Apple Orchard in Medina County, Chief Beaver Hat had a village of Chippewas on Chippewa Lake.

On the upper Cuyahoga, near Streetsboro, Chief Big Son, brother of Stigwanish, had a village of Senecas before he moved. Prominent in its leadership were his two sons John Hanur and John Mohawk and his three sons-in-law, George Wilson, Nickshaw, and Wabmong.

Traces of many villages have been found along the Indian trail which ran across the northern border of Windham township in Portage County to the Seneca village near Streetsboro on the Cuyahoga.

Bath had a Mingo village which considered Logan its chief.

A half mile north of Boston on the west bank was a village called Ponty's Camp. These were Ottawas who looked to Pontiac and Ogontz. These Indians in Boston were believed to be fairly good farmers. Mature apple trees were found here by the first white settlers. The valley had some little-known, but sophisticated English-speaking chiefs. Net-a-wat-wees of the Delawares was a chief of high stature here and was included in every major treaty meeting. Ogontz of the Ottawas was a plain chief, but a man of great responsibility. He was educated by the French in Canada and became a prominent churchman.

Polemic Hopacan, better known as Captain Pipe, was less educated. Tough, wily, predatory, he was important to the Indian communities in making gentlemen of some whites.

The valley tends to overclaim the two great chiefs, Pontiac and Logan. They spent little time on the Cuyahoga, but they did leave faint marks on it.

Pontiac, tiger of the Northwest, spent much time in early manhood at Ponty's Camp on the Cuyahoga. On Lewis Evans's map of middle British colonies, it is called "Tawas."

Pontiac later became chief of vengeance for his race and was little seen on the Cuyahoga. But his son, Blackbird, the Ottawa chief, was educated with money paid by Mr. Bissel of Twinsburg, Ohio, and was seen a lot in the villages on the Cuyahoga before he became busy as Indian diplomat, scholar, and author.

Blackhawk, born prior to 1772, was reared on the Cuyahoga, but moved to larger Indian affairs in the west. Captured at the end of the Black Hawk War, he was being brought to Washington through Cleveland. There he asked permission to visit his mother's grave on the Cuyahoga, which was granted.

Mingotown on the Cuyahoga considered Logan its chief, though he was seldom there. He was an Indian of national importance and one of the best Indian friends of the white man, up until Colonel Cresap murdered all Logan's relatives. When Logan turned on the white man, he started the second bloodiest war in the Ohio country. And when it ended, Logan made his famous speech under the Logan Elm which shamed Lord Dunmore's staff and nearly every thoughtful white man who has ever read it.

Wabmong is the object of some funny stories by casual historians who have him cavorting around like a chicken thief, unaware that he was heading 500 Senecas, and personally prevented the massacre of the white population of Stow Township at the outset of the War of 1812, when the Indians in the Cuyahoga valley had to decide between the Americans and the British.

Wabmong's village of Senecas was just south of Silver Lake. Like Stigwamish, this chief had complex loyalites and elected to move his Indians under the British flag. But his people had been bribed by the British to wipe out the village of Stow upon departure. Wabmong learned of it and advanced the removal date by a surprise announcement. He moved them out in a single night.

In the evening gloom beside the mouth of the Cuyahoga, Carter and Seneca discussed these things. Seneca expressed concern about Moravians still wandering from river to river in search of ground they could keep. More importantly ... Seneca needed and sought Carter's word that Williams and Darrow would be brought to trial.

The failure to bring two white men to trial would prove to be crucial in Seneca's thinking. In 1807 a David Diver in Canfield was shot by an Indian. Two men from Canfield, Darrow and Williams, set out to track down the murderer.

In midwinter, an Indian, close friend to Seneca, was shot. His name was Nickshaw or Nicksau, and he was rather well known along the Cuyahoga, being impressive in appearance.

The Indians suspected Darrow and Williams of killing Nickshaw in the belief that he had murdered David Diver. Darrow and Williams claimed self-defense. Meanwhile it became strongly possible that the man who killed Diver was an Indian named John Mohawk. Seneca presented his conclusion to Major Carter — Darrow and Williams were murderers and the killing of Nickshaw was a not needed murder.

Carter knew Darrow and Williams were claiming self-defense but Seneca did not believe them and told Carter he too would be convinced if he would accompany Seneca to bury Nickshaw.

Carter and Seneca went up onto the escarpment together. Nickshaw lay in the snow. The wound was in the back of his head. He had fallen face down. There were no scuffle marks in the snow, and no new snow on top of Nickshaw.

Carter conceded. There was no fight. No self-defense.

General Elijah Wadsworth of Canfield wrote to Judge Samuel Huntington at the mouth of the Cuyahoga:

Dear Sir: Since I last wrote you, we have information from your quarter that Nickshaw was killed instead of John Mohawk. If this be true, and as Mohawk was the one shot Mr. Diver, ought not Mohawk be demanded of their chief, Ogontz, and delivered up for trial?

Your serv't
Elijah Wadsworth

To General Wadsworth, Canfield:
Dear Sir:

As the deceased was not one of Ogontz's nation, he said he would not like to lead in obtaining redress, but would be satisfied with whatever Seneca agreed to.

Seneca said he wanted the same measure of justice dealt out to Indians as white men. He said he was not content to see all the exertions of our civil authority used against those who had shot the white man while we were asleep as to the murder of an innocent Indian. He concluded by saying that he would be satisfied if both the Indian and white aggressors could have a fair and equal trial. And only then.

I gave him assurances that the law would be put in force equally against both, and persuaded him to remain peaceful until court should meet at Warren. My expectation was, and still is, that the Court of Common Pleas would issue a bench warrant for the apprehension of Darrow and Williams.

But it is said that the magistrates of Hudson have been deterred by threats from securing the offenders. I hope for the honor of the country that the majority of the people there do not countenance such atrocities, and that some of the civil authorities will have firmness enough to put the law in force.

But Mr. Allen Gaylord told me that the first man to arrest Darrow or Williams will be shot, and the constables do not dare issue a warrant against them, and that if Seneca wants war they were ready for it.

Major Carter agrees with me that the best way to give the Indians satisfaction in this is to do them justice.

On the same day I saw Seneca again, who said he had been threatened by some Hudson (Ohio) people. But he told me he did not wish to start war, and would deliver over John Mohawk for trial voluntarily, but only when Darrow and Williams were secured for trial.

He and Major Carter agree. They went up to the place where Nickshaw was killed and buried him. There was no appearance on the snow of a fight or scuffle and no club near. Nickshaw appears to have been shot in the back as he was running, and fell dead in his tracks.

Seneca observed, "The Indians might lie, and the white men might lie, but the snow could not lie." He is well convinced it was an unnecessary murder" ... under this conviction justice demands and our own interests require that he should be gratified.

In case it should be necessary to force the delivery of John Mohawk under the treaty, the regular course is to get affidavits to the facts, transmit to the governor and request him to make the demand, using militia.

But Major Carter and I believe this unnecessary ... We have no doubt that Seneca will deliver John Mohawk when we can assure him that Darrow and Williams are arrested for trial.

Meanwhile, I think you can assure your friends that for the present none of the Seneca nation among us will harm your citizens of their property.

I am sir, respectfully
Sam'l Huntington

However, Carter charged Seneca had never delivered John Mohawk.

Seneca countered — since the hanging of John O'mic, Seneca could no longer trust the whites. He would only deliver Mohawk after the arrest of Darrow and Williams.

Carter quickly reminded Seneca that he had seen the trial and its result — O'mic was found guilty of murder.

While Seneca agreed, he knew Carter missed the heart of his concern — dignity was very important to a defeated people and the white men had made of a feast of the hanging.

There was no question in Carter's mind that the trial had been fair. John O'mic, a fine-looking young Indian, had been one of three Indians who had murdered a family of three whites and stolen their property. Two Indians escaped.

Yet it seemed to Carter that Samuel Huntington or Sheriff Baldwin or Alfred Kelley or some of those being paid for law execution in 1812 could assume the responsibility for the prisoner. But they felt the Indians might mobilize to free O'mic, and no one had the respect of the Indians as Major Carter did. So O'mic was in chains in Carter's house.

O'mic asked Carter to explain how it would be tomorrow on execution day. Carter did not feel he should have inherited that job either, but explained it forthrightly.

Afterward, O'mic asked if Carter would accompany him up to the platform. Carter explained someone else would do that but O'mic pleaded and Carter agreed.

The Indian voiced one final request, that he not be blindfolded, "I will show the white faces how an Indian dies."

Major Carter poured the Indian some whiskey and sat with him the night. The next day on the way to the execution, young O'mic sat on his coffin on a wagon.

An eyewitness account by the Honorable Elisha Whittlesey describes the scene in Cleveland:

He was a fine looking young Indian and watched everything that occurred with much anxiety. The gallows was erected in the Public Square in front of where the old courthouse was erected.

144

After the religious services were over, Major Jones attempted to form a hollow square of militia so the prisoner would be well guarded. He rode back and forth with drawn sword, epaulets an scabbard flying, but he didn't know what order to give.

Carter said to Sheriff Baldwin, "Get that damn fool off that horse and out of the way."

Arriving at the gallows, Mr. Carter and the sheriff and O'mic ascended the platform by a ladder.

A rope was put around the prisoner's neck with a loop in the end. Another was let down through a hole in the top piece, on which was a hook attached to the rope around the neck. The rope with the hook was brought over to one of the posts and fastened near the ground.

As the sheriff brought down the cap, O'mic was the most terrified being I have ever seen. Seizing the cap with his right hand ... he stepped to one of the posts and put his arm around it. The sheriff approached him to loose his hold, and for a moment, it was a question if O'mic would throw him to the ground.

O'mic asked for Major Carter. (Again) Carter ascended the platform and a negotiation in regular diplomatic style was had. It was in the native tongue, as I understood at the time. Mr. Carter appealed to O'mic to display his courage, narrating what he had said about showing the white faces how an Indian could die ... Finally O'mic ... said that if Major Carter would get him a pint of whisky he would consent to die.

Carter sent to his tavern for a full glass tumbler of the fine Monongahela ... O'mic drank the whisky in as little time as it took him to pour it out of the glass.

Mr. Carter came down, and the sheriff again drew down the cap and the same scene of terror was reenacted. Again he asked for Mr. Carter.

Mr. Carter ascended the platform, and O'mic gave him the honor of an Indian pledge that he would no longer resist the sentence of the court if he could have another half pint of whisky.

Carter sent for the whiskey and stood with O'mic. When the whiskey came, he held it to John O'mic's mouth while he drank. The sheriff tied the Indian's arms back and tied the rope to prevent the prisoner from going to the side post again, avoiding the trapdoor.

Humanity at its worst — people who had known O'mic and his father — stood and watched.

The execution took place. To quote Elisha Whittlesey again:

At that moment a terrific storm appeared suddenly and came up from north north-west with great rapidity, to avoid which, and it being doubtful the neck was broken ... the rope was drawn down with the design of raising the body ... so that it would fall several feet and thereby dislocate the neck. The body was put into the coffin and the coffin into the grave.

The storm came on heavy and all scampered away but O'mic.

The real disgrace occurred later that night. A doctor and a group of medical students barely waited for dusk when they converged on the grave, dug up the body and carried it to a dissecting table.

Although through many decades the raising of bodies for study by medical students has seemed a fit subject for jokes among thick-skinned, thin-souled doctors, this particular grave robbery was to cost the Cuyahoga communities.

Once again Americans abused Indian trust.

"So I'm leaving, Major, and taking them all with me, Ogontz, Big Son, Mohawk, Pipe ... the Ottawas, Senecas, Chippewas, Andastes."

Carter nodded.

Seneca put out his hand, "But, Major, if you ever want to join us, you could be ... you could be ... a Seneca."

While the local militia companies were arming to fight the British, the chiefs on the Cuyahoga marshaled all their men and marched them off to join the British. Not one remained.

After the war, five came back to the Cuyahoga valley. Four of them were shot by Captain Delawn Mills's men. After that, a handful came back for a short time. But by 1817, it was hard to find an Indian in the Cuyaboga valley. And today, if you stand looking at the massive signal tree on the Goudy farm on Peck Road in Cuyahoga Falls when the wind is blowing through its branches ... it sounds like a sad *a cappella* Amen.

10

Decision at Station Hope

As he rode into Cleveland along the Lake Erie escarpment, mornings, Ashbel Walworth was used to having the wind sting his right ear, but not talk into it.

So the morning the wind started talking, Walworth turned his horse slaunchwise down the cliff to the Cuyahoga to look. He found himself gawking down at a strange confrontation.

On the east bank facing west a well-dressed Southerner sat a fine horse. On the west bank facing east a large and ancient-looking black man sat on a fallen tree.

Between them, on the black man's side of the river, but closer to the water, Major Lorenzo Carter stood broadbased and feather-edged to both of them. Cradling a long gun like some forest judiciary, Carter turned his head from the Black to the Southerner and back as each spoke. Not a benevolent-looking referee, he seemed superior to both and eager to be shut of this.

Of course most people spoke politely when Major Carter was around. Still Walworth was struck by the mildness in the Southerner's voice as he addressed the Negro to ask about his treatment. Did he not think Mr. Young had used him well for a negra and given him good treatment on his place?

Carter watched the Black think, then heard him respond with a thoughtful yes.

The Southerner continued questioning ... wouldn't the negra be physically better off in a warmer climate with his crippled foot?

The black man took even longer before he reluctantly agreed. Ben's toes had frozen on a cliff one day and the resulting rheumatism had twisted his legs making it almost impossible for him to walk right — especially when the weather turned cold. Of course, the warm southern weather had been a big part of his decision whether or not to go north.

But the Southerner saw the opening and poured out his trump card: If Ben would return, Mr. Young would give him his own cabin!

The Negro turned to Carter for confirmation.

What men most feared and admired about Carter was direct fairness and this time was no different. Carter looked Ben eye to eye and put the decision back on his shoulders.

The Negro grasped his forehead as if to squeeze out a decision. Ashbel Walworth tied his horse and found himself edging closer, eager to hear the runaway's decision.

Seeing Ben's struggle, Carter suggested he remember the man making this offer was a slave catcher who would only get paid if Ben returned.

When the gentleman from Kentucky had first ridden in, inquiring for "a nigra named Ben," he found his way naturally to the Major's cabin, the capitol west of Ft. Pitt.

The Kentuckian had heard up river that Ben was in Carter's town. He asked Carter very politely but pointedly if this were true.

Spitted on Major Carter's stare, the visitor felt constrained to explain, somewhat nervously, he had been sent by Mr. Young according to the law.

The Southerner had not yet learned — Lorenzo Carter was all the law they had here at the Cuyahoga's mouth. Cleveland was still just a scraggle of cabins astride a mud road a rod wide and a foot deep. It was the Republic's only toehold on the Great Lakes country. But Carter already acted as if it were the seat of a new civilization even though no local laws were written.

The Kentuckian politely persisted hoping the Major would not let sentiment color his actions in a matter of property.

When Carter said flatly he had no sentiments toward Ben one way or another, the Southerner smiled. To discharge any possibility of misunderstanding, he restated the obvious — his mission was to see to the safe return of Mr. Young's property; anyone interferin' would be subject to a $500 fine.

Carter had no good answer.

The Kentuckian recognized the stalemate asking only to see the property face to face.

Carter eyed the Kentuckian for a moment, then laid out his plan: the Southerner should be on the east bank near the foot of Huron Road the following morning. Carter would deliver Ben on the west bank; but the river would stay between the two. Any talk would go across the water.

As the next sunrise lit the village's eastern escarpment, Ben hobbled down to the ferry bank where Carter was waiting. It wasn't long before the Kentuckian arrived as directed and sent a patient inquiry across the water ... did not Mr. Young have good quarters for Ben? Never raised a whip to him? Even at this distance the slave catcher could see Ben's twisted legs. And wasn't the weather more agreeable to your health?

Carter's thoughts drifted back to spring when Ben had been a passenger in the canoe of a Mr. Hunter who was paddling his wife, daughter and a small black boy from Michigan to Cleveland. They had just passed the mouth of Rocky River a few miles west of the mouth of the Cuyahoga when a storm wailed in out of Canada and slammed the canoe against the American cliffs that front the lake east of the river.

The children perished first; finally only Ben was left. French traders discovered him clinging to the frozen tree. They brought him to Major Carter's at the mouth of the Cuyahoga.

Runaway slaves were just beginning to find their way to the shores of Lake Erie, guided by no more than the North Star. The long valleys of the Blue Ridge and Cumberland mountains formed a natural trough to the Ohio. Once across there was an easy path up the Tuscarawas, across The Portage and up the twisty Cuyahoga to Lake Erie.

150

All through the summer, Carter nursed Ben back to a kind of health. By fall, Ben was barely able to totter his bulk around the cabin and to a practical man like Carter who would not keep somebody in town who could not help the settlement, it went against the grain. From the trail of rumors the Kentuckian had followed up the Tuscarawas, it was obvious that the Major was anxious to be rid of "poor Ben." In fact he had even made the statement, "Niggers are no good up here." Ben knew that.

The Kentuckian called again across the water … and weren't the people better down South as well?

This was not a yes or no question … some were, others were not.

Then why, the catcher wanted to know, did Ben run away at all?

Here at least was an easy question … Freedom!

Carter studied Ben. Freedom! Remember Carter … remember back in Vermont when you had a farm, friends, and civilization to keep you company? What made you want to blaze a trail through a thousand miles of woods to chop a cabin out of the forest and fight malaria and disease and hunger on a frontier river with no doctor within a hundred miles?

Freedom! you wanted. That's all the black man wanted. A man would walk the shoes right off his feet, and the feet right off his legs for that. Carter took a new look at Ben.

Carter did not at that time know that Ben was the first of an endless line who would be marching north, in spite of laws and fines, to reach this port on the lake.

The Kentuckian fired the ultimatum: Did Ben want to stay here or come back home?

Walworth inched closer to hear the reply.

Freedom or slavery? Ben was on his feet now. He did not look like a man who had made a decision. He looked more like a hound dog that had been called off the rabbit chase. He stumped up and down the shore.

Several times the Southerner was about to add one more argument. Carter thought it was wily judgment that he each

151

time withheld. He had Ben rocking back and forth on the knife edge of a decision. Anything he added would probably lose for his client a $2,000 property.

Now the Kentuckian sent his final attempt across the river … Mr. Young had asked his catcher to tell Ben if he decided against going back, Mr. Young would forgive Ben for gettin' enticed away and he would be welcome home anytime.

Carter recognized the Kentuckian's telling stroke. Could he detect a smile on the Southerner's face? He could not.

Ben looked over at Carter as if to ask advice, but did not. He lowered his head and trudged slowly toward the ferry raft Carter kept tied up for crossing the river.

Walworth watched the Major paddle the little craft back across in silence while Ben stared at the approaching east bank. The Kentuckian was already at the landing as the boat scraped ashore. Ben climbed out painfully and stood before him. The Kentuckian smiled and put his hand on the big black's shoulder.

The Major shook his head and strode up the riverbank to his cabin. Ben was already becoming one less thing the Major had to do.

But some in the settlement did not forget Ben so easily. No doubt the Major told the settlers in the tavern what the slave had decided, and he probably let it go at that. But even though more than a century separates us from that day in 1806, perhaps the Major did not forget that easily.

There is a sequel.

Next day, Ben and his captor made their way up the Old Carter Road through Cleveland Mills. Ben was riding and the Kentuckian walked alongside, chatting amiably. Suddenly two men leaped out of the woods pointing their rifles at the Kentuckian like two unblinking eyes. The Kentuckian stared back.

The riflemen shouted to Ben to escape.

Ben slid off the horse. His twisted legs carried him like a scurrying crab into the woods.

The Kentuckian never protested or tried to find Ben again. The account of Ben's history recorded by Ashbel Walworth tells us that only three people knew about Ben's "escape." They were described as "two hangers-on" at the Major's tavern named John Thompson and James Greer. The third person was Lorenzo Carter.

Perhaps it would never have been known that Thompson and Greer had set Ben free again. Their motives are still obscured by a veil of years. But their part of the adventure came to light that winter.

A son of Major Spafford and a young brother of Nathan Perry were out hunting in the west bank wilderness one day and became lost. After tramping about aimlessly for some hours, they stumbled upon a horse's track which led them to a rude hut hidden away in the forest. There was only one person living there — Ben.

Ben was the first Negro resident of the Cuyahoga.

Eventually the twisty Cuyahoga became a main road to freedom. Slaves from all over the south found their way along its banks, later following the towpath of the canal that led them to the lake and Canada.

And all along the way the fugitives impressed strong men like Lorenzo Carter to help them in their journey — men who came to call themselves station masters and conductors on the road to freedom.

Later when the network of roads to freedom were established with such cunning and secrecy that they became very efficient from station to station, the network became known as the Underground Railroad.

And the station that operated at the mouth end of the twisty Cuyahoga was named Station Hope.

11

The General

IF YOU should ever find yourself driving over Portage Road, City of Akron, County of Summit, State of Ohio, pull over out of the rush of today. Get out, put your feet right on that road, and walk into the 16th century. It is worth a half hour of your life, and it will jar you a little.

Over the rumble of fast traffic on brick you'll see the trees still meet over the street, nodding smugly of old events. The road you will be walking over is almost surely the oldest main artery in America.

It appeared on the earliest European maps of North America. It's still the same length, and it still bears the same name that it has carried in every language from Erie to Iroquois to Delaware to French, Spanish and only recently, English — Portage Path.

For centuries when the continent lay sleeping as far as white men knew, there was a steady flow of traffic over the Portage Path. Who knows what maps and compasses primitive men used? But they had found, perhaps by centuries of trial and error, the gateway for the water route between the Gulf of Mexico and the Great Lakes.

When the continent was solid trees, you could hardly travel from the lakes to the gulf by land. But Indian tribes found they could come by water up the Mississippi to the Ohio River, then up the Tuscarawas which gave them an easy route up to the formidable slope of the Continental Divide that splits the continent laterally, water off one slope flowing to the Gulf, off the other to the Great Lakes and the St. Lawrence.

Now if upon reaching the head of the Tuscarawas, an Indian walked overland to the north only eight miles, he came to the Little Cuyahoga which flows north. If he put his canoe back in and followed the current, he plunged down 300 feet in 30 miles to Lake Erie, which would take him down to the St. Lawrence.

The main key to this 2,000-mile trip was this short eight-mile portage; and the white man found that generations of Indians had beaten a groove about nine inches deep, one man wide, and eight miles long.

This Portage Path became, in 1785, the Western Boundary of the United States. Forty years later, the white man took it over and for the same reason the Indians had used it. He wanted to move his boats from the Great Lakes to the great Gulf by water. But these were big boats 80 feet long and 30 tons heavy, and there were hundreds of them.

Where he needed to lift his canalboats 300 feet, practically straight up from Lake Erie to the Portage, they had to build 42 locks. To service the canal mules and horses, feed the passengers and unload the boats during the six hours of locking up the escarpment, a city grew at the high place, what was known as the Summit.

The Summit would have been nothing but a lock tender and tavern keep to the canal if it hadn't been for the Cuyahoga tributary, the Little Cuyahoga, mightiest creek in America.

Lost in a gigantic gorge 40 sizes too big for it, like the uncomfortable kid whose mother buys coats with "growing room," the Little Cuyahoga is undignified.

In some places it chatters down over stairsteps of shale. In other places it is a turgid swale of stained bubbles, carry-off from a chemical city. In many places, it bubbles literally *under* Akron today, fighting for a look at the sun between factories, only visible now and then blinking under a street bridge just before hurtling down into a culvert, emerging later in a gush only to duck under another plant. Kids mistake it in places for a big storm sewer.

Yet, without any qualification whatsoever, this little creek literally built Akron. The land, before it was Akron, had not the first thing a city needs, and its growth defied the laws of economic gravity. Akron was started by four men who wanted both navigation and hydraulic water so badly that they hand-made it.

Not traditional frontiersmen, these four were the last of the great colonial leader breed, giant patriots of the all-'round type who did some farming, law, science, politics, and a lot of nation building. They were Dr. Eliakim Crosby, Judge Leicester King, Senator Alfred Kelley, and General Simon Perkins.

Now when a man is put to a lot of extra trouble over a low-paying project it sticks in his memory — and even in his affection.

Perkins as a young surveyor back before the War of 1812 had a lot of grief surveying for a client a thousand torn-up acres between the head of the Tuscarawas and the loop of the Little Cuyahoga. Therefore, years later, when Perkins saw a notice that this tough thousand acres was going for taxes, he paid $4.03 and was certified to the land; and then he forgot it for 18 years. It was to become one of the all-time bargains of history.

By 1825, Simon Perkins, a handsome, rugged 46, was living in Warren. He heard that land surveyors were driving stakes through his thousand acres over by the Little Cuyahoga. He mounted and rode 52 miles west of Warren. It had to be the canal fellows surveying, so he tried to figure how high a price he could charge the canal, for Perkins was above all a financial man. He was in on the founding of several businesses, including the famous Western Reserve Bank.

Upon arrival, though, at the Little Cuyahoga, he made a surprising move. Two men had cabins near the big bend in the Little Cuyahoga, Paul Williams and Major Miner Spicer. They'd come together in 1810. Perkins found them both and traded reports of what had become of the men of the 7th Ohio Volunteer Infantry; then Perkins suggested that instead of charging the State of Ohio for their land, they all three *donate* it for the canal.

Williams and Spicer understood the move, and instantly donated a wide strip. But to complete the strip, a parcel was needed from a Charles Brown, a carpenter from Connecticut. He answered, "I'm not a moneyed man, General. I need to sell, and sell dear."

"Then The Canal will never buy it." Like a few other ambitious men, Perkins was beginning to speak of The Canal in capital letters.

"They've *got* to come through here, so they've got to buy it."

Perkins explained to Brown the state did not need to buy his land. "They can go to the west, come upstream alongside the Maumee and down the Miami. Miss us completely. If you'd give up a strip, The Canal will turn your remaining land into gold."

Brown warned that could be a long time off.

Perkins said — not long after the canal reaches the top.

Brown countered — if Perkins believed that, why not buy Brown's land and give a strip of it to the canal?

Perkins said the delay would be enough that he could not tie up cash that long. However, he offered a trade — 45 acres in the Little Cuyahoga Valley or a hundred farther out.

Brown chose the close-in 45.

Perkins figured that the spot where the Pittsburgh-Columbus stage crossed the right of way of The Canal, which climbed up the other side of the escarpment from the Cuyahoga and down would become a kind of center of things. Being a surveyor, he measured out a township, with an area in the center for a business district surrounded by 300 cabin lots.

He did the work alone, because looking at that heavily timbered, fully gouged ridge, few others got the picture of tomorrow.

When he took the plat to Ravenna, county seat of Portage County, the clerk said, "To file townsite papers, General, you have to have a name for the place."

Perkins took off his great fur mitts and studied the ceiling. Educated in the tradition of the great colonials, Perkins had studied Greek. As he stood envisioning the highest place on the escarpment in his thousand acres, a place known to Indians and settlers as "the summit," a place for which he now had high plans, a lofty Greek word came to him meaning *high place*. He reached for the quill, and he wrote ... *Akron*.

However in 1825, Akron was only a name on a plat in the Portage County clerk's office. Yet word drifted out that on the Portage Path, at The Summit, land had been measured off for sale for a village. Those who wanted work on the rumored canal inquired how to get there.

The general took it that far. And it might have stayed that way if it hadn't been for the doctor and the judge. But before they could do much good, a 33-year-old man had to come along, named Kelley, Alfred Kelley.

12

Kelley's Canal

THE *village* of Akron was built by the Cuyahoga and General Perkins; the *town*, by the Cuyahoga and Dr. Crosby. But the *city* of Akron — quite another matter — was built by the Cuyahoga and the toughest little giant who ever rode down this valley in the sleet and hail — "Mister Kelley."

The Mister was because — well — with his linen soaking wet from rain and sweat, standing calf-deep in canal mud, he was a Mister — that's all.

Lonesome from a soaring intellect, dyspeptic from a gnawing canker of duty, Kelley was driven, and he drove the valley to the largest engineering earthwork in the then history of the world — the Ohio and Erie Canal.

The fact is that building the Cuyahoga or Akron or Cleveland was way beneath Kelley's sights. He was out to save the whole frontier from financial disaster. On his way to that, it just happens he left in his wake a chain of major and minor cities.

A whip-figured man with the winkless eyes of a fighter, Kelley's was not a comfortable presence. His forehead was broad above a high-boned face. The mouth was a thin-lipped slash, and the eyes impatient.

He was out of pace with the slow land. It was not ideal equipment for the hundreds of miles of human hurdles and digging that lay ahead of him.

In dealing with his 62 legislative colleagues, his heavy sense of destiny, unrelieved by any flash of humor, threw away the fatherly indulgence he could have had as the youngest senator in the state's history.

159

The feathers he really ruffled were on legislators whose counties would be bypassed completely by the canal. Kelley expected them to rise above sectionalism and vote for the good of the region, all the while insisting the canal should parallel the Cuyahoga. Damaging was the fact that along the river lay his own personal real estate and that of his brothers.

Kelley's brisk manner caused other men to slow their response to him. Representative Beardsley drawled his group's objection, "Mr. Kelley, this hard times extend all the way from the Maumee River to the Muskingum. Why will digging a ditch from Cleveland to Cincinnati lift that whole patch?"

Kelley worked for the canal like a man afraid for his life. Actually he was afraid for the people.

Kelley reminded men that the state was only an ax throw from bankruptcy. The bank notes of not one regional bank would pass at face value. Some were discounted 75 per cent. Things were so bad that by 1819 trade stopped, land sales stopped, immigration stopped.

Alfred Kelley and Governor Ethan Allen Brown knew what was the matter. There was good money in the east, but it would not flow west.

The trouble was you couldn't get a barrel of, say, Ohio flour to New York overland without paying a dollar a hundred-weight drayage every hundred miles to push it across the Appalachian barrier. That put a barrel of Ohio flour on the New York dock for about $11 — and there she'd sit. Of course you could ship it down the Ohio River to New Orleans. But the problem was getting it to Cincinnati from upstate, so it could make the trip.

Now if there were a north-south canal through Ohio from Lake Erie to the Ohio River, that barrel of flour could travel from just about any place in Ohio, up to Lake Erie and across New York State's proposed Erie Canal and down to New York City for $1.70 a barrel, shipping. It could sell for anything over $5.20.

Eastern dollars would then flow west.

On the floor of the General Assembly the anticanal men brought everyone back to what they called *reality*. "With only $133,000 in the state treasury, Mr. Brown and Mr. Kelley talk of spending five-million. The taxable value of all the land in the state is only fifteen!"

As legislator and as governor and as U.S. Senator, Governor Brown personally labored eight years to pass the canal bill, using all the considerable negotiation skill at his command, "Alfred, the word *canal* has become a fighting word. Let us change the designation to the *Internal Improvements Bill*. It's hard to be against *Improvements.*"

But many were, "Let us not be confused. This new bill is for the same old canal. This impoverished state is supposed to build a canal longer than the wealthy state of New York is building, and with twice as many locks."

Alfred Kelley inherited the leadership on the canal drive as it passed down from Thomas Jefferson to Governor Worthington to Thomas Morrow to Governor Ethan Allen Brown. But Brown went off to the U.S. Senate. As the new leader of the canal movement, Kelley came up against the leaders of a hundred local revolts. If the canal plans left out a town, that town set out to kill the canal by passing resolutions to declare they would not pay taxes if any part were to be used to pay the interest on money borrowed to dig a canal.

They sent copies to New York newspapers in paid space, because Governor Brown was at that very time in New York trying to borrow construction money from John Jacob Astor and other financial firms. These notices showed the financiers that the governor did not have his state behind him on this project.

Kelley was not a strong speechmaker. He couldn't stump these towns, but he sought out the leaders.

General Simon Perkins was a natural leader in Warren, and he was thrust to the head of the Trumbull County anticanal movement. The canal was not planned to go through Trumbull County.

DAILY LINE OF OHIO CANAL PACKETS

Between Cleveland & Portsmouth

DISTANCE 309 MILES IN 80 HOURS.

A packet of this Line leaves Cleveland every day at 4 o'clock P.M. and Portmouth every day at 9 o'clock A.M.

T. INGRAHAM,	Cleveland	
OTIS & CURTISS,	do.	} AGENTS
G. J. LEET,	Portsmouth	

NEIL, Moore & Co.'s Line of Stages leaves Cleveland daily for Columbus via Wooster and Hebron.

Cleveland Directory 1837

Muskingum River
Elev. 700'

Slackwater Navigation
91 miles to Marietta
& Ohio River

Walhonding River

DRESDEN
ROSCOE
ADAMS MILL
COSHOCTON
NEWCOMERSTOWN
Muskingum River
Tuscarawas River
PORT WASHINGTON
CANAL DOVER
NEW PHILADELPHIA
ZOAR
Milton Dam
Sugar Creek

LOCK 33

Sugar Creek

TABLE OF DISTANCES		from Cleveland	from Dresden
CLEVELAND LOCK 42		0 MILES	149
BOSTON		19	130
PENINSULA		21	128
LOCK 1 AKRON		35	114
BARBERTON		42	107
WOLF CREEK LOCK		44	105
CLINTON		50	99
CANAL FULTON		54	95
MASSILLON		63	86
NAVARRE		68	81
BOLIVAR		77	72
ZOAR		81	68
CANAL DOVER		91	58
NEW PHILADELPHIA		94	55
NEW CASTLE		97	52
TRENTON		101	48
EASTPORT		105	44
PORT WASHINGTON		109	40
NEWCOMERSTOWN		116	33
COSHOCTON		132	17
ADAMS MILL		143	6
DRESDEN		149	0

profile

io Canal

BARSTOW & CO.

FORWARDING
AND
Commission Merchants
AND DEALERS IN

PRODUCE SALT,
Ashes, Staves &c.

RIVER STREET
OHIO CITY.

AGENTS FOR
Pilot, Traders, Erie & Ohio Lines
ON THE ERIE CANAL

AND PROPRIETORS OF

WASHINGTON LINE,
OHIO CANAL

Portage
Summit
Elev. 968'

Lake Erie
Elev. 573'

OHIO
CITY

BRECKSVILLE

BOSTON

BARBERTON

PENINSULA
Aqueduct

CLEVELAND

AKRON

Portage
Lakes

CUYAHOGA FALLS

Cuyahoga River

Little Cuyahoga

Old Portage Path

N

Kelley knew from previous land transactions that Perkins was land wise. He would know that the canal would make his Cuyahoga-Tuscarawas land valuable. Yet he fought that route.

So Perkins was sincere in believing the canal should route itself through the larger communities, like Warren.

Kelley argued that even if that were true, one would have to consider the shape and cost of a canal that would go through Warren, Columbus, Chillicothe, Circleville, Dayton and Cincinnati.

As a former surveyor, Perkins agreed. But when he came out in favor of the Cuyahoga route, he was bitterly attacked by the anticanal camp. "He's as selfish a man as exists," said the Sandusky *Clarion*, "which will account for the liberality of this weathercock."

The canal bill needed friends from wherever. There was another stubborn, unsocial, dedicated man in the legislature who wasn't doing very well, Nathaniel Guilford. For as long as men had been trying to pass a canal bill, Guilford had been trying to pass a school bill for public education. He had inherited it from Caleb Atwater and Ephraim Cutler.

Kelley studied the record of voting on the previous canal bills and the previous education bills. Then he went to Guilford with an observation: in the areas where education is weak, the canal is strong, and where you're strong we are weak.

Guilford, after many years and many deals, was not enthusiastic. He addressed himself to his ale. But Kelley made Guilford a proposition — if Guilford's education people would vote for the canal, Kelley would persuade his procanal legislators to vote for the school bill.

He had Guilford's attention.

Fighting localism all the way, Kelley had to bend. In fact, to run the canal past the most votes, they split the canal in two: one from Cleveland south to Portsmouth; one from Toledo south to Cincinnati.

Even so, the canal bill went through an ordeal of committees. Sandusky and other irate areas continued to fight it bitterly

164

and effectively. Nevertheless, on February 4, 1825, the canal bill passed the Ohio legislature.

The bill was so poorly seated that Kelley rushed the state into beginning construction before the law could be modified or hogtied by enemies of the canal who now set out to elect an anticanal legislature.

Kelley was under fire because the very first section of the canal to be built was in his own area — the 38-mile stretch from Cleveland to the summit (Akron) — so that shipments to New York could begin early from a large part of Ohio, bringing revenue to settlers and townsmen and toll revenues to the state, which would be evidence to eastern banks that the balance of the canal construction money would be well lent.

Micajah Williams suggested, "It might be well if you would be at pains to inform widely, particularly in the south and west towns of Ohio, why we have begun the canal in your part of the state. I am told Daniel Heaton on the Mahoning River and James Kilbourne on the Sandusky are saying that Canal Commission members are favoring their own regions."

"I agree with the usefulness of your thought," wrote Kelley, "but as the false rumor will be apt to travel like a bird while any correction will travel like an ox, the latter will never overtake the former. It would do best to get the canal dug fast and bury the false rumor in dollars."

But for the human hurdles Kelley had to cross, it wasn't necessary to look to his outright opponents in southern and western counties, nor to the millions of cubic yards of mud to be moved at ten cents a yard, nor the 800 miles of timber four feet across at the stumps, nor to the 300 feet of lift up from Lake Erie to Akron in 42 locks.

Look right beside Kelley at the man appointed to be the other active commissioner, Micajah Williams.

Kelley was full of duty. And Williams was full of frolic. At 36, Kelley was a precocious young man. At 28, Williams was even more so, and ambitious and able in a different way. Politically they were opposite. While Kelley was for Adams and helped organize the Whig party, Williams helped organize the Jacksonians.

Williams wanted to build an organization, delegate to it, and make it function. Kelley wanted to see everything himself, in person.

But in the face of laying 300 miles of slack water through a nearly unbroken forest and building 42 locks up to Akron and 33 down the other side to the Tuscarawas, they worked together against the overwhelming enormity of the thing.

After the legislators and money men, Kelley's biggest human hurdles were the contractors.

He organized a very sound and elaborate bid-evaluation system. And as soon as the news was out, professional contractors from New York's Erie Canal began moving onto the scene. To Kelley's surprise, many of the best ones weren't bidding. They were hiring on as foremen to local men who hastily organized contracting companies.

This disturbed Kelley. He called in Ephraim Johnson, a long-time successful contractor off the Erie, and expressed surprise because Johnson had not bid on any sections.

Johnson explained. He had heard that local contractors had submitted bids ten to 15 percent under Kelley's own estimates for various sections. Regular contractors — such as himself — would not get any work until half of those men went out of business.

The professional canal contractor was a special breed who came on from the Erie, the Chesapeake and Ohio, the National Road, the Connecticut canals. They knew more about canal building than Kelley. Tough, cynical and extremely able men, they knew what their first competition would be, and that these local contractors would hire local farmers to do the digging. So the professionals knew that while initially they would probably have to hire out as foremen, when hard weather sent the farmers home, then the professionals would take over.

They would bring in the sad-faced, glad-voiced sinewy Irish who could push dirt 12 hours a day on 30 cents, slumgullion, whiskey, and the durable hope that in three years they would have "worked off the dead horse" — paid off the contractor who had paid their passage from Ireland.

These were the tough, determined, great Gaels of Ireland whom the gods made mad. Contractors who knew how to keep them mad enough to dig — but not mad enough to quit — had special secrets no local contractor would match.

They could take a strip of wilderness full of ague and shoulder-smashing timber and rain and cold and slate and clay, and, come hell or high water, they could cut through it a hundred-foot wide swath containing a canal ditch 24 feet wide, four feet deep, and as straight.

They could leave a graveyard every ten miles, and know that was the cost, and say an Irish prayer and get the ditch moving again.

Kelley needed this.

Johnson explained his bid would be higher than any local contractor because, beyond paying each of his men $12 a month, he would pay a dollar a day extra to any man who would work in water.

The professional contractor calculated the rise in wages and materials which he knew would begin when the job got moving. He also worried about smallpox and canal fever in his bidding. He explained he would not know how to bid until he saw exactly how Kelley's resident engineers worked … were they good engineers who could judge a canal lock by more than how the face stone is dressed. And he needed to know if they carried enough weight to get a foolish specification changed.

This offended Kelley who emphasized that all specifications were drawn carefully.

Johnson pointed out a few other things that were too tough about Kelley's contracts: holding the fall to one inch per mile, holding to hammer-dressed lock facings, insisting on clearing two rods wide on each side and allowing only $250 a mile for timber clearing, insisting on 90-foot oak timbers in dam construction.

There was a long list of grievances against Kelley's tough

specifications and rules. The amateur contractors accepted all these docilely. The professionals fought them. So the local contractors won most bids. Their enthusiasm and conscientiousness got the work off to a big start in July 1825.

Five thousand men attacked the forest and the earth along the Cuyahoga through Cleveland, Independence, Northfield. The canal was heading for Boston, Peninsula, Ira, Cuyahoga Falls, Akron. And they did good work.

But in the second summer, the rains came and the heat. It dropped Western farmers on their faces in the mud by platoons. Smallpox ran down the right-of-way. For every one buried, three went home.

Now the professional contractors came, and the great, flat-muscled, stone-faced Irish. They chopped 42 giant steps into the rising shale-clay escarpment from Lake Erie to The Summit, which became 42 locks with massive, oak plank gates on iron hinges and stone walls.

Sullen ... silent ... strong, and organized, they dropped the trees and grooved the land; 50 barrows running behind a leader from the canal bed to the spoil bank for a towpath and back from dawn to dusk, relentlessly.

"Holy Mither!" Irish foremen fractured the air, "ye roll them barrows like my granny's granny on her way t'church! Call yoursilves Irish! Arragh! A disgrace to the race!"

But even the toughest Irishmen were amazed at a tougher one, Alfred Kelley. In all weather he was out on the canal, night and day at three dollars per diem. Contractors tested him by building some parts of the towpath with a cover of clay over piled trash timbers. It saved them from burning the timber and hauling fill. Kelley carried a four-foot iron rod as stiff as his spine. Before accepting a section for payment, he'd walk the towpath and jab the rod into it every so often. Sometimes the rod would go in too easily.

"A shovel please, Mr. Johnson."

"Never mind digging. We buried some timber scrap in there to fill that cut. But it's big trunked stuff. It'll hold."

168

"It'll settle in five years, Mr. Johnson."

"By then you'll need to resurface anyway."

"The contract says stone fill and clay surface, Mr. Johnson."

"Look, I've got to get paid to meet payroll."

"I'll come and re-inspect without delay the moment you're ready."

Some contractors couldn't stand up under Kelley's stern inspections and his driving timetable. They absconded with funds, leaving their Irishmen stranded without pay.

Kelley instituted the system by which contractors had to prove they'd paid their men. Kelley held contractors so brutally to the letter of their bids that they turned to confiscating materials: stone, timber, lime, from adjacent lands.

Always inspecting, Kelley broke his robust health, but he rode anyway, through the mud and rain and heat, always attired as if for the legislature.

Kelley missed the birth of one son as he married the bitch public, and reduced his legal marriage to an affair of lonely letter writing ... "even you my wife much as you wish to see me would not have me leave so important a work at which I have been so long engaged when apparently so near consummation ... besides you know it would be inconsistent with our character ... (January 21, 1825).

But the work owned Kelley.

Simon Perkins, who had come over to Kelley's side at first reluctantly, now demanded a piece of him. He wrote him asking him to rest after a severe illness, "... because I do not see how your substitute is to be found elsewhere if you should get sick again."

But he did get sick, again and again, in contractor huts, in inns in Akron, in settler cabins along the route. Doctors were sent to find him.

Micajah Williams wrote Kelley, "to preserve yourself for the balance of the work you must depend upon your resident engineers and spare yourself the long hours in saddle and on the work site."

Kelley lost a son. And by now even those who had hated his stringent rules and laughed at his dedication would not release him.

In anticipation of the opening of the Akron-Cleveland part of the canal, boxes and barrels and bulk shipments of goods were piling up beside the locks at Akron. So the public would not let Kelley break off with it and return to his family.

In fact, upon the death of Kelley's young son, Micajah Williams wrote: "You will not fail to remember that your friends and your country yet have a right to expect your energies and intelligence to be exerted in their behalf." The letter then went right on with canal matters.

As the contractors worked their way north from the Portage Summit and simultaneously south from the mouth of the Cuyahoga, the first step was grubbing and clearing to a width 20 feet beyond either side of the excavation, stumps to be no higher than 12 inches.

Excavating, south from Cleveland, the men were constantly digging under water. Work animals were useless on long hill stretches where they could get no footing.

The arduous swamp work was killing, yet little worse than the laborious lock-building by which the canal climbed up the escarpment to Akron. In late autumn, men and animals slipped on the steep frozen face of the ridge. Falling shale slid down from the higher locks to the crews carving out the lower locks.

Lock 1 at the top (Exchange Street, Akron) was at the 968-foot elevation. From there north the locks butted together down 21 steps to the beginning of the Portage Path. The canal ran level for a short distance to Lock 23 at the junction of the Cuyahoga and the Little Cuyahoga, then it stepped down three locks to Number 26, Mud Catcher, at Ira, Lock 27 at Everett, 28 and 29 at Peninsula, Johnnycake Lock and Pancake Lock. At Peninsula, the canal crossed to the east side of the Cuyahoga by aqueduct. In the next few miles to the north, the canal walked down many locks. Number 32 at Boston was difficult. Thirty-six at Brecksville was a hard one, built in conjunction with two aqueduct crossings, including the long one across Tinker's Creek.

By 1827, the trail of the Irish across northern Ohio could be followed by their personal marks on the land: from Irish-town in Akron through two Irish cemeteries to the north, and three Irish settlements, on up to St. Mary's-of-the-Flats at the Cuyahoga's mouth.

They dug a reservoir hole at the summit that you could lose a village in. But most of all, they left a 39-mile straight cut on the earth that would hold slack water and float billions of dollars of commerce.

On July 4, 1827, Kelley trudged down the bank of the Cuyahoga to board the grand opening canalboat, the *Allen Trimble*, which would run south to meet the northbound *State of Ohio*.

Wracked from illness, his face was drained of expression. People stepped out of his path and turned and hushed.

"That's him. It's Mr. Kelley."

He recognized a face here and there and nodded. He

paused beside Ephraim Johnson, "Are you lowering the miter sill on the first lock so the boats can enter the river when the lake level is low?"

Johnson removed a cigar from sun-cracked lips and smiled. "Godalmighty, Mr. Kelley. Work right through the ceremonies?"

"We'll hurry the ceremony." Then Kelley inquired how the contractor would lower the sill with six feet of water standing on it.

The ceremony was that the first vessel to float on the canal, the *State of Ohio*, built by the Wheeler brothers in Akron, came floating down to Cleveland bearing a distinguished load of Ohio statesmen to band music.

But the important event that day was the *second* boat which floated into Cleveland after the band music had stopped. It carried wheat in on July 4, 1827.

No one seems to know the name of that vessel. But overnight, on July 5, 1827, wheat that had sold for 25 cents a bushel jumped to 75 cents.

Northbound on the canal floated flour out of Akron,

wheat, pork, whiskey, flax, ginseng, coal, potash, walnut timber. Southbound over the canal, headed for the hinterland at the canal head, floated iron, brass, glass, plaster, iron nails, tools, books, millstones ... and settlers. Instantly, the moment the water filled the canal.

Henry Newberry dug some coal out of the Cuyahoga bank at Tallmadge, loaded it into a canalboat, hauled it to Cleveland. He wagoned it house to house, but nobody wanted the dirty, black stuff, so he gave away a free sample.

Then John Ballard saw it burn pale orange hot in a blacksmith shop. That year he built an iron foundry on the Cuyahoga where Henry Newberry's coal could float right up alongside. He told Newberry to pile the coal beside the kidney stone iron ore.

But in 1830 when the canal reached the Ohio River at Portsmouth, Alfred Kelley and Micajah Williams had won their fight to float Ohio produce to paying markets — New Orleans and New York.

13

The River's the Doctor

WHEN THE staircase of locks had been built from Akron down to the world, boats began to walk back up loaded with wonders that were not of the Western forest: real glass for windows out of Pittsburgh via Portsmouth and the canal; plaster dust for cabin chinking out of Buffalo via Cleveland and the canal; whale oil lamps, china plates. And converging on Lock 1 from the Akron hinterland for transshipment to the world came bulk from the land, outbound via the mouth of the Cuyahoga.

The land beside the locks at Akron became stevedore, warehouse, terminal, and tavern to the canal, and Akron thought itself doing very well. But Dr. Eliakim Crosby didn't.

He began telling Akron they were missing the chance of a lifetime. "A town has got to *make* something to ship out. Can't just be a place people go *through*."

But Akron had no outstanding farm land, no minerals. Timber, yes, but the whole Northwest Territory had timber.

What *did* they have?

Dr. Crosby finally found something. But it would require tremendous amounts of work, a ton of money, and, most of all, some long-sighted men. Crosby sent messages over to Trumbull County to General Simon Perkins and Judge Leicester King to meet him in Akron a week from Sabbath.

They arrived with the superiority of busy men being imposed upon. But Crosby being Crosby, you couldn't afford at least not to hear him out.

The doctor took them out to Lock 1 on the canal just south of where the Little Cuyahoga joins the Cuyahoga. The men could look down on heavily cargoed canalboats crawling both north and south. It gave Judge King an idea, which irritated Dr. Crosby at the moment. King was overjowled and had never become a part of these woods. He was still Connecticut. He said, "Look at that traffic! If we only had *another* canal now from here to Pittsburgh, Akron would become-"

But Crosby interrupted. "I want you to look down there at the Little Cuyahoga."

Crosby finally got their attention.

He took a map from his saddlebag, squared it with the land, and showed we don't have any large river. But look what we could do here. The land rises so gradually between here and Middleburg that you don't notice there's a vertical difference of almost a hundred foot.

Now suppose we tapped the Little Cuyahoga right here — the doctor's finger stabbed the map at a point of high ground (near Case Avenue) — and built a millrace to divert water over here, then run it down the face of this valley to Lock 5 on the canal. Between these two points, with a drop like that, the water would run twenty mills. Put twenty dams and a millwheel at each dam, twenty factories.

The doctor looked up at General Perkins and Judge King.

"By God," Perkins breathed.

Studying the requirements, they found the sheer digging to cut a river down the steep sides of the valley was enormous. The job of acquiring the land from the owners along the route of the proposed new river would be in itself a major project. They would not have the governmental right of eminent domain. And if owners figured out the purpose, land prices would shoot up, particularly if it was suspected that King, Crosby, and Perkins were involved.

It would take a wagonload of borrowed money. But King and Perkins had a lot to gain in improved valuation.

Crosby would build the millrace, Perkins would lay out another town at the junction. Judge King drew the delicate job, buying a strip of land for the millrace without kiting the price.

Some very careful regional writers record that Judge King asked Crosby to "Mark the line for the millrace at night."

Trees are too thick to work at night, but a full moon was due in a week. However, under cover of oak the moon would not light the work enough for running a straight line, Crosby feared.

"Then run it crooked, Doctor, and just straighten it day-times."

People will still see our survey blazes, King objected.

Don't use blazes. Put out hunting traps with a stake to mark them but close the unbaited traps.

Judge King went over to Ravenna Courthouse to study the land deeds. And he went to the tavern beside Lock 1 to study the owners. With whom would he be dealing in buying the right-of-way? He hoped he wouldn't find any absentee owners living back in Connecticut. It would be costly to acquire such titles. He found only three of those, but he found one name that alerted him — Charles Brown.

King went to Perkins, "You traded a lot on Little Cuya-hoga to a Charles Brown to get him away from the canal right-of-way?"

"Aye."

He's now standing right across the right-of-way of progress again.

Perkins shook his head as he remembered the deal he had made with Brown. "How could it happen?"

King explained.

Men who have good land sense are always choosing the same pieces of ground.

If they asked Brown to move *again*, he'd know that *again* there was a good reason. Brown had now had a chance to see that Perkins had been overwhelmingly right about the canal. It had succeeded; it *had* raised land values.

King suggested Perkins might have a better chance of get-ting Brown to reverse the trade. Perkins agreed to try.

Regional scholar Hugh D. Allen records the Perkins-Brown exchange:

Perkins said, "You made a good trade with me before, Mr. Brown; I think you were satisfied, but now I would like to have it back."

Brown clearly remembered the last time Perkins had asked Brown to move ... the big canal came through. So this request reassured Brown that something else big was coming. It seemed even more certain when Perkins offered 56 acres in exchange for Brown's 45.

But Brown was intrigued enough to ride out and look at the proferred land. He was pleasantly surprised at what he saw in the 56. He agreed to the exchange.

However, Judge King discovered a title mix-up. Perkins did not own it. The 56 acres, although *technically* owned by Mehitabel Barston, were *legally* owned by her husband. And Mehitabel Barston's husband was a tough burr.

When Judge King approached him about the purchase of 56 acres, Barston was suspicious that anyone would want such a small part of the Barston land. A verbal skirmish ensued ending in a proposal: King could buy the *entire tract* including the stony hillside — all for $14,000.

The Judge hesitated. Raising that much money would take some time.

Barston wrote up a five day option at $14,000 ending at midnight on the fifth day.

It took Judge King four and a half days to raise the money, and a half day to get papers to prove it, and the evening to ride back to Barston's and lay the papers on the table. But when midnight chimed on Barston's Connecticut clock, Barston did not appear.

Judge King pulled out his pocket clock. Barston's clock was accurate. He rose and paced the kitchen. Suddenly a door opened from the shed and Barston walked in proclaiming that since midnight had passed, King's option had expired. Barston wanted to raise the price.

But King stood firm in his claim — because the money was placed on the table five minutes before midnight, the option was fulfilled and the land now belonged to King.

Barston consulted his lawyer who confirmed the land had legally passed to Judge King.

Leicester King worked quickly. Curiosity rose about his purchases, so he did not buy in a straight line, but bought first on one end of the line, then the other, avoiding the middle. As speculation became more acute, he even bought a few parcels far away from the river so that they destroyed any pattern or shape which might be becoming apparent.

He did his work so well that not until he had finished did the sellers of the land get together and discover the pieces they had sold fitted together in a strip that paralleled the Little Cuyahoga and obviously were part of a major plan.

When that plan became known, it started the biggest drinking laugh that had been available at the Summit. "Crosby's going to build a river!"

When the digging of "Crosby Creek" began, the men sweating up on the ridge behind shovels looked down at the canal. They could see themselves being pointed out by the canal captains as local curiosities. On hot quiet days, laughter would float up to them. They knew the laugh was spreading south to every lockside tavern between there and Portsmouth and north Cleveland.

Cutting the millrace along the ridge, sometimes through solid rock, chewed up men and money faster than channel. Crosby, Perkins, and King had to find new loans.

It took two years. But when they were finished, Little Cuyahoga waters plunged downhill laden with kinetic power enough to turn 20 large wheels. The millrace flowed down along Main Street to Mill Street, then turned into the canal. Immediately the building of what came to be known as Old Stone Mill began. It turned its wheel in 1832. That date could be called the real birth date of Akron.

The mills which now grew up along "Crosby's Cascade" forced people to take a new look at Eliakim Crosby. People who used to call him "Doc" when he was a doctor, called him "Doctor Crosby" now that he had stopped practicing medicine. He was the surgeon who amputated a slice of river, grafted it to a town, and brought into the world a city.

It remained for General Perkins to complete the town plat around the split-off waters of the Little Cuyahoga. He platted Howard Street, paralleling the canal as the main street, named it Howard for Dr. Crosby's son-in-law who started the first store at the corner of Market. The store was built by Seth Iredell, the Quaker, and first mayor.

The new town became North Akron, a mile from the "old" Akron. They were divided by a gore-shaped tract — and a thousand acres of jealousy which would in its own way later rock mid-America. But we must stick to the river.

The water power from the Little Cuy's left hand, grabbed later by a stubborn Dutchman, made Akron the flour and cereal capital of the world, starting with Old Stone Mill.

But Crosby, Perkins, Kelley, King, and the Cuyahoga had ahead even greater destiny for Akron, and a bigger fight.

Judge King started it. He began a campaign in the legislatures of both Ohio and Pennsylvania for another canal to link Akron and Pittsburgh. Then he went out to raise the money.

14

The Luck of Jedediah Brownhead, Esq.

"TAKE THE PISTOL, LANE." Frost nudged an old-fashioned brass single barrel across the desk at his sharp-jawed friend. "One of those blacklegs is going to start shooting. Then what'll you do?"

"Same as last time." Lane squint-smiled with his one good eye. "Run."

Sam'l Lane was not a man to accept a fight unless it was worth it; and along the lower Cuyahoga in the 1830s, a fight could be for keeps. Specifically, he saw no gain in a physical fight. Unfortunately, his character, principles, and devil-take manner stirred up enemies in his wake like dry leaves after a fast horse. The Cuyahoga valley echoed with the damning of Sam'l Lane.

The damners wanted action, not debate. And Sam'l Lane's only weapon was his pen. He became the first biographer of the Cuyahoga.

To fill in the profile of Brownhead's life, one needs to use what he wrote of himself, what others wrote of him, and assume the language that must have been used between Brownhead and his loyal friend, Henry Frost — which follows.

Scarce 19-years-old when he came to Akron in 1834, Lane was already well-traveled. Therefore, the finely attired strangers who inhabited the canal taverns did not impress his worldly eye as they did the local settlers. He'd seen them before in every big town from his home in Connecticut to New Orleans, which pumped these blacklegs up the Mississippi river arteries. To Sam'l Lane, the ruffle shirts, plug hats, kid gloves, and bejeweled fingers were the plumage of gamblers, counterfeiters, and thieves.

Four years in canal-bustling Akron grew Lane's first fringe of chin whiskers and his first head of real anger. While still practicing his trade of sign and house painter, he took up the pen to write a little semiweekly newspaper that voiced his opinions of blackleg activity and life in general.

While Lane's pen flushed out coveys of blacklegs, it was a poor defense against their bullets, bludgeons, and bare knuckles.

"Dammit, Lane, you were lucky to get off with only one buttoned-up eye!" exploded Frost. "You're tweaking the nose of every gambler, saloonkeeper, counterfeiter b'hoy, thief, pickpocket, and ..."

"... con man," added Lane.

"And to top it off," bellowed Frost, "you even dig at law-abiding citizens."

"Now, Henry," Lane rasped in the harsh Connecticut dialect that characterized his articles in the *Buzzard*. "Uncle Jed sez that a real jolly, nothin'-tu-du-with-polyticks, anti-blackleg, respectable paper will du well here, an' that's jist what I'm goin' tu print."

"Lane, that phony accent and the false name, Jedediah Brownhead, Esquire, won't protect you. They know who writes it. Half the town calls you 'Jed' already."

This time Frost picked up the heavy little cannon and held it out to his friend. "Careful. It's loaded."

Lane squinted down the sights, lining them up through the window at a stem-legged stranger across the street who was ushering an awkward giant farmer into the saloon.

"Bang!" he said. "There goes another blackleg, compliments of Sam'l Lane."

A smile crinkled the wide mouth. With the fringe of whiskers framing the smooth-shaven upper lip, the mouth and jutting cone of a nose, Sam'l Lane came closer to being the clownish Jedediah Brownhead, Esq., than the sophisticated editor of Akron's much talked about newspaper. Lane gently laid the pistol on the desk.

"Henry," he drawled, "I was raised to the occupashun of teechin' the young idear how to shute. But seein' as how that's rather poor bizness in this secshun, I've concluded to try my hand at editerin' awhile."

Frost sat as stone faced as the blacklegs did when they read Lane's humor.

In booming Akron, blacklegs made no attempts to front their professions, or purpose. It was every man for himself, and while all communities had their reform groups, the general attitude toward transients, upon whom the blacklegs preyed, was that "he who gets fleeced should have kept his coat buttoned."

The traffic through Akron was heavy. Inland farmers from as far south as the big bend in the canal at Newark shipped north to Akron. They accompanied their farm produce that far north, where it was transferred to boats bound for the mouth of the Cuyahoga. The farmers stayed in Akron to make purchases of goods imported from New York via Cleveland. Very often these men had with them most of their savings. Sometimes they brought with them their land payment money.

Now these were lonely men who had licked a hundred acres of hardwood and supported with their bare hands life amid nature. For some, it had been several years since they had been among strangers or seen a woman wearing new cloth and bracelets. The big U turn on the Cuyahoga was a bright new world to them, and they were not expecting it to be peopled by predatory blacklegs. They fell easy prey to the friendly smiles of the handsomely clothed people.

When the witty pen of Jedediah Brownhead, Esq., went after them in his strictly reform paper, the *Buzzard*, it made good reading. And when people read, they sometimes acted. So with half the state's blacklegs concentrated right here in the new canal city like gaudy green horseflies on slow-melting sugar, a man could stir up a lot of trouble with hardly tossing a name.

Along with their dazzling display of high fashion finery, the blacklegs presented an elegant friendliness which bored travelers on the canal packets found overpoweringly attractive. Boston and Peninsula were already favorite haunts during the blackleg working hours. There the boats began the laborious stair-step through the locks to the summit.

To eat, the passengers often had to disembark and cook their own meals over open fires. This, along with the practice most canalboats had of carrying their spare horses on board, led many passengers to accept the hospitality of the well-dressed strangers, ride with them into Akron for a friendly glass or two to wait until their boat caught up with them on the summit ... *"And perhaps a hand of cards or two."*

This was part of what Sam Lane was determined to clean up. This was what moved the pen of Jedediah Brownhead, Esq., and kept the brickbats flying at Lane's head. Plain, hard-headed luck kept them from doing damage.

"Sum folks may think, perhaps, that I've got a curious name for my paper," Jed quipped in one issue of the *Buzzard*. "You see, a buzzard is a kind of hawk, an' my Buzzard is near of kin tu the turkey buzzard that I've hern tell on way down South where it's a fine tu kill 'em, cause, you see, they remove all the filth and carin from the streets. Now, you see, I calku-late to make my paper prodigous handy in this way. If there's enny thing wrong goin on, I calkulate to tell on't, an expose, an endevor to remove newsances and so forth from the city."

The *Buzzard's* sweeping forages on blacklegs were extremely successful. But Lane had many close squeaks. Pelt-ing with rotten eggs was common. Once he was cowhided for his commentary on a local drunkard and cohort of the black-legs; but the whip wielder was relatively easy to outrun. She was the drunkard's wife.

The buttoned-up eye Lane now displayed to his friend Henry Frost was still tender from the fist of a notorious Negro pugilist and dancer named John Kelley who had attempted to obtain possession of a hall for a "distreputable exhibition" and had been severely criticized by the *Buzzard*. Having been knocked to the ground on this occasion, Lane had been saved from a lethal stomping by his own agility at pivoting on his back while keeping his feet toward his attacker — and the timely intervention of bystanders.

Lane was constantly being lured by invitations into dark alleys, secluded back rooms, and lonely woods by irate blacklegs. It wasn't common sense that saved him. This was why Henry Frost now pushed the pistol toward Lane, more insistently.

"Lane, you've proved you don't show the white feather. But you've also proved wit and words aren't going to help. Take the pistol."

Lane stared at the miniature cannon, fingering his beard.

"I was a barkeep once," he said. "Only way I could earn a living." His right hand reached for the dull gleaming pistol. "The meanest of all occupations," he continued, "is that which requires a man to dole out whiskey at three cents a glass when he knows perhaps a whole family is suffering for the bread which should have been bought with the coppers."

Lane was idly checking the primer. Suddenly he leaned forward, roughly clattering the pistol to the desktop. "Say," he exclaimed. "That'd make a good temperance item. 'Man's most miserable occupation.'" He reached for his pen.

Henry Frost started for the door. "Promise me you'll carry the pistol?"

The scratching of his pen on paper drowned out Lane's soft answer. "Like the barkeep, Henry, a man's got to live."

Only a few days later, with the brass pistol pulling at the skirt pocket of his overcoat, Sam'l Lane called at the Hall Hotel, on business with the landlord's brother. There were no threats to his person this day — no rotten eggs, no horsewhips, no fist-swinging pugilists.

Just Dwight Spooner.

Through drink-puffed eyes, Spooner, a leader, watched the editor bustle through the taproom. Dwight Spooner rubbed the stubble on his face and nodded to other men.

Half a dozen lounging blacklegs caught the look, and waited with him.

Lane didn't keep them waiting long. As he picked his way through the taproom toward the door, Spooner's hulk rose and blotted out the light. A fist like a hand of bananas knotted around Lane's collar and he was yanked into mid-air by a yard of beef. Sam's hand instinctively flew to his hat, keeping it squared on his head. The other dipped into the coat pocket.

A well-manicured hand, trimmed with starched cuff, fell on his elbow, a hand decorated brightly with several razor-sharp diamonds that can slash a man's face. A voice hissed in Lane's ear, "Don't pull the pistol, Jed, or it's the end of you."

Lane managed to roll his eyes enough to make out the town's most notorious blackleg. He could also see Spooner's other fist suspended.

"Landlord!" choked Lane, quietly withdrawing an empty hand from the pistol pocket. "Give me protection!"

The landlord smiled, pushed open the front door and turned to Lane who still dangled limply from Spooner's grip. "If you are going to fight, gentlemen, do it outside."

Lane was dragged out.

"Go ahead, Spooner — mash the polecat!"

Lane's right hand sneaked into the coat pocket again.

Spooner's eyes glistened. "How 'bout it Jed Brown-head," he taunted, "shall I strike you?"

Lane's hand came out of the pocket, the pistol cocked. "Shall I mash yer face for you?"

The pistol was against Spooner's belt buckle.

"You can do as you please about it, Dwight," Lane gasped as calmly as he could. "But you may feel bad about it afterwards. Real bad."

Another hand linked into the crook of Spooner's arm. "Now hold on, Dwight," drawled a friendly voice. "You could get into serious trouble mashin' up a prominent citizen like J. Brownhead, Esquire, here." Spooner's fist wavered. A howl went up from the blacklegs.

185

Another friendly voice drifted into Lane's now pounding eardrums. "Lay off, Dwight. There's nothing to gain by mashing *our friend.*" The emphasis was threatening. Spooner's fist dropped a little and his eyes circled the ring of bystanders. The circle was complete — blacklegs on one side, friends of Jed on the other.

The clamp that bunched Lane's collar relaxed and, slowly, the pistol was uncocked and slipped into the pocket again. Apparently no one had even seen it.

But Sam'l Lane had only half an hour to recuperate from big Dwight Spooner. He returned to his office, taking care to place the pistol on a convenient shelf above the editorial table.

Dwight Spooner was herded into the tavern by the blacklegs. There he filled up with more corn courage and a few proddings.

Jedediah Brownhead looked up from his editorial as the stumbling thumps scuffed up the stairs to his office. He laid the pen down and took the pistol from its shelf just as the door banged open.

Spooner swung on the doorframe eyes glistening, "Lane! You gonna buzzard me any more?"

The pistol cocked. Spooner saw it this time.

"Get out of my office, Spooner, or I'll buzzard you so you'll stay buzzarded!"

Spooner got. Lane stood at the office window, watching the giant disappear down the mud street.

He chuckled. So, Sam'l Lane — the pen can start a fight, but it takes a pistol to finish it. You might even run for sheriff one day and put some of these pen-scratched principles into action.

Lane looked hard at the pistol. No need to keep it primed now that danger's over. With his pen, he pried the wadding from the barrel and shook the charge onto the desk. Out tumbled four large shot, three slugs of lead, and a pile of powder which even to an unpracticed eye was a large mouthful for any pistol, not to mention this one with its old-fashioned brass barrel.

Sam'l Lane shuddered. In his great concern, Henry Frost had tried to double the protection for his friend. But if the trigger had been pulled, it would have backfired Lane off the earth. Sam'l Lane had been carrying a bomb.

If the experience of very nearly blowing himself from the lives of the blacklegs was any lesson to Sam'l Lane, he never showed it by future caution. His long and varied career was a continual oscillation between the pistol and the pen.

He served as editor of several publications alternately with terms as sheriff, probate judge, and finally mayor of Akron.

The same bravado characterized both his pen and his pistols. But he never actually fired. He just used it to protect his pen ... and this was what people remembered.

In later years, Lane helped Akron's *Beacon-Journal* make a name for itself that continues today; and he wrote perhaps the most detailed book on the embattled Cuyahoga — to which most subsequent regional books are indebted, including this one.

15

The Biggest Financial Man on the Cuyahoga

THE MOST BELOVED, most exciting money man on the entire Cuyahoga shore from 1800 to 1850 was James Brown at Boston.

While many doers of good works are scored as cowards, Mr. Brown in his vast larceny was a symbol of unbelievable gallantry. Heroically molded, he stood straight as a promise, six foot two, unbooted. Feature by feature, the face was not carefully handsome, but it had slashing good looks under blue-black hair and a luminous smile.

Even his most effective enemy, Sam'l A. Lane, sheriff of Akron, conveyed well on 2,000 *Reward* posters that Brown's frame and deep-set eyes were commanding. He described Brown's voice as genial and his manner courtly.

Clothes hung on him as on a tailor's dummy. His drinking was correct and his marriage to Lucy Watrous Mather, of Cleveland's then first family, was the stamp of social distinction.

Brown's friends, who were many, often complimented Lane on the accuracy of the written descriptions of him on the *Reward* posters and on the pages of Akron's reform newspaper.

As editor of the *Buzzard*, Lane had flushed out of the Cuyahoga valley scores of corrupt and fraudulent men. As sheriff he jailed them. But with neither portfolio could he make a case stick against the towering prestige of James Brown. While in the same breath sincerely complimenting Lane on his descriptive prose, the people said of course they had no information leading to the conviction of Mr. Brown; and, if they did, they would certainly have no part in the downfall of such a fine man. "In fact, you ought to write a book about him."

Being both experts of the world, Lane and Brown recognized each other as formidable. It was not lost on Brown that Lane was one of those wiry enduring men who never tire. Lane's humor he knew was not the jolly unguarded type. He laughed a split second too late.

Lane himself admired Brown, but he was committed to arresting and convicting him.

"I'm going to tell them in print what you're doing."

"Why? They already know."

"But see what they say when I print it all."

"They'll say I'm doing more good printing money than you're doing printing the *Buzzard.*"

When the *Buzzard* came out it carried a complete story on James Brown.

Brown built a house on the west bank of the Cuyahoga. In 1825, he built on the same land a storehouse, laying in $1,200 worth of merchandise and keeping tavern in the same building.

Many men in the commerce of coal, iron, whiskey, hogs and brass awaited the opening of The Ohio Canal in 1827 to ship their cargoes, [wrote Lane] *but none waited so eagerly as James Brown who was planning to ship money — in bulk.*

Haven't Brown's neighbors, the Buzzard *asked, noted that the colleagues he has assembled are very well dressed and well spoken for the operation of mere store and tavern?*

Have any wondered how it is that Mr. Brown needs such impressive help in the running of a store which stocks under $2,000 in merchandise?

For your own protection, you should note the stature of the men who have taken up storekeeping in the little neighboring town of Boston. They are William G. Taylor of Cleveland; Abraham S. Holmes; Col. William Ashley of Boston; William Latta of Bath; Jonathan De Courcey and Thomas Johnson of Norton; Joshua King and Joe Keeler of Portage.

James Brown has a very able brother, Dan, who is very like him, except more handsome but less statesmanlike in crime.

These men are counterfeiters; and on a vast and damaging scale.

The next morning, Mr. Lane's editorial office was a pile of broken glass and wood. While he was inspecting the debris a courier came up to give him "the compliments of Mr. Brown and will you meet him at Hall's Tavern?"

Lane rode to Pittsburgh instead for a bag of type, leaving a workman to clean up the *Buzzard* office. When he returned in four days, the press was upright and cleaned. It was not damaged.

The courier repeated the invitation. Lane went to Hall's Tavern. Brown greeted him from the center of a table of men without rising, but with courtesy, proffering a draft of Cuyahoga neck oil.

Lane accepted, but insisted on paying with his own coin.

"Fine, Mr. Lane. But the proprietor finds *my* money very acceptable," Brown spread U.S. bank notes on the table.

"I don't. You wanted to talk to me."

"To tell you your paper spoke to my disadvantage, Mr. Lane, and I incline to get mad."

"So do I, Mr. Brown. And you're going to jail, if it takes forty years."

"It will take longer, Mr. Lane."

It was extremely difficult, however, because whenever Lane caused Brown to be arrested, a crowd gathered around and accompanied the genial Brown to the jail to see that he got out on bail without delay.

When Brown's cases came to trial, they were arranged for bad weather, when possible, to prevent overcrowding. The crowds came not only to see Brown, but also because such distinguished and colorful attorneys handled his defense.

Jim Brown was eager to have his brother, Dan, come in with him on a full-time basis. But Dan was then in the lucrative business of droving horses east to Pittsburgh — other people's horses. Jim argued with him that horses were a long roundabout way to make money. "Why go through those middle steps when we can make money direct on the press?"

A special condition of the times made the counterfeiting business especially workable and especially direct. It was an era when 40 different wildcat currencies were abroad in the west, the bank notes issued by local banks. These currencies were different colors, denominations, and discounts. Much of it would not pass at 25 percent of face value, and the actual value fluctuated day to day, even hour by hour.

Many a settler, just paid for pork he had canalled to the Cincinnati market, heard that the $400 he had received was in a tender fast falling in value. While he scurried around the waterfront trying to convert it to a more stable coinage, the $400 had turned to $100 in his hands — or to ashes. Such settlers never knew that their own frenzied effort to convert actually cut the value of their money in that immediate vicinity.

But the point is that if a counterfeit dealer was available in such moments of panic, he could easily exchange his counterfeit for legitimate currency. Of course he must make sure that the real money was worth more than his counterfeit, before trading.

Brown saw his biggest opportunity in the one currency which stood up very well any place, United States bank notes, issued by the Philadelphia branch. Naturally, these became nearly as scarce as hard money; and hardly any of them flowed west.

It was this money shortage which Mr. Brown proposed to relieve. He was determined to run a strictly quality operation. He acquired some very fine plates hardly to be distinguished from U.S. bank notes. He had good engravers and printers with him. However, to make the notes in commercial quantities, some expensive printing equipment was needed which required the sudden raising of capital. Brown always insisted on paying his bills in good money.

Now the way Brown raised good money when he needed it made him legend up and down the Cuyahoga.

Two assets particularly permitted him to *do* what other men only dreamed: a personal effrontery and an uncommonly powerful black horse named "Old John," procured for him by Dan.

Brown caused to be forged a bank draft on the Bank of Pittsburgh. Being scrupulous in financial affairs, he also had it marked "certified."

He then took five horses from his shed on the bank of the Cuyahoga and rode east at night with the string toward Pittsburgh. He dropped Old John off first at a stable in Warren. The other horses he dropped off at about 30-mile intervals, telling each hostler to feed it well, but leave the saddle on. The last horse, he rode into the Pittsburgh area.

Resting during the day, he sauntered casually into a bank late in the afternoon, and with the easy boredom of a man of large affairs he placed forged credentials before the banker along with the certified bank draft.

"It's a large one," the banker said. "But should be no trouble on that bank, sir. What currency you want it?"

"U.S. bank notes, if convenient. Small denominations."

"There'll be a twenty dollar charge as we'll have to send an armed man when we collect from that bank."

Brown unrolled some bills. "Very well."

When the draft was cashed, Brown thanked the banker, and strolled casually out the door. But once the door shut behind him, casualness stripped off him like a sweater. He ran down the steps, jammed the legitimate bills into his saddlebag, untied the mare, and jumped on. His heel raked the mare's flank as he headed her west through the cut in the Allegheny escarpment.

At Aliquippa he leaped off, threw the lines of the lathered mare to the hostler. "Get me the Virginia Red!"

The change-over was under five minutes, and he was westing toward the Cuyahoga. When he reached Warren, he was exhausted, but the giant Old John pounded the trail west. Dawn was lighting the sky when Brown crossed the Cuyahoga. He went into his shed long enough to get water for Old John and himself and to change his clothes and grab an ax.

He went back outside with the ax, over to his boundary line where he began splitting wood loudly under his neighbor's window.

The neighbor's wife came out and Brown asked her, "What time is it?"

"I don't know."

"Since my clock is broken, would you go into your house and look?"

She came back out, "Half after seven, Jim.

When the extradition officers came from Pennsylvania, they talked to Brown's neighbor's wife who said, "It's impossible; I remember talking to him at half after seven the next morning."

The Pennsylvania constable mounted his horse and flapped on his hat. "It's not him then. No horse could do it from Pittsburgh in one night."

When Brown's own press was operating, it turned out good quality U.S. bank notes.

Now you must understand the scope of Brown's thinking. It was no part of his idea to go around personally handing off bogus money at the retail level. Nor would he permit his agents to do so. Instead he marketed the bills in volume, *as counterfeit*, to dealers at 20 percent of face value. The men who bought from Brown and from Brown's men knew what they were buying. They almost never saw Brown, the head of "Moneyshop Hill" who seldom so much as touched a bogus bill. In his own pocket, he liked to carry genuine U.S. bank notes.

Brown's shipments of queer went aboard canalboats northbound for New York State, southbound for New Orleans. Cargoes were substantial. He would, with some regularity, ship quantities of as much as $1,500,000.

Besides U.S. bank notes, Brown printed a considerable number of mortgages on property in eastern cities, and he printed some bonds of western states which he sold in the east.

A major part of his management ability was acquiring the plates. In addition to commissioning the finest engravings, he would sometimes steal the original plates in daring maneuvers in which he was very lucky.

Lane printed in the *Buzzard*: "How is it that small packages come in over the canal for Brown's store in Boston, but only large shipments go out?"

Brown would personally set the pattern for opening a new territory. When he did, few could emulate his boldness or brilliance. To open the money market in lower Canada, he rode out of the Cuyahoga valley on Old John before the thaw one spring. He established several dealers, but Canadian law officers picked up his scent, and by the time he reached the middle of the north shore of Lake Erie, they were in full pursuit.

Brown's escape from them and from Canada was the subject of admiring talk up and down the Cuyahoga valley for decades. The Canadians were so close behind that time was counted in heartbeats. He was heading west along Lake Erie, but he suddenly reversed and headed Old John east over thawing Canada soil for the east end of Lake Erie where it narrows. Soon he arrived at the place where he saw the spring ice breakup was beginning at the edge of open water.

He rode still eastward along the shore, picking the exact spot where he judged the ice to be thawed to just between slush and ice. Then he rode south across the breaking ice. Old John's hooves sucked slush, and once broke through. Brown whipped him on.

Canadian officers were still testing the ice at various points when Brown crossed the U.S. border in midlake. By the time they found sufficiently firm ice for crossing, Old John and Brown were clattering up onto the United States shore near Silver Creek.

Brown's Canadian outlets over the years dispensed several million *Made-in-Boston, Ohio*, dollars — U.S. bank notes of high quality, but not legally negotiable.

One of the greatest threats to Jim Brown was the dangerous admiration of his own colleagues who yielded sometimes to the temptation to brag of their leader to their drinking companions.

Except for this, he might not even have been arrested for his perfect execution of the Boston, Massachusetts, "transaction." He had forged a very large draft on a bank there. He proceeded from Boston, Ohio, to Boston, Massachusetts, and negotiated the draft. Then he used the same trick as in the Pittsburgh "transaction": a prearranged relay of horses to race back to Boston on the Cuyahoga. He made sure to be seen there immediately, sauntering casually down the road as church let out.

His own colleagues were so amazed that word of the feat seeped out and spread. Sam'l A. Lane sent the lead back to Massachusetts. Brown was extradited by Massachusetts authorities, taken to trial in Boston. However, the court ruled, that "With the fastest mode of travel known, no living man could have performed the journey in the time intervening between perpetration of the crime here and Mr. Brown's thoroughly proved presence in Boston, Ohio."

Thereafter, Ohio sheriffs riding after James Brown could put no heart into their work.

But Sam'l A. Lane pressed relentlessly. He had been able to convict many of Brown's *customers*, but Brown himself had an immunity to conviction. Such crowds of admirers gathered 'round him at trials now that even judges were affected and leaned toward acquittal.

One judge summed up: "Even the prosecution concedes that Mr. Brown did not personally misrepresent to anyone that the bills were real. In fact, he aggressively stated to the purchasers that they were *not* real. The man who passes a spurious bill off as *real* is guilty. But a man who announces it is *not* real has not passed a counterfeit bill because his statement has stripped it of its counterfeit quality."

Arrested and tried often, Brown still stood so high in the estimation of citizens of the Cuyahoga valley that in April 1834, they elected him Justice of the Peace of Boston. He administered this office with such authority and conscientious attention to detail that he was twice re-elected.

While he held office, it was known to all that he headed the Cuyahoga valley money syndicate. Many were in fact grateful to him for freeing the money-tight economy, not inspecting their cash too carefully. If it passed from hand to hand, what mattered?

In 1837, Samuel A. Lane, through the *Buzzard*, started a new editorial drive against Brown. He avoided butting head on into Brown's born-lucky popularity by addressing his newspaper campaign not directly against Brown, but against counterfeiting in general.

The campaign was so forceful that it incited the law of three counties to go on a rampage. With a concentration like that, they were bound to apprehend dealers who bought counterfeit bills from Brown and who were inept in passing the money. Arresting the dealers led the officers to Brown's own confederates, some of whom bought freedom by reluctantly giving information about Brown.

Brown was therefore arrested and brought to trial approximately a dozen times in the next two years. "Going to Mr. Brown's trials" became a thing to do.

The state often had to ask for a continuance in order to assemble witnesses, letting Brown free on $10-to-$20,000 bonds. In five such cases, when the new trial date was set, the many witnesses were suddenly unavailable, missing, or relocated.

Many of Brown's colleagues and customers were put in the penitentiary during this drive, but "Old Jim" as he was now called, remained chief of bogus banking in the west.

In the early 1840s he moved farther upriver and was elected Justice of the Peace at North Hampton in October 1845.

But in 1846, Brown's distinguished defense attorney, Judge Rufus P. Spalding, lost an examination on a charge that Brown counterfeited coin. Judge McClure on the bench bound him over to U.S. District Court in Columbus, letting him wait at home on $20,000 bail.

The trial in Columbus, August 1, 1846, was presided over by Justice John McLean, the later admired Ohio Supreme Court justice and U.S. Postmaster General. Brown's defense attorneys were Hon. Rufus P. Spalding and Hon. Noah M. Swayne (later U.S. Supreme Court).

Nevertheless the case went against Brown, and his sentence was ten years in prison.

The three barns which burned down in the following week had only one thing in common. They all belonged to witnesses against Brown.

In prison, Brown's great spirit shrank like a caged eagle. Yet his commanding presence even there won him the respect of the officers and prisoners. Within a few months, he was made file leader of the first platoon in the lockstep march of the prisoners between dining hall and shops.

Sheriff Lane who had worked hard for Brown's arrest and conviction went to visit the prison. It shocked him to see how gaunt and unsmiling the giant had become.

Mr. Brown was later given special charge of the prison hospital. While he held that responsibility, cholera broke out. Brown was a bulwark of strength, in constant motion day and night nursing sick prisoners. The prison officials credited him with personally saving scores of lives.

His work was so dramatic that prison officers assisted Brown's only daughter, Laura, in forwarding a request for a pardon for Brown. President Zachary Taylor granted the pardon and Mr. Brown walked free July 22, 1849, after two years and 11 months in jail.

But once out of jail, Brown's property was dissipated and Lane had jailed and scattered most of his gang. He was forced to a lower level of operations. Going downhill, Brown was finally arrested and convicted on a lowly charge of passing a counterfeit bill.

In the years following, he was in and out of jail on counterfeiting charges.

While serving one three-year term, he had a visitor, Sam'l A. Lane, ex-sheriff and ex-editor of the *Buzzard*.

Brown did not rise. "It's too early for the buzzards. I'm not dead yet."

Awkwardly, Lane explained his mission was to open

negotiations for the publication of Brown's biography to be written by Lane with Brown's help, the profits to be equally divided.

Brown's handsome, shaggy head went back in laughter. The black hair was salted with gray, but still thick. The voice was grainy and vibrant, "I'm your whole life, aren't I, Lane?"

Lane walked to the gate and signaled for the guard.

"Lane!" Brown had risen. "I'll let you write my story on one condition. You spent your life getting me *in* here. Now if you want to write my story, get me pardoned."

They stared at each other many seconds.

Finally Lane turned and trudged out of the cell.

16

Oilbow on the Cuyahoga

SELDOM CAN the surge growth of a city be traced to one cause and one day. But in the case of Cleveland, real growth began in the hour that the *State of Ohio* tied up in Cleveland in 1827, having dropped down from the Akron summit.

The frontier period ended abruptly with the canal opening. Now came that flood of goods pouring down the Cuyahoga valley on the canal, fed by Cuyahoga water. These shipments brought cash to the west, which started a stream of commerce to and from the east. This commerce gave rise to a row of commission houses lining the east bank of the Cuyahoga, men who learned the sources of all products.

Construction of houses drew heavy imports from the east. A few ironmongers were getting started, using the red kidney ore found on the surface along the Cuyahoga. Coal came down the Cuyahoga valley by canal from Massillon for heating Cleveland.

A good shipping trade developed between the mouth of the Cuyahoga and Buffalo. The commission houses on the east bank of the Cuyahoga stretched farther south from the mouth as long slender warehouses grew there.

And by the time of the Civil War, the Cuyahoga stage was set for a vast national commerce.

When you break partners with a man in a close-out showdown, you suddenly realize from then on you will have to fight the very same strengths you once wanted on your side. But by ten o'clock on the morning of February 4, 1865, the three Clark brothers hadn't taken the breakup that seriously.

All six of the men in the showdown that morning on the east bank of the Cuyahoga near the mouth of Kingsbury Run did understand that the outcome today would tell whether the three Clark brothers and their lawyer had more nerve than the young partner they were trying to dismiss.

It was also understood that the whole of the Andrews, Clark & Company should go to the high bidder. However, *none* of them understood that the outcome would affect the lives of millions of people over the next 100 years, and turn the banks of this river shiny black and iridescent.

Maurice Clark knew the young partner best. They had been very close friends. That's why it jarred Clark now as he stared across the table into the coldest blue eyes on the river. What had attracted Clark in the first place was the young man's unbelievable calmness in the face of business panic, and his humorless sense of destiny.

Even now, as the business was about to break up, the young partner sat facing them as calm as ice, just as if alone he was an even match for the three Clark brothers and their lawyer.

Maurice snapped, "John, the Clark Brothers bid five hundred dollars for the business."

Rockefeller bid a thousand. The young man's expressionless bid echoed so fast it looked as if he would go all the way to $10,000.

Clark knew he would have trouble panicking his young partner because of the spartan discipline under which John D. Rockefeller had been raised.

When he was a boy his red-haired, blue-eyed mother praised him highly for diving into the river to save a drowning boy; then she immediately whipped him for being on the ice without permission. It would take a lot to shock him after that.

Maurice Clark jumped the bid suddenly. $5000.
The young partner did not hesitate. $5,500.

At an early age the young man developed a canny way with a dollar. His father spread it all over town that "I trade with the boys and skin 'em, and I just beat 'em at it every time I can. I want to make 'em sharp."

So John probably knew the true value of the business. Maurice Clark figured the bidding might as well get up there. $10,000 was the Clark's bid.
$10,500 came the echo.

However, if John had to borrow to pay, he'd probably drop out next round. As a boy the young partner had lent out $50 from his turkey-raising money to a farmer for a year at interest. At the end of the year he got his fifty, but in addition interest — $3.75.

He saw how easily that $3.75 came compared to worked-for money he had just received for three days of potato digging at 37½¢. He wrote in his diary, "The impression is gaining ground with me that it is a good thing to let my money be my servant, not make myself a slave to money." The young man liked to *get* interest, not *give* it.

$11,000 ... cash! Clark bid.
$11,500 Rockefeller countered.

Another unnerving thing about bidding against this calm young man, he could lose all but the last hand, and still win. He had that shot-with-luck bearing. His sister had said, "When it's raining porridge, you'll find John's dish right side up."

$12,000, bid Maurice Clark.
$12,500, Rockefeller bid.

The Clark brothers stared at their partner gauging his stubbornness.
They knew of his famous stubborn job hunt. When he

graduated from high school, John went to Folsom's Commercial College for three months to learn "bookkeeping and business ethics."

Then he laid siege to Cleveland for a job. The 16-year-old boy made a list of all the *large* companies in Cleveland. He wanted training that would lead to his own business. He started right down his list — canals, banks, wholesale merchants.

He got all the way to the bottom of his list. No job. So he started at the top of the list again, making a second round of calls. Some of the employers who recognized this as a second call became very unpleasant. They were shocked at his reaction. It was as if he hadn't even heard them. Just thanked them, and walked out.

When he hit the bottom of the list for the second time, without a job, his family and friends stepped in. They told him to try smaller places of business. John thanked them and started at the top of his list, third time. He said that he was not the least discouraged, "Because I'm every day at my business, the business of looking for work. I put in my full time on it."

Halfway down his list on the third go-'round he walked into Hewitt & Tuttle, commission merchants on Merwin Street on the Cuyahoga River. Mr. Hewitt offered him the job of bookkeeper-clerk in Hewitt & Tuttle on the morning of September 26, 1855. Salary was not mentioned.

That same afternoon John Rockefeller hung his hat on a peg beside the high desk which contained the ledger, the letter press, and the blotter on which he was to record every transaction. He put his foot on the rung of the high chair like a man who had finally got the toehold he was looking for, and he swung onto the seat like a man taking charge.

He never did ask the salary.

As Maurice Clark studied his partner, he knew that a man who'll go without work until he gets the job he wants, won't shake out of this bidding at $13,000.

And a man who has so little regard for money that he doesn't even ask the salary is hard to bid against.

The Clarks bid $15,000
$15,500, echoed the partner.

The position at Hewitt & Tuttle relieved the young clerk's family, but it worried a friend of his that he still didn't know his salary. It even worried Mr. Tuttle, the other partner in Hewitt & Tuttle.

"Young man, if you ever have occasion to procure goods for this firm, always inquire the price before buying."

"Yes, sir."

"Now your salary is three dollars and fifty cents a week. Why didn't you ask before?"

"I cared very little about that. My real pay will be learning business."

Tuttle stared at the young man. "I'll write your first week's check. How do you spell Rockefeller? Everybody'll have trouble with that one."

Many have, including Maurice Clark. But along the Cuyahoga there was little trouble with it, and principally because of Mr. Tuttle and Mr. Hewitt. They were so pleased with the ultraprecise, ultracareful work of young J. D. Rockefeller that they talked him up in the trade. He was raised to $25 a month, then $500 a year. But his real pay was much greater. Hewitt & Tuttle was a commission merchant firm and a whole university of business education, if you knew what the ledgers were saying.

What they said to the young bookkeeper was that bushels of corn located downstate in country counties were worth fifty cents. But floated north to the 44,000 people of Cleveland, they were worth a dollar and a quarter each. But *how* you moved them was important, in what kind of containers or vehicles. It was also important to be able to store them — to wait for favorable market prices.

He learned the value of an item is *where* it is located. He learned that the science of *moving* the item to where it is worth more is an art. You can use up the margin or preserve part of it.

Shortly Rockefeller was given great freedom and authority

to arrange complex transactions involving transshipment of goods over various carriers — canals to the Cuyahoga to dock, to railroads or lake vessels or wagons.

In 1858 he was raised to $600 a year.

That year he took some of his own money and bought 80 barrels of pork on his own account and resold them at a profit. Then he bought some flour and hams and resold.

Isaac Hewitt noted the young man's innovations and adopted some of them.

Rockefeller asked for $800 a year. Hewitt would like to have paid it, but felt he couldn't. He offered $700.

In the auction, Maurice Clark, who remembered how recently Rockefeller had been earning $700 a year, knew that his next bid would seem like a lot of money to the young man.

$20,000 was the bid to shame John out.

$20,500, John bid.

Clark of course, knew that John Rockefeller had been accustomed to big financial responsibilities. His mother had looked to him since late boyhood as the head of the household. There were two brothers and a sister to support.

The father, William Avery Rockefeller, was an excellent businessman in early life, but the opposite of his son John. A handsome black-haired giant, he had a smile like the sun coming out, and charm to burn.

However, he unfortunately had overcharmed Anne Vanderbeak, a part-time housemaid, who explained it to the sheriff. William Rockefeller was indicted. And from then on, he took longer and longer trips away from home; his business, on the fringe of medicine, became vague, mysterious and slightly suspect.

Mrs. Rockefeller therefore leaned on John D. At 15, the lad was a man in money matters. At 26, he probably couldn't be frightened off at the $25,000 level.

Maurice Clark looked a query at his two brothers and his lawyer. The brothers nodded. Clark bid $30,000.

The six men in the room focused on John Rockefeller who stared out the window at the Cuyahoga. Without looking away from it, he said, "Thirty thousand five hundred dollars."

Clark now figured Rockefeller was up to where he'd have to borrow not only from friendly banks, but some from more hostile money sellers.

Yet he remembered Rockefeller had an almost swaggering nerve when it came to borrowing money. Clark, of all people, had reason to know that.

In 1859, when John had been turned down for a raise to $800 a year, or $15.30 a week, he felt it was time to "go for himself."

Along the river were several other commission merchant and produce shipping firms. In one of them was another ambitious clerk, Maurice B. Clark, highly capable, and highly discontented with his pay. Clark and Rockefeller had talked a lot about forming a partnership as commission merchants in grain, hay, meats, miscellaneous goods.

Now was the time. They figured they needed $4,000 to start, $2,000 apiece.

Clark, the senior of the two, had saved $2,000; Rockefeller only $900. Clark said, "Well, let's start with that. And you can owe eleven hundred dollars into the pot."

"No. We should be even. I'll borrow."

"How can a bank lend you money on a business that isn't even working yet?"

Well, they couldn't. But John Rockefeller went to his father, "You told me you'd have one thousand dollars for me when I turned twenty-one, sir."

"Aye. But you're a long way from that."

"Only sixteen months, sir."

"And you want the money sooner?"

"Yes, sir. Tomorrow, sir."

Rockefeller senior stood up. "Tomorrow!"

"Yes, sir. But I mean to pay you interest on it for the sixteen months before I'm twenty-one."

The Senior relaxed and said, "Very commendable. Six and one-half percent."

"Five and a half, sir."

Rockefeller senior smiled broadly and sat down, "Very good. You're ready."

Two days later John Rockefeller, with money in hand, said to his friend, "Maurice, I'm ready."

The Clark & Rockefeller Company opened its doors on the Cuyahoga at 62 River Street. Rockefeller was young, but working on rented money matures a man fast.

In the auction, Maurice Clark knew that now at 26, after all they'd learned together, John wouldn't hesitate to borrow a large portion of $30,000. The bid must be much higher, $40,000.

Young Rockefeller had already developed a habit of laying both hands side by side over his face, as if staring into the future. When the hands came down, he bid $40,500.

Maurice said the bidding had gone past the point of faith in the company. "We're up to where you need tremendous confidence in the industry."

"Yes."

However, Maurice Clark, of all people, should know the confidence John Rockefeller had in the industry.

The firm of Clark & Rockefeller started off so strong that in their first year they sold $450,000 worth of other peoples' hay, wheat, pork, stone, and coal. Shipped it up the Cuyahoga or the canal or out over the five railroads along the river. Took out a net profit of $4,400.

Clark did most of the searching for new shipments to handle. Rockefeller ran the office, arranged the transports and the loans from banks to buy merchandise for resale. The partners already had their eyes on the extra warehouse space available along the river at Nos. 39-45 River Street, and some space on the dock.

This prosperity was based on the buying, selling, forwarding of good, solid, age-old commodities. But in the matter of *confidence*, the firm was about to take a sudden change that required confidence in the new and untried.

One morning at dawn in 1860, John Rockefeller looked out his office window on the east bank of the Cuyahoga to the black west shore as river commerce awakened.

The sun behind him ignited the bottoms of the clouds, then the tops of the trees. The waters remained dark except that suddenly a shaft of sun sliced between two warehouses to illuminate a cross-current strip of the turgid surface of the Cuyahoga.

But this morning the river did not burn iron red, nor coal black. It shimmered iridescent, a sparkling scum of rainbow that would color the economic history of America.

It caused John Rockefeller to call his partner. They stared at it.

Aye, John, petroleum.

It came out of the ground crude at fifty cents the barrel, sold for eighty cents the *gallon*, refined.

But there's so many in it, the spread is dropping fast.

John observed they must be careless businessmen that so much of their profit floats by our window.

Clark explained that he'd been approached by a fine young chemist from England, Sam Andrews, who had experience in illuminants. Although Andrews had no money, he wanted to get into the petroleum refining business. Maurice discouraged him. Maurice and John didn't have $250 to spare.

John thought, "Perhaps we ought to listen to him."

In 1863 Clark and Rockefeller put up half the capital to establish a small petroleum refinery on the south bank of Kingsbury Run where it emptied into the Cuyahoga. It was three acres located right on the track of the Atlantic & Great Western Railroad. The rest of the capital came from Clark's two brothers, James and Richard. Sam Andrews was in charge of production.

The company was named Andrews, Clark & Company.

In the auction, Clark bid $45,000. There were three Clarks drawing a living from the company. They could bid pretty high to retain the jobs of three men.
$45,500 was John's bid.

Refining was simple. Crude was strained into a tank and flowed to a still to be boiled. The first distillate was gasoline, practically a waste product. Next benzol or naphtha; next kerosene, which is what you were after for lighting and cooking.

Except for the time John Rockefeller took to ride his horse up past the Spelman house, hoping for a glimpse of Laura Celestia Spelman, he spent his days and nights on the Cuyahoga shore tending two thriving businesses.

Rockefeller believed that when a business has natural buoyance, *that's* the time to help it grow. Put money in it.

He began borrowing money to expand the petroleum facility. Even started another small one upriver a few miles, as part of Andrews, Clark & Company, called The Standard Works. It meant Maurice Clark had to co-sign the bank loan notes.

Then Rockefeller suggested to Clark that they hire a plumber by the month instead of by the job.

It meant a steady expense, but it worked out all right. Then Rockefeller pushed again. He proposed buying their own pipes and joints in quantity. Not from the jobber.

They saved half the plumbing costs. But it meant Rockefeller had to ask Maurice to co-sign with him another bank loan note.

Maurice was nervous about borrowing. But Rockefeller was beginning to realize he could make better use of the money than the banks could.

Next it was the barrels.

Maurice objected — let's stick to the business we're in.

John countered — to do that we'd have to borrow. John reasoned for the difference between .90 and $2.50, they could pay the highest interest in town.

Maurice wanted to know just how much they would need to borrow to build a cooperage.

But John knew that hardly mattered if they were going to stay in petroleum!

Maurice Clark co-signed the increasing loan notes with increasing reluctance.

Rockefeller meanwhile was crosswise daily with Clark's brother. Big Jim Clark did the buying of crude for the company; and he fretted under Rockefeller's tight bookkeeping. Jim Clark was tough and profane. Their feud broke out in the open.

Clark bid $47,000. Rockefeller — $47,500.

About the time that Maurice Clark became openly worried and Jim Clark became resentful, Rockefeller saw that in buying timber for their barrels, they were paying top dollar. He proposed buying a timber tract.

Maurice signed another note reluctantly.

Soon after that John pointed out that meant hauling green timber to the cooperage, paying freight on a lot of sap. Needed was a kiln on the timber tract.

Maurice exploded, too many loans to extend this oil business! Over *$100,000!* But John said they should borrow whenever it would safely extend the business.

Maurice threatened to break up the business right then and there. Rockefeller smoothed it over. He privately concluded, however, that if any of the Clarks ever again suggested breaking up the company, he would not smooth it over. So that he would know how to handle the problem if it ever came up, he reviewed his personal credit around town. He found, to his surprise, that he could muster $50,000 in loans.

In the bidding, Jim Clark tapped Richard Clark on the

arm. Richard Clark consulted some papers in a notebook from his chest pocket. He snapped the book shut, and nodded to Maurice. Maurice bid $50,000.

The figure silenced the room. Half of a $100,000 was a figure to command great respect.

John Rockefeller had a wife, a baby, a sister, and a mother to support, and a pair of brothers to help get started after the war. At $50,000, you stop to consider these things. Besides he needed time to raise funds for the Erie Street Church, and he wanted to keep ten percent of his own income free for his charities.

But, after all, the refinery was earning well. It was big as refineries went along the Cuyahoga. And even without the Clarks, Rockefeller would still have Sam Andrews' excellent engineering ability.

$50,500, John Rockefeller said.

A week after Maurice Clark had threatened to break up the company, John Rockefeller challenged Jim Clark on a couple of items of his travel to Titusville and the Pennsylvania oil regions to buy the crude oil for the refinery. John wanted a better accounting for Jim's expenses and also for the oil he bought.

Jim Clark vulgarly abused Rockefeller, and scathingly referred to him as "the Sunday School Superintendent." It was true that Rockefeller was a Sunday School Superintendent. But he knew he was not being complimented on it.

He endured a profane blast suggesting that it was time to get the Sunday School element out of the business. Then John said quietly, "Jim, I better tell you not to try to scare me with a bluff you don't mean."

Jim said he meant every word.

John asked if he spoke for his two brothers.

"Yes!"

John said good. Remember this conversation, Jim.

In the years ahead, Jim Clark would remember it many times.

John Rockefeller walked out of the refinery.

The next morning the three Clark brothers were stunned to see a notice of dissolution in the Cleveland *Leader*, signed by Rockefeller. After the initial surprise, they rallied quickly, realizing there were three of them, and in a buy-out showdown they should be able to raise more money. They asked Andrews where he stood.

He stood with Rockefeller, but he could not command important dollars.

The Clarks needed to shake Rockefeller out of the bidding quickly now as they approached their own top limit.

$60,00, Clark bid.

There was a pause, and then a quiet voice — $60,500.

None of these men had expected numbers like this. The attorney was stunned.

Jim Clark told Rockefeller not to bid what he could not raise in cash.

John said that anything he bid, he could pay.

Incredible as that was, more so was what happened from that bid forward. Jim Clark announced that the three Clarks could each go bond on hired money so they could run this up as high as they wanted.

Rockefeller reminded Jim that he had once warned him not to bluff.

Jim said they were not bluffing — $65,000.

John bid $65,500.

Maurice warned they were now beyond faith in the company and the oil industry.

Rockefeller agreed totally. He said they were now up to faith in ourselves. He said his bid was $72,500.

Maurice Clark stood up, "The business is yours."

The next day's Cleveland *Leader* carried an advertisement

for carbon oil, benzene, and lubricating oils from the new firm of Rockefeller & Andrews.

That same issue of the Cleveland *Leader* was exciting if you worked along the shores of the Cuyahoga. It explained that there were now 50 refineries, large and small, on the Cuyahoga. They represented an invested capital of $3,000,000, and they were putting out about 6,000 barrels of refined oil per day. Two thirds of it was shipped to New York and other ports for export.

And on one refinery there was a new sign: The Rockefeller & Andrews Company. Shortly after that there was another sign at the head of Kingsbury Run:

THE STANDARD WORKS
Owners:
J. D. Rockefeller
Samuel Andrews
William Rockefeller

Just about that moment, the Gilded Age began — and it seemed to run on iron and oil, which turned the Cuyahoga iron red with an iridescent scum of oilbow colors.

There were some in carriages going over the bridge who looked down at the red and the rainbow and said it was a shame to dirty the river that way. But those who were right down in the waters in boats and barges and scows thought the red and the rainbow were the sweetest colors a river ever had.

And a young man named J. D. Rockefeller was just on the point of becoming a legend among the bankers of Cleveland — in fact, of the world.

John would leave the river. That story is known to school children. John's competitive shrewdness turned cruel — demanding excessive rebates from railroads hauling oil — price cutting in competitor's back yards until they agreed to sell out to him.

John left the Cuyahoga for New York City where the banks were bigger.

His name came to stand for greed.

As a billionaire, he continued his boyhood habit of ten percent for charity.

17

The Quaker's Oats

THE MAN WHO made the Cuyahoga one of the most influential rivers in the United States was a short, tough, strait-laced German, Ferdinand Schumacher.

But before he arrived some preparations had been made. While Cleveland evolved with the opening of the canal, Akron sprang into being. And it grew not in a gently rising curve, but in sharp steps like the stairway of land locks to its summit. Most of these steps up resulted from the canal's reaching new major shipping towns on its way south and finally cutting through into the Ohio River in 1830. Akron's population jumped to 910.

The completion of Dr. Eliakim Crosby's Cascade Millrace using the waters of the Little Cuyahoga was the next big step up.

Then as each of five grinding mills was built at each of five dams one above the other, climbing the side of the Little Cuyahoga valley, Akron became 2,336 people.

In 1840 the city took an extra large step up. Leicester King had always wanted to connect Akron to Pittsburgh by canal. General Perkins and Dr. Eliakim Crosby helped on this one, too, but King spearheaded the politics and financing.

King had ten years of saddle time invested before Ohio agreed to make available one dollar for every two dollars raised by private investment. Pennsylvania voted $50,000 to the long canal from Pittsburgh to Newcastle to Youngstown, Warren, Ravenna, Akron. King needed $840,000; so again he took to the saddle, riding hundreds of miles on the byways along the right-of-way, raising funds.

Despite the financial panic of 1837, King was successful, and the Pennsylvania and Ohio Canal came into Akron in 1840, using for its last leg the runoff spillway of Dr. Crosby's mill-race. That connected it to the Ohio and Lake Erie and from the moment of that connection another major phase of Akron's growth began as the city became terminal, tavern, warehouser, and stevedore to a three-way waterborne commerce.

Now within the city other industries grew, particularly clay products, farm machinery, wool, leather goods, and boat building.

But the Little Cuyahoga was about to make Akron into the nation's headquarters for one of mankind's basic staples with the help of an unsmiling little German storekeeper.

While Ferdinand Schumacher was becoming Akron's largest industrialist, the young pioneers who furnished the waterway foundations for his industry had become old men.

General Perkins was the first to die, in 1844.

Dr. Crosby, encouraged by the success of Cascade Mill-race, set out to build an even greater one at Cuyahoga Falls. But he ran into trouble with financing, then he ran into harder digging than he anticipated, then he ran into the financial panic of 1837. With his fortune and his health smashed by the project, he moved west in 1853 and died in 1854.

Judge King built a fortune and died in 1856.

The general, the doctor, and the judge left their names on streets, schools, and the pages of history.

Dr. Crosby had been right when he said Akron would not grow into a really great city just by being a warehouse and a tavern for the passing canal traffic. He said they had to *make* something to ship out. And they could not do that until they had power for manufacturing.

To furnish that power they built Cascade Millrace, a controlled sluice split off from the Little Cuyahoga on such a course that it came down the escarpment over a series of dams to turn five enormous water wheels. At these damsites five mills grew up: The Aetna, a distillery; the Center Mill, north of

Market; the Cascade, near the bottom of the hill; Perkins Mill, wool; and the City Mill.

These weren't little village mills where you took your grain to be ground while you waited. The Little Cuyahoga's waters ground the grain, 50 barrels a day, then went over the spillways into the canal and floated the flour north to Cleveland, south to Cincinnati. That made Akron a very large flour center. But that was about to seem small.

Even at 29, Ferdinand Schumacher wore an older man's beard, squared off severely below the chin, heavy on the sides but with the smooth ecclesiastical upper lip. Above it sat a Quaker's shovel hat which shadowed a stern face set against relaxation, tobacco, and liquor.

In 1851 he came from Hanover, Germany, to Akron, and there he started a small grocery on Howard Street.

The only reason that is important to the Cuyahoga is that Ferdinand did not like to see his customers buying such deluxe and fancy foods. He thought it was a little sinful. Back in Germany in the grocery business, he used to sell a lot of oats, good solid grain that grew good solid people, and cost very little. America ought to be eating it. So he put in a stock.

However, Akron people did not bring oats to the table. Oats were for the stable. Oats were for horses.

So the oats did not sell. But Schumacher was a stubborn man. For three years, he worried about people not eating oats; and in 1854, he invented a chopper to make tiny cubes of oats. He packed them in one-ounce jars.

Akron people took a liking to these little cubes of oats, bought a lot of them. In five years, Schumacher built a small factory near Market and Howard. It was referred to as the German Mill. He did so well that in five years he needed a second plant. The railroad had arrived. Since he had one plant on the canal, he built the new one in the triangle formed by Main, Market and Exchange Streets.

In the next ten years, Schumacher's business grew like wild oats. When you consider that Akron left the oat strictly for the horse until Schumacher chopped it into blocks, the growth was dramatic.

The oat is something to which you must apply quite a lot of ingenuity to make it marketable. Now in 1876, the stubborn Dutchman found a way to precook the oats and run them between rollers so that they flaked off — rolled oats. I can't go ashore far enough to show you all the excitement this caused. But even from the banks of the Little Cuyahoga's Cascade Mill-race, you could see that the whole United States liked Mr. Schumacher's rolled oats.

More Schumacher plants went up alongside the Cascade and the canal — and now alongside the railroad. Schumacher mills occupied an entire city block, and turned Akron's skyline into towering elevators for grain storage.

The eight-story Jumbo Mill was the biggest enterprise in Akron. Ferdinand Schumacher had become far and away the nation's greatest miller. In addition to making rolled oats, he also made flour; and he marketed all the way from Boston to San Francisco.

He was not a leader in the sense of drawing men to him or organizing them or stirring them. He *was* a leader in the sense that men said, "Look what Schumacher's doing; let's get some of that, too."

Following Ferdinand Schumacher's success, many others in and beyond Akron went into the rolled oat business and into the flour business. It had been a mill town ever since Dr. Crosby built the Cascade. But by 1880, there were ten large mills along the Cascade and Little Cuyahoga, and 11 smaller ones.

Strangely enough, the big trouble that started now was because of a wise Scotchman in Canada who was looking down upon the American milling picture from north of the Great Lakes. It seemed to him that American flour mills were too far from their best source of grain. He thereupon built a large mill in Cedar Rapids, Iowa, in the heart of the wheat and corn country. He made flour.

The instant that happened, nearly every mill along the Little Cuyahoga switched instantly from flour to oatmeal, Schumacher's special domain.

Cummins & Allen, owning two mills, built a third right under Ferdinand Schumacher's nose beside Old Stone Mill.

Crowell & Andrews over in Ravenna had bought up the Old Quaker Mill there. They were two powerful young Clevelanders with a lot of nerve and drive. They built this mill up so that it made a strong challenge to Schumacher's mill.

When Schumacher reached the age of 64, he faced a very rugged test. Just as Crowell & Andrews were hitting him hardest in the market place, a fire in the night hit his mills.

For a deeply religious man like Ferdinand Schumacher who looked for the hand of God in nearly every action about him, this was a double blow. The fire caused dust explosions, instantly followed by implosions. And by morning, the mightiest mills in America were ruins.

While smoke still curled up from standing blackened posts, word spread through the crowd which was almost all of Akron, "Well over half a million damages."

"He'll never make it back."

"Who? Schumacher? He'll be rebuilt in six months."

"Nope. No insurance. He says death, storms and fire are God's punishing us. To insure against Him is blasphemy."

Ferdinand Schumacher was crushed. But he didn't whine. The only sign to the town was that hour after hour Schumacher's small figure paced the blackened site of his mills.

He would stop and retrieve a trinket here and there.

This made the population nervous, because in this town, no matter what business you were in, you were in the milling business. If you weren't *in* the mill, you were serving or selling to those who were.

Seeing its largest employer wiped out set Akron scurrying to put him back on his feet. But Schumacher was hard to help.

The men from the brewery walked over into the charred ruins. When they found him, they pointed out to him that the huge piles of grain on the surface were only water damaged. "We can use that. We'll pay cash. It could bring you enough to start construction."

But the little purist would have no part in corrupting youth with alcohol.

Albert Allen of Cummins & Allen, the stiffest competition, walked over onto the burnt acreage, "If you say the word, we'll supply your customers until you can rebuild. We'll ship it in your bags. Hold your trade for you. Be glad to do it."

"I should think ye would," Schumacher said, "you have a fine new mill and no business. I have business and no mill."

The town worried, Schumacher's brutal abruptness was driving off all those who would help them save the business of Akron. They watched him walking along the banks of the Little Cuyahoga, then along the canal with his hands clasped behind his back, thinking.

One morning the gate guard at Cummins & Allen sent a runner to the outer office saying unless he was losing his mind he had just admitted Ferdinand Schumacher though the man would not give his name. He had brushed right by.

The outer office told the inner office, and Albert Allen had all cigars and cuspidors removed from his office.

The man with the spade-cut beard who walked in snapped, "You were good enough to offer your assistance."

"Yes." After his recent rebuff, Allen answered in lean language.

"I accept your offer," said Schumacher, "but different. I have thought this over very long. When Alex Cummins died last year, he made you sole executor of his estate, without bond. That means he thought you an honest man; he ought to know. I understand you increased the value of his estate substantially, so you be also a good business head. I'm proposing to you — your company and mine should merge."

Allen could have been surprised, or he could have been reluctant. But he said nothing.

"P'raps you're wondering," continued the great miller, "what is to gain you should merge with a company with burned down mills."

The old man now took paper from Allen's desk and a pencil from his vest, "Here is your plant along this canal. You cart your grain four blocks up and down the rise to gain the rails. Here is *my* loading platform alongside the railroad tracks.

"I believe we could lay pipe under the road — with a blower here — und blast our grain from the cars direct to your mill."

Allen studied the sketch and fingered his chin.

"Appraisers can value the two properties," Schumacher said. "We let that set shares."

Within the month, Schumacher Milling Company was incorporated for $2,000,000. Work began on a great trench and three large pipes, ten inches, eight, and seven.

To the amazement of Akron, it worked.

Akron went back to work.

Many today who can find the Little Cuyahoga cutting in and out underneath Akron don't know that the pipes were still at work under there, blowing grain between the Quaker Oats elevators on the hilltop and the mills down over the canal.

Now the oatmeal business appeared to do so well for Ferdinand Schumacher that 21 vigorous competitors had crowded in by 1886 to glorify the oat — and to chop the price. The weaker companies kept cutting the price to survive. Chaos sct in.

To stem the falling prices, an enormous association of oatmeal millers formed. All but one company joined. Schumacher, the stubborn, stayed out.

The association had problems. The marginal members quietly accepted a shaved price now and then. Buyers knew that you could approach certain association members with a price deal. The association failed in a year.

Another was formed; this one levied severe fines on any member company which cut prices. But what this did was hold prices protectively high to allow 20 new nonmember companies to form and sneak in under the association price to undersell them *all*.

H. P. Crowell stepped forward. He was one of the young industry leaders who had begun with Andrews in Warren and moved to the Little Cuyahoga. He called a meeting of the industry and he made a blunt proposal. How can the public favor the miller who uses the best grain and the best processes when it's sold in bulk? If we put it in a package with a name on it, the customer could tell the good from the bad.

He proposed the formation of a big new company which would intensively advertise a brand name. "And I'm sorry, Ferdinand, but it shouldn't be *Schumacher.*"

Seven out of the 21 companies were willing, and they merged to become American Cereal Company.

Ferdinand Schumacher thus became president of the largest cereal company in the world, without even liking the idea.

He did not believe in Crowell's ads and his fancy package. "I built the biggest business in the whole country without advertising. And this foolishness in putting oatmeal in fancy boxes is a waste. Let them scoop it out of the barrel like before. Cheaper, too."

The name they put on the package was picked by Crowell. Quaker Oats.

Schumacher tried to continue as before, supervising every detail of the business himself, including reading all the company's mail, personally. Not only that, he answered it all in person.

They had to move the offices to Chicago to be central to their western plants and Akron. When the Dutchman left the Little Cuyahoga, he walked out of our story. But not until he had fulfilled Dr. Crosby's prophecy that if the waters of the Little Cuyahoga were made to furnish power, it would make Akron.

18

Giants on the Little Cuyahoga

ONE EXPECTS the mighty and overpowering rivers to influence the destiny of the people on their banks. Indeed rivers of barely controllable brute strength like the Ohio, the Colorado, the Columbia, are so totally imposing they force conclusions upon their shores and their men.

But the short, winding Cuyahoga is exciting for the opposite reason. It makes men loom large because they took her small breadth and currents and through man-made works amplified the Cuyahoga's power and reach and navigability.

The tremendous national flour and cereal industry headquartered in Akron and made possible by the millrace which Dr. Crosby split off from the Little Cuyahoga vastly exceeded the expectations of Crosby and his colleagues. Yet Cuyahoga waters were about to start another chain of events which would make Akron the center for an enormous international saga.

When C. A. Barnes, Akron hat store owner, returned to visit his home town of Jamestown, New York, he met a frail young doctor who had ceased practicing medicine and was carrying around an idea too large for most men to see.

Benjamin Franklin Goodrich had started to practice medicine so young that people had no confidence, so he wandered into other vocations, at one point real estate. In this business, he came into possession of a failing Hudson River rubber plant which he could not sell. He felt his only way out was to operate it.

He was not able to halt the failure; but he became deeply involved in the mysterious personality of the witch, rubber. Soft and resilient when given its freedom, if captured in a mold only a little smaller than itself, rubber would crack iron to get out. Sometimes sticky, it could also be hard and glassy.

But Benjamin Franklin Goodrich could make it do his will rather predictably; and he could think of a thousand uses for it. He knew the process had to be different from that dictated by the equipment in his old shop on the Hudson. He needed big money and a lot of water to cool hot rubber.

Goodrich had married a Jamestown girl, and he was there looking for capital when C. A. Barnes came home to Jamestown from Akron. Goodrich was still not the confident type of man one pictures raising substantial capital. Yet when he discussed rubber all could see he had a mind with an upstairs in it. Listeners could picture him in the laboratory, if not behind the ledgers.

C. A. Barnes heard him. Barnes too was a quiet man, but in his work of fitting hats to the leading heads in Akron, he had come to know the soul and mind of his adopted town with a strange sureness.

From the back of a small drawing room Barnes watched Goodrich conclude an impromptu but earnest presentation of the potential in a rubber factory. Though Goodrich's earnestness had captured the concentration of the man, his forthright statement that he was seeking capital started men edging away.

Barnes caught Goodrich's eye and beckoned. Natively courteous, Goodrich required several minutes to disengage himself from the question period. But when he finally did, Barnes said to him, "Akron. Akron, Ohio, is the place you want. It has water from the canal and the Cuyahoga River."

"I have water on the Hudson. What's needed is—"

"Men who need a business that needs water. Akron people built water channels to encourage manufacturers."

Goodrich studied Barnes with the natural suspicion of the oft disappointed. Barnes continued as if he spoke for all Akron, "Write down these names: Colonel Perkins; George Crouse; Schumacher; Seiberling; David King; Buchtel."

Goodrich's face was puzzled. Barnes went right on.

"Those men will understand, and if they believe you, they'll find the money."

Goodrich made a trip to Akron.

Perkins and Crouse listened first. Colonel Perkins, son of General Perkins, then traveled to New York to look at Goodrich's rubber shop to see if there was some machinery there and to see what he could learn of the rubber business.

When he came back to Akron, he called a meeting at the Empire House near Lock 1. Perkins looked around the taproom mentally taking attendance: Miller and Buchtel from farm machinery were there; Schumacher, Cummins, Hower, Allen from rolled oats and flour; Christy, a banker; David King, son of the Judge; and J. Parke Alexander, a professional town builder. The action men of Akron had come.

It was a formidable and an able court. Perkins said to young Goodrich, "Tell them your mind, Ben."

Ben Goodrich rose. He explained the vast, varied market he saw for rubber. "I plan to start with fire hose. Leather hose leaks or breaks just when you need it most. Then I'd go to other lines. I'll bring some of my machines from New York; and give it all my time. Everything else must come from somewhere."

The most able of men can get their feet through their collars when confronted by a showdown like this one. Goodrich's earnest, but modest delivery, coupled with his too varied biography, caused a silence in the room as Akron studied him.

But one of the leather men — a square-shaped block, George Crouse — stood and faced the group. In a slow, deep voice that vibrated windows, he said, "This young man has something Akron needs. We've got to keep him here. I subscribe one thousand dollars now."

Perkins said, "Put me down for a thousand."

In a half hour, there were notes for $13,500 on the table. It was a pivotal moment at Akron. In view of what happened, of course, this was pin money, but it came from some men who had never seen a piece of rubber.

Goodrich needed more. So the fund raising continued,

and he took in as partner his brother-in-law from Jamestown, Harvey Tew.

For availability of water and transportation, he located his plant near Lock 1 on the canal. The canal swaled out here to form two wide basins with sluice gates to release more water. Goodrich's new neighbors on that site were mostly houses except for Mr. Ohio Columbus Barber who was building a new match factory there.

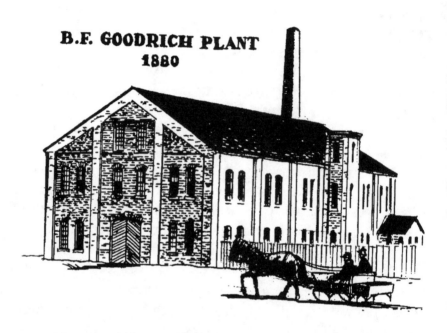

**B.F. GOODRICH PLANT
1880**

So beside the waters of the Ohio Canal inherited from the Cuyahoga rose Goodrich's two-story brick factory, 50' x 100'. It would change the economy of the midwest, spawning ultimately thousands of suppliers to the rubber industry. But at this moment, it housed a rusty jumble of iron which wilted the enthusiasm of the backers.

As they watched, however, the slender, balding young man, with large intense eyes and a wind-catching mustache, move with new poise and purpose. They figuratively exhaled. What the doctor lacked in committee he made up for in motion.

When the first shipment of Brazil Para rubber came up (at

$1.17 a pound), Akron went down to Lock 1 to poke it, smell it, taste it, and shrug. "Too supple to build much on.

And when the stench of vulcanizing sulphur floated down the canal and the Cuyahoga, noses turned up. When the silver coins turned black in cash drawers along the canal from Goodrich's sulphur, the shrugs became a nose pinch and a thumb in the direction of Lock 1.

But one day coils of fat black snakes were stacked in front of Goodrich, Tew & Company — fire hose. The shrugs changed meaning. "Who knows? Stranger things have happened."

The young company had no sales force. It had to write letters to city governments to sell fire hose. City governments didn't buy much through the mail. So Goodrich, Tew & Com-

pany made rubber machinery belting, fruit jar rings, valves for pumps, and tips for billiard cues.

It took in $50,000 in its first year. That was remarkable, but what bothered Goodrich, he needed more money. For five years there were no profits. Backers who had lent money became nervous. Harvey Tew was losing faith.

Ben Goodrich finally said, "Harvey, it looks like a buy-or-sell matter. You want to buy me out or sell to me?"

Tew thought a while. "I'll sell."

The settlement figure was $12,500 for Tew's one-quarter interest in what became the B. F. Goodrich Company.

Tew's withdrawal naturally drew unfavorable attention. The other subscribers now pressed Goodrich. He talked to Colonel Perkins about the future of the industry and how close the company was to profits. "But I need *more* money to get into more product lines."

Perkins came away convinced all over again. He raised enough dollars to pay off all the nervous subscribers. Before paying them, Perkins offered each man the option of converting his loan to stock. Almost all took the cash.

Even with Perkins's help, another money crisis struck in 1878. Perkins couldn't help this time. So George Crouse stepped in and countersigned company loan applications up to $45,000. Crouse and Perkins were now stockholders.

The former subscribers, now very much relieved to be out of it with a whole skin, could afford to be cordial again. But the grins froze in 1880. B. F. Goodrich sales reached $319,000. Profit was $69,000, and the company paid a ten percent dividend. This meant that Dr. Goodrich was able to draw $4,000 over and above his $2,000 salary. Colonel Perkins and George Crouse also drew their first returns in 11 years.

While most of the world considers such a return slavery, a man starting his own business feels blessed. On the strength of it, Dr. Goodrich built another building beside the first. It cost $9,000.

After another eight years of rather slow, smoldering growth came the brush fire bonanza. A veterinarian in Scotland, Dr. Dunlop, wound a piece of rubber tubing around the front and back wheels of his boy's bicycle to take up the shock of cobblestones.

The rubber tire had arrived.

Everything that rolled could now roll faster. It was the second birth of transportation. Production of all vehicles increased — and the demand for tires. On the Little Cuyahoga stood Ben Goodrich — ready.

Well, you know the rest of the story.

The waters of the Ohio Canal and the Little Cuyahoga were about to spawn a giant industry, because here and there across the country now the air was rent by an occasional series of four-banger explosions and blue smoke as a succession of angry black beetles began blatting over the roads, scaring horses.

They needed soft wheels. Akron was ready.

There came now to the banks of the Little Cuyahoga a Bunyanesque parade of Goodrich competitors: Ohio Columbus Barber, Frank Seiberling, Arthur Marks, Stahdelman, Litchfield, O'Neil, Goodyear, Harvey Firestone — tire builders.

But men along the Cuyahoga should pause and tell their children of Eliakim Crosby and C. A. Barnes. Because of them, three quarters of America's rubber products were made in Akron and nearly everything that rolls — from bicycles to 200-ton off-highway mining trucks — rolled on Akron rubber.

That is no longer true.

The great rubber brand names moved south and west and abroad. Some of the most famous faded under dominant foreign trademarks of mergers.

Some Akron tire logos are weathering on empty factories.

Goodyear continues some operations in Akron. And Dr. Ben Goodrich's name still stands as the B.F. Goodrich Chemical Company.

A previous chapter chronicles the widening circle of employment trauma rippling out.

That swift transition forced Akron to find a tire industry substitute — which it did.

19

The Iron Men

THE CUYAHOGA VALLEY is iron country. It all began way upstream south of the big U-turn in the river in the mind of "Crazy Dan" Heaton.

He was Crazy Dan Heaton because he was always flying in the face of what many called practicality; never crazier than when he announced that he could make iron in the Ohio woods and save the wracking trip to Pittsburgh, which was the western-most point at which a man could buy bar iron.

But Dan Heaton had found rocks in the bottom of Yellow Creek, kidney-shaped rocks flecked with gray, the kind that he and his brother James had not seen since they left Winchester, Virginia, about the year 1800. The Heaton brothers had been ironmasters and they knew iron ore when they saw it.

These good-sized boulders weren't more than five percent iron, and a modern ironmaster wouldn't give them furnace room; but to men a hundred hard miles from iron bolts, ax heads, and plow blades, they looked good in 1803.

Dan and his brother acquired land and mineral rights on both sides of Yellow Creek in the Western Reserve in what is now Struthers, Ohio. That's a long way from the Cuyahoga, and yet you will see in a way that it's the main current of the Cuyahoga story.

The brothers built their furnace with stone walls 20 feet high. To get a blast, they pumped water into a long wooden trough, compressed the air in the box, then forced it into the furnace.

Cast-iron plates an inch thick could be carted west to the

portage and floated down the Cuyahoga at $180 a ton, perhaps the first sign of civilization in the Western Reserve.

Cuyahoga Steam Furnace started up in 1835 on the west bank of the river opposite Cleveland. They built cannon. Whittaker and Wells followed these by the river in 1839. Geauga Furnace opened near Painesville. Elyria and Dover had furnaces. Coal began to come down the Cuyahoga so that furnace men didn't need to burn up acres of timber to get charcoal for the furnaces.

The area grew an appetite for iron — for gun barrels, bolts, screws, ax heads, chain, singletree attachments, tools, wheels. They had, by now, quite a few men trained to make iron. But it was harder and harder to find the rocks. Where would the ore come from?

Answering that question created an iron community peopled by Cleveland-Cliffs, Pickands-Mather, Oglebay Norton, Hanna Mining, the Columbia Fleet, Republic Steel, J&L Steel, and others along the Cuyahoga River.

In one sense all the stories go back to a pile of iron and rock slabs at a fork in the road outside the city of Nagoma, Michigan, on which is a plaque which reads in part: "... to mark the first discovery of iron ore in the Lake Superior region. The exact spot is 300 feet northeasterly from this monument to an iron post. The ore was found under the roots of a fallen pine tree in June 1845 by Margi-Lassa Gesick, a chief of the Chippewa tribe. The land was secured by a mining permit and the property subsequently developed by the Jackson Mining Company, organized July 23, 1845."

United States Deputy Surveyor William A. Burt and his company were surveying this unexplored territory for the United States government. Strangely enough it becomes important that the day was cloudy. Burt was having trouble with his magnetic compass needle which suddenly started jumping all around as reported elsewhere in this volume.

It is a revealing moment in history, because what chiefly

interested Burt was not the cause of the failure of the magnetic compass, but the fact of it. He was himself the inventor of the solar compass, and he was now confronted with proof of the importance of his invention in the surveying of these lands where the magnetic compass would not hold true.

On one page of his field notes is an observation by the young and brilliant head of the survey and exploration party, Douglass Houghton, "Spathos and magnetite iron ores may abound on this T-line."

On the morning of the 19th of September, 1844, Burt's field notes show that at one point one of the magnetic compass-men yelled, "Come and see a variation that will beat them all!"

The survey party was astounded to see the north end of the needle swinging a few degrees to the south of west. Burt said, "Boys, look around and see what you can find!" The party scattered and returned in a few moments carrying iron ore. This was on Teal Lake.

Young Douglass Houghton died on the survey, killed in a storm on Lake Superior when his boat upset. His work was carried on by William Burt, who wrote a full and complete record of the survey.

The most exciting thing for Burt continued to be the justification for his solar compass, but the excitement caused by his published reports was something completely different. Since the reports and maps were made in full detail, they revealed to the nation when coupled with the reports published by Jacob Houghton, brother of Douglass, the rich iron deposits of the Michigan country. Immediately thousands of permits were filed requesting permission to explore and exploit.

From that moment, the race was on. Many men came into the Michigan iron country and began prospecting, mining, building furnaces.

In Cleveland, a group of men had founded the Dead River and Ohio Mining Company. They hired a distinguished Ohio scientist, Dr. J. Lang Castles, to go up to Michigan and have a look. He had been head of the Western Reserve Medical

School, head of a chemical laboratory, and had one of the few microscopes in the west. Up on the south shore of Superior at the Carp River, he was staggered to find a hill of red dirt a thousand feet high and a mile long. He named it Cleveland Mountain, secured the permit, and rushed back to Cleveland to explain that Cleveland Mountain contained enough iron to make a railroad all the way to the Pacific Coast.

W. A. Adair and ten associates listened, formed the Cleveland Iron Mining Company, and issued stock. What was to become extremely important was that one of the stockholders was a young attorney who had just moved to Cleveland, Samuel L. Mather, descendant of Cotton Mather.

A few of the men went up to look at the hill of ore. They found themselves in a forbidding land, so they returned to Cleveland and turned in their stock for cash. Then the company sent Tower Jackson up to Marquette in 1852 as its first resident mining agent. What he found there would have sent most men home. Furnaces which were already established were rapidly going out of business. The climate and the lack of fuel made ironmaking impractical. It was necessary to get the ore down to Cleveland, but transportation was impossible. Jackson wrote back to Cleveland demanding the wherewithal to make a plank road like Euclid Avenue to bring the ore from Cleveland Mountain to where it could be floated downlakes into Cleveland.

Building that road is a whole story in itself as the carts careened out of control and killed the mules; but in 1855, Jackson managed to ship downlakes 1,449 tons of ore.

The job of getting this ore downlakes and around the falls at Sault Ste. Marie was unbelievable. So it is an important part of the Cuyahoga story that Charles T. Harvey, a 24-year-old salesman for the Fairbanks Scale Company, was at the Sault trying to recover from typhoid fever. He observed men struggling to transfer iron ore from decks of vessels onto wagons to be hauled around the falls of St. Mary to be loaded into other vessels below the Sault and sailed south to Cleveland. Young Harvey could see what was needed — a canal at the Sault. He decided he was the man to do it. Two years and two-thousand heartbreaks later, on June 18, 1855, Charles Harvey personally opened the sluice gate to let a vessel through from Lake Superior to Lake Huron. Two months later, the two-masted brig *Columbia* passed down through the lock carrying the first shipment of iron ore, 120 tons consigned to the Cleveland Iron Mining Company at the Crawford & Price wharf on the Cuyahoga River. The brig *Columbia* was later to give its name to a great fleet of boats on the lakes.

When that vessel tied up, the Cuyahoga River became the center of another industrial revolution in the United States.

But only a few men could see it. Samuel L. Mather was one of them. He was the young attorney in whose office the company was formed. Having attended Wesleyan University in Middletown, Connecticut, he was sent to Ohio to look out for the Mather real estate holdings in the Western Reserve, and he was swept up in the iron fever which formed the Cleveland Iron Mining Company. While the fever extinguished in a flurry of depression as the stockholders sold out their stock, Samuel L. Mather held his.

Then the panic of 1857 shut down the iron mills in Pittsburgh, Youngstown, Cleveland, and spread disaster all the way up to the Michigan iron range. The company needed $50,000 more cash to keep its Michigan range in action. Mather went to New York and Boston bankers to borrow. The answer was "no."

That's when Sam Mather invented "iron money." Unable to get real money, he came up with a system of issuing small drafts on nicely printed stock against the treasure of the Cleveland Iron Mining Company. These notes were sent up to Cleveland Mountain where they were used to pay miners, teamsters, cooks, and hardware stores where the company bought supplies. Due to the confidence in the Cleveland Iron Mining Company, these notes circulated freely and were in no hurry to float back to Cleveland to be turned in for cash. This delay was enough to let Mather and the company officers sell more stock.

In this manner, the company inched its way up until the

demand for iron increased in 1861. The Civil War needed cannon, rifles, rails. Now came the ships.

Captain Alva Bradley, then of Vermilion, Ohio, built a fleet of schooners and brigs to carry the ore. It was an 800-mile trip that demanded the utmost seamanship, but the unloading on the Cuyahoga was perhaps the most challenging dock operation in history.

Captain Bradley, one of the earliest in this type of navigation, continued to increase his fleet. In 1858, he launched the *London*. Soon after that the *Exchange*, and then the *Wagstaff*, which carried iron ore for a quarter of a century. In the year 1873, he launched six new ships, and at that point he began to build steamships. In 1867, the Cleveland Iron Mining Company bought a half interest in the *George Sherman* for $14,000, capacity 550 tons of ore.

In 1869 came the big leap forward when Captain Peck built the *R. J. Hackett*. In 1872, when Cleveland Iron Mining Company was bringing down nearly a million tons of ore, the company bought into the Cleveland Transportation Company, a fleet of steam vessels and schooners especially built for iron: The *Geneva*, the *Vienna*, the *Sparta*, the *Havana*, the *Genoa*, the *Verona*, the *Helena*, the *Sumatra*. These vessels each carried a thousand tons per trip to Cuyahoga docks.

To this point, the Cuyahoga's merchant navy was wooden sail, but now iron vessels began to enter the trade. The first iron freighter built specifically for this business, and not a converted passenger vessel, was the *Onoko* built in Cleveland in 1882. She was 287 feet long.

In 1888, the directors of the Cleveland Iron Mining Company commissioned two steel vessels, $400,000 each, capacity 2,600 tons. These giants dropped the cost of transportation from about $3.00 a ton to $1.22. That year, Cleveland Iron Mining Company brought down 5,000,000 tons.

Now the locks and channels and harbors were getting too small for the vessels. The Poe Lock opened in 1896; it was 800 feet long, 100 feet wide and 22 feet deep. Cleveland Iron Mining Company now built a 426-foot steel ship, the *Cadillac*, with an 18-foot draft and a capacity of 6,000 tons. Along came the *Choctaw*, the *Andaste*, the *Centurian*, the *Presque Isle*, and the *Angeline* at 455 feet. And now the ships were too big for the unloading equipment and the stage was set for a new race of mechanical men on the Cuyahoga shore.

In 1890, Sam Mather, who had guided the Cleveland Iron Mining Company, died. His son, William Gwinn Mather, was vice president of the company, which in 1891 merged with the Iron Cliffs Company to become Cleveland-Cliffs Iron Company. William Gwinn Mather became president of the combined operation and remained so for 42 years.

But it's time to flash back to another beginning. The most exciting year in the history of the Cuyahoga was 1883. By then a plethora of iron companies, working out of the Iron Trades Building at the mouth of the river, had founded such a complex of mines and vessel companies that they had run out of people. One man might be sales agent for one company, mine supervisor for another, vessel coordinator for another. Iron had become a Cuyahoga way of life. Families grew up in it, married into other families who were in it, and compounded the complexity of this burgeoning business.

Many wished to straighten matters out so that a man could be clearer about whom he was buying from, whom he was selling to, whom he was competing with, and who were his partners. But there was little time for that because of the industry-shaking events which crowded in with more urgency than the desire for organization. The congress had just passed tariff legislation protecting the iron industry, thus attracting more men into the building of furnaces. The Bessemer process was just showing men new uses for lower grade ores; power drills were coming into use so that less attractive deposits could suddenly be worked. Cornish pumps were being installed in the pits and, as the shafts sought deeper levels, new hoisting machines were coming in. A new and longer lock was opened at the Sault, the 300-foot *Onoko* had been built with a capacity of 3,000 tons, promising even greater speeds and capacities. Explorers were moving beyond the Marquette Range into the area north of Lake Superior, opening up the Vermilion Range. The Steel Age was dawning.

Many men saw that to push into this new era some clearer organization was needed in the industry. Samuel L. Mather was in the process of merging to form Cleveland-Cliffs; Hewitt & Tuttle was consolidating into Tuttle, Oglebay and Company, the partnership of M. A. Hanna and Company was forming from the Rhodes and Carter Iron Ore and Pig Iron Agency; but to most, action was more interesting than organization.

The young son of Samuel L. Mather, and brother of William Gwinn Mather, was a shy and thoughtful man who saw that a ton of finished steel was the result of such a puzzle of separate and individual coal, ore, furnace, dock and vessel companies that there was a strong need for an integrated company efficiently coordinating installations all the way from Lake Superior mines to Cuyahoga mills to the Allegheny coal fields. He was working for the Cleveland Iron Mining Company, having served a long apprenticeship in the mines of Michigan. There he had formed an especially strong attachment to two dramatic men: Colonel James Pickands, a Civil War hero now turned mine supply merchant, and a hard-driving iron agent affiliated with a dozen companies, J. C. Morse. These two were men of action, but they had a tremendous respect for the quiet thoughtfulness of young Sam Mather. Morse and Pickands were brothers-in-law, for they had come home from the ranges to Cleveland to marry two Outhwaite sisters and take them back to the iron country.

The three men conducted their dreaming by mail; and then one morning a modest advertisement appeared in the Cleveland *Leader*: "Announcing the formation of Pickands-Mather & Company, dealers in pig iron and iron ore." They had two rooms in the Grand Arcade in Cleveland, with an option on more space, and they had an office boy named Henry Dalton, with a jovial smile, who loved to sell. In 1884, this infant firm brought down 1,022 tons of ore. Two years later, they brought down a quarter of a million tons. And then, as they carried out Sam Mather's plan, Pickands-Mather & Company grew from three men and an office boy to thousands of employees working from the Mesabi Range in Minnesota across vessel fleets, blast furnaces, steel mills, reaching far east into the Allegheny coal country, with the Cuyahoga valley being the nerve center. It was a flaming hot, smoking, clanging Vulcan's workshop.

That Cuyahoga valley leadership continues today. For example, on the shores of the Cuyahoga, Joe Slater brought about one of the technological breakthroughs in the thousand-year history of iron and steel.

In 1943, the United States government begged for more blast furnaces for the war effort. Now the blast furnace, one of the basic inventions of all time, had remained very much like the furnace Dan Heaton built in Struthers, Ohio. It had grown, of course, so that by 1943, it stood 100 feet high, 28 feet across; and it could cast 1,400 tons of pig iron a day. But Joe Slater, chairman of Republic Steel's blast furnace committee, wanted to get more iron out of a furnace.

A Mr. Julian Avery, who had never seen a blast furnace, but had a large inquiring mind, had suggested to Joe Slater that the air blast whipped through a blast furnace so fast that not all the valuable oxygen would consume in the chemical reaction inside. He wondered: If you put a throttle valve on the top of the furnace to tame this blast and create a back pressure, could not the chemical reaction be carried out more completely?

While it sounded rather simple to Mr. Avery, furnace men were not keen about any procedure which would turn their smokestack into an explosive pressure cooker. A blast furnace is an awesome monster to tamper with. Its stack contains a tumult of gas, coke, and metal at 2,500 degrees; and the whole is aggravated by a turbo-driven hurricane coming in at the rate of 85 cubic feet of air per second.

But Joe Slater, a patriotic man, was under the pressure of war. He wanted to try putting in the *entire* 100,000 cubic feet of air needed to make a ton of iron, or what he called, "A hundred of wind a minute." If you could hold it in there without blowing your stack, that should give you twenty percent more steel. If it didn't work, "there'd be a hell of a mess on the cast house floor."

On the morning of July 7, 1944, Joe Slater and Walter Montgomery, his furnace foreman, pumped in a hundred of wind, holding it in with a pressure top. A long working day later, the pressure top had not blown, and Joe Slater was making more iron from one furnace than anyone in all history. The company president, Charles White, asked Joe if he thought the furnace would take it on a regular basis. Joe Slater replied, "If I can run two weeks, I can run two months. If I can run two months, I can run forever."

Slater tortured his furnace with pressures no other furnace had endured. He found he could also reduce the coke use by 13 percent, and lower the entire cost a dollar a ton. The furnace could use poorer coke and leaner ore. He died on the job shortly after, but he made the Cuyahoga valley put out more steel for World War II than was possible before Joe Slater managed his hundred of wind a minute without blowing up the melt-house.

Meanwhile, Cuyahoga vessels drained the Michigan and Minnesota mines so deep that they were down to lean ore, and ore that was costly to recover. The steel industry in the center of the United States was suffering from competition of richer ores nearer the surface in many countries. That's when the men at the mouth of the Cuyahoga made their next big moves: opening a vast new Labrador iron ore country and benefiting low-grade domestic ores with the development of taconite.

The drama of the iron men continues.

20

Peck's Big Boats

STRANGELY ENOUGH at mid-century, mid-America needed a special kind of hero — a ship. The design of that vessel was trying to be born in a lot of men's minds.

While the iron men from the mouth of the Cuyahoga were opening up the Michigan iron ranges with nerve and muscle, Mark Hanna and others were opening up the coal fields south of the Cuyahoga and floating coal down the canal to feed the ironmasters' furnaces.

But it took a whole navy of three-masted schooners to bring down a little iron, and a cavalry of mules to unload it.

A ship was needed unlike any other. It must be narrow enough to clear the locks, but big enough to bring downlakes acres of the Michigan Peninsula and Minnesota. The ship needed to be deep draft for iron ore capacity, but shallow enough for Cuyahoga navigation. It needed quarters for a large crew — quarters that would take up no space. It needed so many conflicting characteristics that marine architects couldn't design her.

At the age of 25, Eli Peck built his first ship. She was graceful, shiply, and shapely. In 1847, he built one with a graceful name, *Jenny Lind*; but she was a slightly ugly boat in front, scowlike.

"What's Peck up to?" people asked of the shipwrights as they watched it build over the months.

Peck was sneaking up on the design for the most unusual merchant fleet in world history.

Even among shipping and boating people of the world, few know that hundreds of miles from salt water, the mouth of the Cuyahoga headed the nation's most unusual and massive merchant navy in a single trade. This was the Great Lakes bulk fleet — iron ore, coal, limestone, some salt, cement and cereals. Its enormous vessels have decks designed for fast unloading of bulk cargoes, hulls designed against the tantrums of the inland seas, drafted for the shallow channels and rivers. They are also designed to the special appetites and chemistry of blast furnaces.

When strangers get their first close-up of these long, low floating monsters beating the waters between the Cuyahoga and Duluth, they often pull off the highway and stare. At first they think they're looking at two vessels passing each other, or, on hazy days, at an island with a house on each end. Waiting for one at a drawbridge is a ghostly experience. They don't move, they loom at you, strangely silent. And as you wait, the ship never stops going by.

Beating the water between the Cuyahoga and Duluth for about 30 turnarounds a year, these great ships do the basic hauling for the midwest's steelmaking complex. To seacoast ship lovers, they don't have the wave-splitting grace; but when you get to know them, these bluff-bowed boxes become truly beautiful.

How they happened is very much the story of Eli Peck, who was as blunt-bowed and relentless as his most famous ship.

At the age of 25, Captain Peck set up his own yard in among already existing shipyards, dry docks, and related establishments near what is now West 58th Street in Cleveland. It was in 1847 that his *Jenny Lind*, a 200-ton-capacity schooner, slid off the ways and into the Cuyahoga.

The *Lind*'s hull was closer in form to a barge than his other ships. The blunted bow and squared cross section carried much more cargo than the usual boat of the same size.

The cargo she carried was best described as "miscellaneous," neither bulk nor package freight, but bricks, textiles, machinery and milling supplies, and groceries. A real need for the big bulker had not yet shown itself by 1847.

But in the year the Soo opened, Eli Peck and Irvine U. Masters entered into a partnership that bore their names. Peck & Masters was small among the Cuyahoga shipyards which turned out 84,000 tons of shipping, 500 vessels, between 1849 and 1869. Peck & Masters built 50. But it tells you something about them to note that these 50 added up to 27,000 tons, *roughly a third of all Cuyahoga construction.*

Mr. Masters was not a seafaring man; he was a financial partner with other interests, in 1863 being elected mayor of Cleveland. But this capital gave Peck the freedom to carry out his design concepts which built the kind of shipyard they wrote about in the paper:

It will be seen that nearly all the vessels, whether sail or steam, built by Mr. Peck, were of the first class, being mainly barques and large propellers. They will be recognized by those familiar with lake commerce as models in size, beauty and strength, whilst several have made unusually quick trips.

While conventional boats by conventional builders hovered around the 150-ton capacity mark, Peck combined size and design to produce such boats as: *Desota*, 570 tons, barque (1855); *Evergreen City*, 610 tons, propeller (1856); *Northwest*, 628 tons, barque (1862); *Pewabic*, 730 tons, propeller (1863).

And, as he progressed, he knew he was getting closer to the bulk carrier the nation needed for converting the red dirt from Michigan into Cuyahoga iron for shafts, plates, rods, nails, rails, and destiny.

Peck often stood before his work board reflecting. Irvine Masters often rose from the ledgers to look over his shoulder. He would see light pencil-sketch overlays on drawings of a ship already afloat. Detail changes; a plan for communications, oddly from the bow of the ship to the stern; a rudder that could be operated from more than one station. Sometimes, even as early as this, penciled speculations on the layout of the deck — the engine house and pilothouse far separated.

"What ship is that, Eli? Your great S. S. *Maybe*?"

"Yes. With a new idea added. She may never sail."

"Eli, we didn't get a reputation from Buffalo to Detroit for *old* ideas."

"Well, I should be ready with drawings in two months. Can we raise construction money on her then?"

"Not for a speculative boat, Eli. Our loans are too heavy for the next six to twelve months. But after that ..."

But they never did build it together. The faithful Masters died in 1864. For five years, Peck carried on alone with the assistance of his now highly trained workmen and, once, a consultant in the person of Captain Gilbert Knapp, who watched over the government's interests during the construction of two revenue cutters. Although Masters was gone, his name remained in gilt above the offices that prospered under his financial guidance. Eli Peck was a loyal man. He kept Masters' name on everything.

This fairness led him to build speculative vessels for which there were no orders:

> *... A working man himself, he was in thorough sympathy with his workmen, and in the slack season, instead of discharging men and thus entailing want upon them, he built vessels* [not on order, but] *on speculation, that he might keep the men busy and their families supplied. Providentially, these speculations were always successful* [as we will later observe] *thus illustrating the proverb that 'there is he that scattereth, and yet increaseth.'* [Cleveland *Plain Dealer*]

And because of this speculation the Captain's great ship finally sailed.

You see from 1864 to 1869, few ships were built by Peck & Masters. Peck's men operated their well-reputed skills to the repair and upkeep of other men's ships, and Eli took care of administrative and financial matters. In this capacity, he began to diversify. He was active in the formation of the People's Gas Light Company and became president of that organization. He was also made a director of the Savings Loan Association.

This brought to his attention with greater forcefulness than ever the importance of iron to Cleveland, and the need for super-vessels to carry enormous amounts of ore.

It was Eli Peck's final examination for destiny. Standing now in his pattern loft, aged 47, amid a clutter of half-finished drawings, he had in his head all the best of history's naval architecture.

He had the confidence of 22 successful years of shipbuilding; he had the timidity born of repairing shipwrecks. He had the awareness of need. He had the poise to go after construction money. To raise money, he had to talk his ship.

"It will be propeller. Single screw."

"Single?"

"Yes. Two of them, exposed on the flanks, would damage in the shallows. One, sheltered by the rudder, will give as much power and nearly as much control. The engine will be as far aft as she'll go.

"Aft, sir?"

"Aft. To free up cargo space. It'll be bigger, though — more powerful. That's the trouble with these new propellers. Though they burn only a fraction of what the side-wheelers do, they're not as fast. So it needs engine."

The hull's cross section was to be square. And there had to be some sail area. Three masts, gaff rigged. He wasn't through with sail just yet. If the new engine failed, the wind would bring Peck's boat in. But the masts were to be short. When the sails were not set, they would look like cargo booms. But all this was a combination of existing features.

"But what will make this boat a money-maker, the pilot-house is to be way forward over the bow."

"Forward, sir!"

"Forward."

A significant thing was Peck's move for much greater teamwork between the docks that loaded and unloaded.

"You see, they've got those loading chutes at Marquette on twenty-four-foot centers now, and everyone's converting their deck hatches to fit. Loading is fast, but *unloading* is where the tie-up is."

"To discharge these boats fast, the pilothouse and other deck structures have got to move out of the way of unloading. Way up forward, over the point of the bow that you wouldn't use for cargo anyway. Then she'd be clear and free, just a big stretch of hatch covers in the middle."

The plans came in before the money did. Peck decided to plunge ahead on speculation. But it occurred to him that Captain Robert Hackett might be interested. They had spoken on several occasions, and Hackett had always been partial to Peck & Masters vessels. Peck sent a message to Detroit on an upbound customer's boat.

Hackett arrived on the next steamer. He looked over the plans.

"It's boxy right up to the stern, Eli."

"Yes, Robert."

He looked over the stocks and the scaffolding, indicating a ship of mammoth capacity. He asked questions. Pilothouse to engineroom communications? Controls? Where would fuel be stored? What about crew quarters? Calculated draft? Minor changes were suggested and agreed on by both.

Robert Hackett approved.

"Eli, I'll cosign with you."

Captain Hackett now had reason to help sell Peck's new vessel. He had money in it. But he found himself suddenly in a strangely awkward position.

Typical of this awkwardness was the day he made a strong presentation of the vessel to his competitor, Captain Varm Jensen. Jensen listened to the wonders of the new supervessel under construction. He thought a moment, and then he said, "Robert, I'm surprised at you. You've been a tough competitor,

246

but fair (except the time you beat me to the fuel dock by running through the fog). But now for the first time, you lie to me."

Hackett purpled, "Lie? Why say that!"

"Figure it out, Robert. As hard as you and I compete, if that boat would really run faster, load more, and unload quicker, would you *really* offer it to *me* ... of all people?"

Hackett knuckled his jaw thoughtfully.

"In fact," Jensen continued, "would you offer it to *any* other captain?"

Hackett went to Cleveland. "Eli, we can't sell the boat. We'll have to operate her ourselves."

They formed the Northwestern Transport Company to contract for carrying ore down from Fayette Brown's Jackson Iron Company. An agent for that and other iron companies, Harvey H. Brown (the son of Fayette), bought a minor interest in Northwestern.

Construction on the boat went ahead. They decided to christen it the *R. J. Hackett*. No doubt Peck's fair nature first proposed this. The hull was closed in and the powerful engine was ordered.

Dockside critics watched with interest and criticism. If the boat was so advanced, why was it not being built with plates of iron?

Peck probably realized that the age of steel vessels was coming. But what kept Peck and other yards from metal was that their men were good with wood. Oak and cedar timbers were strong, and the price was right. Iron members and plating were a somewhat unknown quantity; they were scarce and very costly. Oddly, early wooden ore boats, from the *Hackett* on, accelerated the change-over.

Came the day for launching, many Cleveland mining and transport men were there. They were immediately struck by the great length of uninterrupted deck between pilothouse and after-house. And the masts were sawed off. But the wheeldeck was ridiculously high.

"Why make her look like a giraffe?"

"He did it so the captain can see down over the bow in close navigation."

"What'll keep her from rolling over?"

"Eli Peck's reputation, y'damn fool!"

What the onlookers couldn't see was that although the

Hackett had rather conventional major dimensions — 200 feet long and 33 feet wide — space available for cargo should hold at least 1,129 tons of iron ore. Ore boats of conventional layout prior to this time had been considered large if they could carry 700 tons.

Everything was ready. The *R. J. Hackett* left the stocks bound for history. Bound to keep Cleveland steel mills fed. Bound to leave her mark on the shipyards not only on the Cuyahoga but all along the Lakes.

She drew the calculated amount of draft, when her holds were full, with room left over to clear all navigable waterways. She steamed up to the Jackson mines, the propeller churning up 12 miles an hour. They opened her 24-foot spaced hatches to the loading chutes there and churned on back downlakes with 1,200 tons of ore for the mills at Cleveland.

Along the Cuyahoga, a lot of loud mouths were silent.

With only one trip to her log, plans were being made for a second ship like her.

The *Forest City* was completed by the following year. For one season she operated as a consort, in tow. In doing this, Northwestern Transport continued a practice begun by oxen and barges, carried on by tugs and schooners operating in restricted waters, and employed later by propellers towing sailers over open waters when the latter became unprofitable to operate under their own power. By the time that season ended, they had already made enough money to purchase an engine for the *Forest City*. Except for MacDougall's picturesque whalebacks, there is yet to be found the ore boat built after these that did not use Eli Peck's design. Boats sprang up all over the Lakes — engine room aft, pilothouse forward, and a long stretch of hatches in-between.

These were the long ships.

There were, of course, improvements. Thirteen years later, the *Onoko* — out of Cleveland's Globe Iron Works — became the first iron ore boat with a hull built entirely of iron. The 1880s saw development of the Bessemer steel process and a material even better for the naval architect. The *Spokane* of 1886, also built by the metal fabricators of the Globe works, was the first Lakes boat with a hull of the new material. The year 1895 saw one of the last holdouts of resistance to metal boats. Harvey H. Brown wanted a boat in the Northwestern fleet bearing his father's name. Captain Peck designed it and it fitted his earlier boats to a tee. With one change. It was iron above the waterline.

But methods of forming and joining sheets and strengthening metal had not yet been perfected, so the idea of composite boats never really caught on. It was merely transitional.

The propeller steamer Peck built in 1869 was to be the mold for the modern ore carrier. With engines aft and pilothouse in the point of the bow, nearly the whole hull was left open for cargo. Loading hatch centers were spaced 24 feet apart for the convenience of standardized loading and unloading equipment.

High sides she had, too, and a square hull section to carry nearly twice the cargo of previous boats the same length.

By this time, the good Captain Peck had retired. Ships carrying the legend "N.W.T. Co." had been sold to the Vulcan Transport Company in Detroit. "Peck's boats" had not retired. They stayed on the Lakes and their image can be seen today in the big ones towed by tugs in the serpentine Cuyahoga.

By that time, ore shipping on the Lakes was over its growing pains. Things got to the point where a landlubber could manage a fleet. Or think it profitable enough to get someone to do it for him.

At this writing (1998), the thousand-footers cannot navigate the winding Cuyahoga. However, Peck's basic design is still there blown up to fantastic size — an office building pilot-house astern; and on the bow an aiming stake and a bow watch station.

The thousand-footer, *Columbia Star* is named for the tiny brig *Columbia* which brought 142 tons of ore down from Jackson Mine to the Cuyahoga docks — starting the inland seas navy.

21

Here Comes the *Mather*!

SOME PEOPLE lit up with recognition when the S. S. *Samuel Mather*'s bow cut the mouth of the Cuyahoga. The name is a Cuyahoga name.

Beginning with the Mather who was on the executive committee of the Connecticut Land Company, there has always been a sobersided, public-conscienced descendant of Cotton Mather silently and firmly at work for the well-being of the Western Reserve and the Cuyahoga valley.

They were thin-lipped men of towering conscience and ability, reclusive during gaiety, tough as iron during trouble. And iron was their business.

The name has always been on one of Pickands-Mather's best boats: there have been four S. S. *Samuel Mathers* — one afloat ever since '87 when the three-masted, sail-and-steam-powered *Mather* was launched.

I don't mean the S. S. *Samuel L. Mather*, but the *Samuel Mather*, named for the Mather most widely known as "Mister Mather."

Thousands who never knew him personally have seen his works, which fanned out like the stern waves off his ships. All along the iron ore route from the Cuyahoga to Port Arthur on Superior you see the name cut into marble on colleges and hospitals; engraved on the letterheads of foundations, being polished in raised brass letters on the fronts of corporations, branches of corporations, and the ownership plaques on vessels running from the Cuyahoga north to the iron ranges.

On the Cuyahoga, the name's part of the spoken language;

the inflections range from a groan to a sigh. The sighs must wait for his biographer since this book hasn't time to go inland. But the groans are apt to be from maritime competitors based along the Cuyahoga, which some feel might be just a fat fishing stream but for Mather.

Even his seniors called him Mister Mather, and in crowds a path appeared to let him through. Closing in after him, they'd recall the mine accident that pinned young Sam Mather under timbers and iron dust, smashing ribs and an arm which he carried bent through the rest of his life, and through several chapters of this book because of his multi-chaptered life. The dignity and lonely ethics of this slight, wiry vessel operator did not quite conceal his awesome dreams of empire.

He made the Cuyahoga boss over a 2,000-mile steelmaking network, stretching over water and rail arteries all the way from the West Virginia coal country hauling coal to the Cuyahoga furnaces on up through the Great Lakes shipping lanes to the iron ranges of the Marquette, Menominee, Gogebic, and Mesabi in Minnesota.

This network involved scores of furnaces, coal mines, iron mines, limestone quarries; and connecting them all, the world's most unusual merchant navy.

Sam Mather built it.

That brings back into the cast the man who made the Cuyahoga shores the nation's oil refinery.

John D. Rockefeller did not set out to get into the iron business big. But Mather's firm, Pickands-Mather, was deep in the iron business, mining it, smelting it, hauling it.

When the financial panic of 1873 struck like a Lake Superior blow, iron companies were hurt badly. Rockefeller was persuaded to come to the aid of the Merritt brothers, the seven wild iron men of Minnesota who owned and opened the great Mesabi Iron Range.

From that instant, he had to throw so much good money after bad that he felt he had to get into the Mesabi and manage it. To manage it, he had to own it.

While the iron world laughed, Rockefeller acquired, piece by piece, control of the little-regarded Mesabi, where the ore was said to be too lean, too powdery, *and too distant for lower Lakes mills.*

Then a strange message crept over the steel world like the shadow of a cloud. It dawned slowly that he had control of the richest ore property known in the world.

The steel world was afraid Rockefeller would build a steel mill. They locked arms against him under the leadership of the then king of steel in America, Andrew Carnegie.

But if they meant to fight, Rockefeller had an advantage — the ore. "I was astonished," he said, "that the steelmakers had not seen the necessity of controlling their ore supply." They had left that in his hands, unwittingly at first, unwillingly later.

Now Rockefeller set out to control his transportation. He wanted the largest fleet of ore vessels afloat. He wanted construction supervised by an expert. To John D. that meant Mather.

Rockefeller, by then living in New York, invited Mather to take on the work. Mather declined; he was not interested in creating a competitor to his own company's vessel fleet nor its iron ore. Rockefeller said he was only going to haul his own ore in these boats.

Still Mather declined. Having married Amelia Stone, he had heard harsh things about Rockefeller from his father-in-law, Amassa Stone.

But when Mather was in New York, a Rockefeller aide asked him if he would come to Rockefeller's house for dinner.

"I'm sorry. I have a dinner appointment."

"Mr. Mather, could you come for just a few minutes before your dinner?" Gates asked. Gates was Rockefeller's number one man. "Mr. Rockefeller said even ten minutes would be enough."

"It wouldn't. You don't purchase a great vessel in ten minutes."

"I suppose not," Gates grinned. "But it's enough time for you to say 'no' again, isn't it?"

Sam Mather was ushered through an ornate residence

into the presence of the unjeweled, unostentatious, plain multi-millionaire.

"Mr. Mather, thank you for coming. I understand your time is very short. We certainly wish you would assume charge of vessel construction for us?"

"Thank you, sir. But I have explained that I have no desire to encourage you into the ore-carrying trade. I'm perhaps your strongest competitor."

"Would I go for help to one of the weakest?"

Mather grinned. "Why go to a competitor at all?"

Rockefeller explained that he wanted Mather's great knowledge and legendary integrity.

Mather explained that a vessel was a very expensive construction, costing more than an oil refinery.

"And it would cost *me* even more than it would *you*. But I feel you would spend my money more carefully than your own."

Countering Mather's objection to building a ship for a competitor, Rockefeller said, "If I'm going to build *anyway*, shouldn't you as well have the commission as anyone else?"

"Well, although I'm honored, the commission for superintendence of constructing a vessel is not really interesting to me."

"Of course, Mr. Mather. But I had in mind twenty-four."

"Twenty-four!"

Mather walked the carpeted deck of Rockefeller's study.

An unheard of fleet! Or was it an *armada* to conquer the iron world?

Construction of such a fleet would upset the entire economic balance of the Great Lakes. All the shipyards from Duluth to Buffalo could not produce it at once. If word of this order got out, the price of shipbuilding would go out of sight. No other ore company or vessel operator could afford so much as one vessel, and might have trouble even getting repairs. Competitiveness to this new fleet could vanish.

In this depression, with the mills already on slow bell, iron could remain locked in the rocks; miners and mills could idle. If such a fleet was to be built, better that it be built by someone who knew the currents and whirlpools of the Great Lakes marine iron world.

Further, they were to be the largest boats on the lakes — 475 feet.

Mather stopped pacing. "A free hand, Mr. Rockefeller?"

"Absolutely."

"I had better build them."

"Excellent."

"One thing. Until I let contracts, don't discuss how *many* vessels I am building for you."

Mr. Gates remembers smiling at such instructions to such a buyer. But Mr. Rockefeller gravely nodded and extended his hand, "Since you can't stay, I hope you are not late for your dinner, Mr. Mather, and that we see you soon."

Mr. Rockefeller dined alone; they never met again.

In under ten minutes, Mr. Mather took the largest single order for vessels ever placed on the Great Lakes. For the knowledge he carried home to the Cuyahoga, any shipbuilder would have paid his soul.

The Great Lakes had ten shipyards, all shut down, except for desultory winter repair work. These yards all together could build 12 vessels simultaneously, if the two largest each built two ships.

When the hull was designed, Mather sent a set of plans and specifications to selected shipbuilders saying he was "interested in building a ship" and asking for a competitive bid on construction. "If bids are low enough, possibly two ships may be built."

Every yard on the lakes wanted that contract.

Shipyards which had been on hard times for five years sharpened their pencils, trimmed to the bone their production steps; they secured tight-belted competitive bids from their sub-contractors on engine construction, cabin trim, steel plates, and rented money.

The bids came back to Mather lean and clean.

Mather was a thorough man. He asked each shipbuilder to come to his office in the Western Reserve Building on a

Wednesday to go over their bids with him individually to see that they were in agreement on quality of materials and certain construction details and completion schedule.

On the appointed day, ten shipbuilders were seated nervously in Mather's anteroom, each hoping to answer satisfactorily Mather's questions on his bid. Several, seeing their competitors close up, suddenly wished they had bid even lower.

The first man had been in Mather's inner office 20 minutes when he walked out. All studied him carefully. He had a swallowed-the-canary smile that took the heart out of the others.

Mr. Mather would no doubt come out now, thank them for bidding, and dismiss them.

But he called in another shipbuilder. He was in Mather's inner office the quarter part of an hour. Those still waiting speculated that probably the two lowest bidders had been called in first.

When he came out, they all noted that he walked right out of the office as if embarrassed by his good fortune.

Mr. Mather had suggested there might be a second ship built. It looked as if both contracts had been assigned.

But Mr. Mather called for a third shipbuilder.

Well, by four o'clock several of the ten shipbuilders went to the Weddell House bar.

By five o'clock, they had discovered that every yard had got a contract. Each had been bidding only against himself.

It's said that at the Weddell House bar that night any seaman could get all he wanted to drink by just walking in.

By nine o'clock, the news had traveled all the way up to the head of navigation on the Cuyahoga.

When the first 12 vessels neared launching, the second 12 were built. Then Rockefeller wrote Mather asking him to run the fleet. Mather felt he could not, to be true to some of his complex partnerships. He thus declined the leadership in 1898 of what became shortly Rockefeller's 28-vessel Bessemer Steamship Company, largest ore fleet in the world. By 1901, it was 59 vessels, including some 500-footers and above.

On the east shore of the Cuyahoga now began rising the towering, red brick Rockefeller Building of 17 stories to house the fleet offices; to house other iron and vessel companies as tenants; and to throw its morning shadows across the crumbling roof of the old Hewitt & Tuttle warehouse which now wore a patina of lichens and green moss.

It was the building where young Rockefeller landed his first job. On every anniversary of that date, Rockefeller raised the flag.

In the recovery of 1900, American mills produced 18-million tons of steel. Rockefeller's fleet could carry ore enough for every furnace on the Great Lakes. He raised the rates to $1.25 a ton from Duluth to the Cuyahoga. Mr. Carnegie had to pay it.

But it scorched his Scotch soul. He immediately began construction and acquisition via Henry Oliver of a great fleet of his own, The Pittsburgh Steamship Company, at the mouth of the Cuyahoga.

The war was on.

Bow to bow, the vessels of these great fleets raced for survival. Their wash lapped the banks of the Cuyahoga night and day, and their unloading spillage reddened the current.

The mills raced each other just as violently. Small mills and small fleets and small mines were getting killed in the fight.

A Mr. Morgan in New York, initials J. P., thought the battle was getting too rough for the good of his holdings, his clients, and the American economy. He set out to bring peace and efficiency by a huge vertical consolidation, putting together a company called U. S. Steel Corporation.

Although J. P. was to pay a multimillion-dollar premium rather than admit it to John D., "vertical consolidation" was the lesson the young Cuyahoga commission clerk had just taught the world.[1]

---

1. Rockefeller got out of iron and the lakes a few years later, but the whole industry had seen the example of organized bigness he and Mather had set. For example, the dozen shipyards which built his fleet soon combined to become American Shipbuilding, headquartered at the mouth of the Cuyahoga.

Rockefeller had seen a rainbow on the river. Following it upstream, it had led him to an industry in chaos, petroleum. He had straightened it out by establishing "vertical consolidation." It meant control your raw stock, control your transportation, own your refinery, make your own barrels, ship it over your own carriers to your own stores.

Young John D. had played the lesson out in a fiery public chapter. But the students weren't all listening. So old John D. ran a make-up semester for the steel business. The tuition would be high.

To make a "vertically coordinated" steel company with its own iron ore mines and vessels and limestone and furnaces and mills, Morgan raised funds to buy out Carnegie's magnificent mills and Gates' wire mills; and then he had to go to Rockefeller, the teacher, to buy his mines and boats.

J. P.'s arrogant pride wouldn't let him walk down the street a few blocks to talk business with John D.

So they sparred through emissaries, haggling a half year, splitting hairs the size of trees. It was much like the auction John D. had been in with the three Clark brothers years before. But the ante was higher. The price went up weekly as the two delicate dinosaurs coyly dickered. Finally they settled on $88,500,000 for John's ore mines and ore vessels.

Putting Rockefeller's boats together with Carnegie's boats, Pittsburgh Steamship Company became a colossus of shipping — 106 vessels!

John rented them some space for their shore captain's office in the Rockefeller Building by the Cuyahoga.

It became the greatest fleet on the Lakes. When a ship from Pittsburgh Steam went by, it was called "a Corporation boat."

Corporation boats of this first great Pittsburgh fleet, rebuilt many times and converted and repowered, beat the water. Some sailed under other ownerships and other flags.

Many were towed to Canada and converted to barges, some were tied up and converted to floating storage silos, some are anchored off Great Lakes cities as breakwalls, some were towed to Italy for scrap.

Corporation boats from that great fleet have changed names ten times, and still hauled cargo. Meanwhile the Pittsburgh Fleet, headed by Admiral Khoury, went to larger, newer vessels, 730-foot supercarriers!

The *Mather*, which opened this chapter, continued working until 1980. Today, she's tied up as the Steamship William G. Mather Museum, east of the Great Lakes Science Center and the Rock and Roll Hall of Fame and Museum at the foot of Ninth Street in Cleveland near the Coast Guard vessels.

22

Man with a Wheelbarrow

ALL FALL and winter of 1847, visitors to Cleveland had to stop and stare. A lonely shovelman was gravely clearing and digging a straight right-of-way from the mouth of the Cuyahoga south. His progress was slow, but you could tell he was following a line of stakes.

One startling fact was that he worked in all weather, and he worked with a sense of mission.

Visitors always asked the Warren-Cleveland stage coachman, "What is he doing?"

The coachman always answered, "Building the Cleveland-Columbus & Cincinnati Railroad."

The coachman enjoyed leaving it right there, and feeding the information out as piecemeal as possible.

"One man? Why?"

"To hold the charter 'til they raise the money."

"Why do they have to hold it?"

"If they don't start building the railroad within ten years of getting the charter, they lose it. Time's almost up. So they started one man to work. Legally, the road is now under construction."

"Why don't they really build it like they meant it?"

And in that question lies the story. Railroading on the Cuyahoga is a history of adventures in canniness and contrivance.

The mechanical part of that history is glamorous and boldly exciting for all to see. Some of it has been preserved for us by Mr. Mack Lawry of Akron. As the traveler drives north up Route 8 from Akron, away from the river, he is surprised to see several cold but once real steam-snorting locomotives by the roadside. A sign proclaims this to be "Railways of America." They are the same trains that once punished the rails from coast to coast, come to pasture now by the Cuyahoga to serve as a sight for tourists.

Mack Lawry was an Akron businessman, but for years his hobby became building and collecting model railroads as well as the old retired locomotives, Pullman cars, and cabooses that stand in front of a red brick station house typical of those that bordered the Cuyahoga for 50 years.

Inside the station house is a museum of railroading and a corridor lined with paintings from the heyday of trains. From there, you will come upon the largest collection of model trains in the world. A single table holds 11,000 feet of miniature track and 300 switches, all built by Lawry.

Solemn-faced, white-haired Lawry, one of those wiry men of deceptive energy, announced, "It's a piece of America ..."

The rails are a big piece of the Cuyahoga story, because they importantly determined the character of its banks. More important, however, were the people.

This story begins with the group of top-hatted, fine-frocked gentlemen gathered on a sunny afternoon in October 1847, at the river end of Superior Street in Cleveland. Alfred Kelley, stoop shouldered and frail from his work on the canal 17 years before, led them, a long-handled workmen's shovel over his shoulder. At a point just beyond the city limits the group paused long enough to survey the peaceful scene of trees and meadows.

Then Kelley began to dig, scooping the earth into a wheelbarrow with determined bites. When it was full, Jim Briggs, attorney-at-law, hefted the handles of the wheelbarrow and trundled it a short distance away to dump the contents.

From a fallen log where he had taken a seat, gingerly, so he would not soil his trousers, George F. Marshall laughed. "Bravo, gentlemen," he slapped his thigh. "Another barrow-load like that and you'll have it flat enough to stand solid and see which way to aim our railroad."

The others did not pause in the work.

Marshall cackled, "How long you think it'll take us to get to Columbus, Alfred?"

Kelley passed the shovel to Mr. Handy and wiped forehead perspiration. "Well, George, since it's only taken us ten years doing nothing, think how much faster the job will go with five of us shoveling."

Mr. Handy drove the shovel deep into the moist earth. "If George'd get off those sitting muscles, we might make it faster." He heaved the clod into the barrow and passed the shovel to Mr. Sargent.

Oliver Perry staggered a step from the unaccustomed activity at the wheelbarrow, "Get to it, George. We've got 200 miles to go."

"Right, gentlemen," said Kelley, "and once begun, we can't stop."

Even Marshall sobered slightly, "Well, it's a comic beginning for a railroad. We've hardly enough money to pay for this ceremony, but we're obliged from this moment never to stop construction until the road is finished — or lose the charter." Marshall laughed again, but the smile faded swiftly as he looked at Kelley's face.

Kelley said, "Mr. Marshall, I do not intend to be associated with a comic venture." He looked toward Columbus. And he handed the shovel to a bona fide workman, "Mr. Teasely, commence building this right-of-way to the south; and do not leave the job for any reason except the Sabbath, without calling for a replacement." He turned to Marshall. "We have money to raise."

The smiling reporter from the Cleveland *Leader* asked, "Mr. Kelley, do I understand the ground for the Cleveland & Columbus Railroad is now officially broken?"

Kelley's responding gaze was steady. The smile faded from the journalist's face. "You do," he said slowly, "and there is little prospect of its ever being mended."

Next morning, the *Leader* reported the incident as a "Railroad Accident." The paper took this sarcastic tone because the first charter for the Cleveland & Columbus Railroad had been granted ten years before when railroad fever was running high throughout the land and every city was determined to get rails first. It would mean the making of a city.

The prize was worth it. Cleveland, which the canal had enabled reaching the New York market, was already a trade metropolis, funneling goods from the midwest and the middle seaboard which extended west and north to Michigan's shores. Railroads, as they were envisioned by the more worldly, would not only siphon off this trade, but also open up the entire eastern seaboard as a market.

The winner in this pit fight to gain the first charters would be a metropolis even greater than Cleveland at the end of the canal.

Sandusky, archrival to the river's king city, was first to petition the Ohio legislature for a railroad. Their charter to build the Mad River and Lake Erie Railroad was refused, understandably enough, because the legislators were concerned more with paying the debts on the completed canal than with financing a new and so far unproven means of transportation.

Thus began the bickering of a score of Ohio towns that had been ignored by the canal, all trying to attract the railroads and feed on the wealth of a nation's trade.

On January 26, 1832, the first charter was granted incorporating an "Erie and Ohio Railroad," but since no terminals were named and the route vaguely implied as "between Lake Erie and the Ohio River," every city that could conceivably became a part of the route joined the melee to be first with rails. Painesville cited her harbor as "susceptible of as great, if not greater, improvement as that at Cleveland."

It must be remembered that while those giants who spun the steel webs that eventually entwined this nation were just beginning to grow in power in the east, the midwest thought only in terms of short line roads.

Each city sought to become a rail metropolis by starting first and, hopefully, linking later with other short lines.

Other cities soon squared off in rivalry. While Painesville was planning a route through Chardon, Salem, and Wellsville, the editor of the Ashtabula *Sentinel* was busy devising a route from his city through Jefferson, Warren, and East Liverpool. Both cities fought bitterly and eventually got their charters.

At this point, Conneaut put in her bid for a railroad, declaring that it was the terminal point of the shortest and least expensive route between lake shore and the Ohio River. On January 11, 1836, a charter was granted for the Conneaut and Beaver Railroad Company.

Clevelanders, seemingly confident of their position as the lake shore terminus of trade, took a smug view of the petty scrapping around them when they eventually chartered their own railroad link to tie the three major cities: Cleveland, Columbus, and Cincinnati.

Saner heads prevailed among the Cleveland railroaders, and it was soon realized that while the Columbus to Cincinnati route would draw upon the midwestern markets, a route to Pittsburgh would eventually open the outlets through the Pennsylvania railroads to the eastern markets. And so it was that on March 14, 1836, the Cleveland and Pittsburgh Rail Road Company was granted a charter.

Now Cleveland may have been a wolf among the bickering scrapping dogs around it, but Cleveland also lacked the one thing that eventually terminated the plans of many short lines in that day — money.

With the financial panic of 1837 already brewing, Pennsylvania refused to support her end of a Cleveland and Pittsburgh route.

Strangely enough, on an eve of panic, the national treasury was choked with money and a national surplus revenue was declared. By an Act of Congress on June 23, 1836, the surplus was divided among the states, a prize of $2,000,000 falling

264

to Ohio. Clevelanders cast a greedy eye on the $120,000 allotted to Cuyahoga County.

But it was up to the county officials to designate the money either to internal improvements which would give the railroad its start, or to private individuals. The dog fight continued in earnest with only two things positive about the prize: it was generally agreed that the state would loan the money with the interest going to support public schools; and, what was most important as fuel to this bitter fight, the United States would never ask for its money back.

The compromise law of March 24, 1837, was almost immediately dubbed, "The Plunder Law." And Cleveland campaigned to raise the two thirds necessary to match their plunder, expecting Pennsylvania to do likewise for her end of the road. Valiantly, the editor of the Cleveland *Herald* exclaimed, "Private investment and state aid combined would have to raise less than a million dollars."

He called for a public meeting to determine where the county's plunder would go. Unfortunately, words weren't enough. No meeting was ever held, and the fund commissioners of Cuyahoga County finally announced that the money would go to private individuals.

While the plunder law was just one more fruitless route to nothing for Clevelanders, it indirectly applied a pressure to the railroad builders that couldn't be ignored.

It seems that the city of Sandusky had succeeded in obtaining plunder from the state and had used it to build their long-delayed Mad River and Lake Erie Railroad.

It may have been a rickety strap-iron, "shake gut" line, plagued, as always, with snakeheads and shifting roadbeds; it may have been horse-drawn and only 33 miles long, but, by Godfrey, it was a *railroad*.

Sandusky was out in front.

Now the railroad interests pitched into the race with a vengeance. In the utter confusion of short-line railroads that were chartered during the 1830s, one of them, the Ohio Railroad, rallied enough support to give Sandusky a good run for its money.[1]

The Ohio Railroad Company set out to build a rail link from Sandusky to Manhattan at the mouth of the Maumee. Unfortunately, this stretch of so-called land had been known from the time of the early frontiersmen as "The Black Swamp." The "walk on the mud" as it was called, was a railroad on stilts sunk in the swamp. It was doomed before it started, but at least it had been started.

The charter for the Cleveland, Columbus & Cincinnati had lain dormant since 1835, and in those days charters were granted with the stipulation that work would begin within a certain period of time and continue uninterrupted. In time, the Big C's charter had quietly expired, but no one seemed to notice. Cleveland still had the canal.

Sandusky extended her rails southward while Clevelanders, who knew these puny, strap-iron affairs could never carry the weight of freight that poured over the canal, were content to wait until someone got up gumption enough (and money enough) to build a real railroad.

On the morning of July 27, 1846, however, an incident occurred that shook the Big C to the roots of its complacency. Fifty passengers arrived in Buffalo, intending to travel by lake ship to Cleveland where they could catch a canalboat for Cincinnati. No doubt ship captains were prompted by the additional fares they could collect by extending their passage to

---

1. The Ohio Railroad was another dream of Painesville organizers. Originally, the charter described a road to link Buffalo with Toledo (then called Manhattan) along the lake shore. The Painesville people were lucky in securing a share of plunder from the state, but it is hinted quite strongly that their luck was tempered somewhat by shady manipulations.

As required by the plunder law, Painesville sold stock in the enterprise to pay two thirds of the construction costs. The directors gleefully announced that $800,000 worth of stocks had been sold, but perhaps glossed over the fact that this was in land, not cash. It was only after the state had paid out some $249,000 that it was discovered the land was actually worth only about $30,000. By then, the Ohio Railroad had squandered the money on one of the most comic fiascos in the history of railroading.

but their argument appealed to the sophistication of the travelers. "Why suffer that plodding canal," they reasoned "when you can take the railroad at Sandusky and get fast, modern transportation all the way to Cincinnati?"

Fifty passengers promptly voted to bypass Cleveland and booked passage for Sandusky.

Clevelanders panicked. It was an omen that couldn't be ignored. In desperation, the old charter for the Cleveland, Columbus & Cincinnati Railroad was revised and the Ohio legislature passed an act enabling Cleveland to subscribe money for the road.

But the directors trying to sell bonds for the enterprise in New York soon found that old canal debts were still hampering investors and the Mexican War was siphoning off most of the extra money available. They returned with a mere $250,000 in conditional stock subscriptions and pledges, hardly enough to resume the project. As far as the discouraged directors were concerned, it would take a genius to make the Cleveland, Columbus & Cincinnati Railroad a reality.

With only a small glimmer of hope, Richard Hilliard of the Big C endured the stagecoach to Columbus and called on Alfred Kelley, who now lived there.

"Mr. Kelley," Hilliard explained, "you're the only man who can do the job. Our second charter is about to run out. If work doesn't start, we'll lose it. There won't be a railroad. There won't be a Cleveland."

No doubt, as they talked, Kelley was remembering the long years he had slaved to bring the canal into reality.

He looked at Hilliard, his firm mouth pinching the words. "I'm sorry, I can't do it."

Hilliard continued the discussion far into the night, but Kelley refused.

Hilliard spent a fitful night as guest in Kelley's house, perhaps dreaming of his report to his fellow directors. At breakfast he greeted Kelley with a bleak good morning and seated himself at the table.

Kelley cleared his throat. Hilliard's eyes snapped up from his plate. He waited, not daring to speak.

"I've reconsidered," Kelley said. "It is a matter of great importance to the interests and welfare of the state. I feel it is my duty."

Alfred Kelley returned to Cleveland by stage as the president of the Big C. He would return to Columbus by rail.

The clock was running. Kelley raced to begin construction before the charter ran out. The surveys were made, the estimates totaled, but on deadline eve not a shovelful of earth had been turned.

And so it was, on October 1, 1847, a solemn group again marched to a spot just outside Cleveland proper, their top hats and frock coats contrasting blatantly with their shovels and wheelbarrows: Kelley, followed by the treasurer of the Big C, T. P. Handy; the engineer, J. H. Sargent; Attorney James A. Briggs; H. B. Payne, Oliver Perry, John A. Foote, and the laughing, slouching, logsitting George F. Marshall.

And it was that fall and winter that a solitary workman was to be seen laboring forlornly in this remote spot, languidly picking at the earth, loading his wheelbarrow and carting it to a spot where the mounds grew bigger and the task more hopeless.

In one last now-or-never gesture of defiance at the lethargy that had stalemated the Cleveland railroad for ten years, Kelley called a meeting in the Empire Hall on the evening of August 1, 1848.

The *Herald* described the audience as "the bone and sinew of Cleveland-Commercial men, Dry Goods, Grocery and Hardware dealers, Mechanics, Capitalists, Bankers, Lawyers, Doctors and even the clergy."

Kelley took the podium gravely, "Gentlemen, we are here to discuss the condition of the Cleveland, Columbus and Cincinnati Railroad." At that moment, a number of men grouped at the doors, prepared for an early exit, were startled to hear the bolts click. Kelley was taking no chances.

"Yes, gentlemen," said Kelley. *"The doors are locked and will remain locked until we have enough subscribers to make sure the road."*

Kelley then launched into one of the most persuasive arguments of his career.

Murmuring grew as Kelley took his seat and John A. Foote moved forward. He pointed directly at Richard Hilliard.

"Mr. Hilliard. Will you raise your subscription to fifteen thousand dollars?"

Hilliard rose as if to a question. But he said, "Yes."

With every "yes," cheers rocked the hall. All told, they totaled $114,000.

Mr. Kelley had his railroad. And he built it with the same shrewd integrity and hawkeye to the future with which he had built the canal.

"Strap iron, Alfred?"

"No. Solid iron. I'll be in Quebec this June to see that seven thousand tons of English iron are delivered promptly."

"That's not enough."

"It'll last the year. By then, I'll be in Wales. I'll get another five thousand tons. Spread the order in thinner piles. A thinner price."

"But the money, Alfred?"

"We'll pay in company bonds."

"The culverts? We'll build in wood?"

"Stone."

"The bridges?"

"Iron."

"There's not enough."

Kelley bit the words. "We'll find enough. We build in stone and iron so we don't do the work twice."

As Henry Clay had observed years before in addressing the Ohio Legislature, "Alfred Kelley has too much cast iron in his composition to be popular."

A scant year from the historic meeting in Empire Hall, the first locomotive puffed up the grade at River Road. Kneebreeched boys swarmed over the wooden flat cars and slowed the train to a stop.

With such a faltering first run, one wonders if the Big C would ever rival the canal in freight. However, on November 22, 1851, the train made its complete run from Cincinnati to Cleveland carrying a full load composed of the entire state legislature, the mayors and city councils of Cincinnati and Columbus, headed by Ohio's governor, Reuben Wood.

Officially, Big C said good-bye to their man with the wheelbarrow who had worked so diligently through the winter of '47, but he was not to be unemployed long. It is said he immediately went to work on the Lake Shore Line.

Railroad fever became epidemic and men sought new rails to carry their money. The Cleveland & Pittsburgh, whose charter had also lain dormant these past ten years, was revived. Rail lines began creeping into the Cuyahoga valley like steel tributaries.

But the Big C Railroad made one decision that was to give rise to a dramatic competitor. It avoided Kent Township's part of the river en route to Columbus. That would not have made much difference except for one thing. That was where Marvin Kent lived.

Kent had settled in Madison Falls where the Cuyahoga's southern course begins its westerly loop toward Akron. By 1850, he was head of a glass works, a woolen mill, and a flour mill. The town changed its name to Kent.

As trains began to roll over the Big C rails, Kent was ready to begin his next enterprise, a cotton mill by the falls of the Cuyahoga. When the Big C avoided Kent Township's part of the river, Kent took it personally. "What's the use for us to build these mills if I can have no railroad to connect us to the outer world!"

Kent voiced the views of hundreds of unrailed towns. Kent, however, did something about it, personally. He stormed off to the state legislature at Columbus and introduced a bill chartering a railroad to run east from his home town, through Warren to the Pennsylvania line, and west from Kent to Ashtabula. Kent was moderate in his immediate plans, but not in ideas. To make sure he would have as many markets at the disposal of his mills as possible, he described a route ultimately running to the southwest corner of the state, to the very border of the south itself.

Originally Kent's name for this road was the Coal Hill Railroad, but to understand Kent's next move, we must understand that this was the era of the great rail mergers and the rail merchants, most of them roughnecks like Jim Fisk and Daniel Drew who used every power at their command to gobble up rivals presuming to be any more than short-line, intercity roads. The history of the big lines is corroded, of course, with cloudy, deals and scandals. Towns and cities which had innocently and sincerely invested money to build rails through their towns often found the charters absorbed by the big roads, their bonds repudiated, their money gone and, in some cases, the rails diverted to other destinations. The merged railroads rushing between the cities made big cities bigger and backwatered the small towns.

But Marvin Kent, with a small railroad charter in his pocket and a big railroad idea in his head, was about to bring the big railroads and the big markets to Kent. Kent's charter presumed a great deal by granting the right to stretch across the entire state of Ohio. It was a juicy plum for the big roads, if they found out about it.

Kent determined that they would not. But the name he had chosen made people wonder about its terminals, and ask. Consequently, Coal Hill was changed to "The Franklin and Warren Railroad," safely mundane. Both towns were well to the east of Kent's prime target on the Cuyahoga. Kent was able to maintain an illusion that his short line was barely long enough to connect two unimportant cities. However, Kent shrewdly kept the terms of his original charter unchanged.

The Franklin and Warren was organized at once and

$900,000 raised in stock subscriptions. On July 4, 1853, Kent stood by the banks of the Cuyahoga and turned the first shovelful of earth. Seven days later, work commenced in earnest to extend the road, not east to Warren or Franklin, but south to Dayton where it would connect with the new Cincinnati, Hamilton and Dayton line.

Kent's so-called Franklin and Warren line was well started on its cut across the state when the money markets plunged again. Drought hit the midwest farmlands, rail building came to a standstill. Kent decided it was time to bring his road into the open and his plan to its rightful place in the commerce of the United States. In 1855, he made a slight change in the name from Franklin & Warren to the Atlantic & Great Western Railroad.[3] Now *there* was a *rail*road!

Over the next ten years, the Atlantic & Great Western grew beyond even Kent's grandiose dreams. Edwin Drake in Titusville brought oil to the road's traffic in 1859.[4]

By the time the Civil War swelled the railroad's traffic to the bursting point, the Atlantic & Great Western, connecting with the Erie Railroad, had the first trains traveling all the way from Salamanca, east of Erie, over 369 miles of track to Dayton, Ohio. By this time, however, Kent was thoroughly disgusted with the mad expenditures, the scandals, repudiated bonds, stock manipulations, bankruptcies, forced sales and the extravagant moneysucking construction which clung like a plague to everything that came near the eastern railroad moguls. In 1864, he resigned.

The Atlantic & Great Western was leased to the Erie Railroad and, although its name remains only in histories and leg-

---

3. Although money was tight in the United States, Europe was bursting at the wallet. It was almost easy for Kent to obtain the necessary financing from James McHenry, an English moneymonger who became the guiding spirit of the Atlantic & Great Western.
4. James McHenry, never one to let the slightest moneymaking opportunity go by, publicized the oil discovery overseas; and, as a consequence, had English investors standing in line to buy the road's stocks. They say that construction of the Atlantic & Great Western proceeded during this period at a pace even faster than the building of the Union Pacific.

ends told by the railroad buffs of today, it had gone far beyond its original purpose in crossing rails with the Cuyahoga.

Into this fantastic garble of railroads that were conceived, born, built, and often bankrupted during the '40s and '60s, we must add one more road — a rather important one in Cleveland's future which led to rails along the Cuyahoga.

While all other roads could take the products of industry and the midwest farmlands out of the port city, the Cleveland & Mahoning was the one road that brought in fuel so necessary for the industrial furnaces. It tapped the heart of the best coal country in Ohio, the Briar Hill deposit near Youngstown.[5]

The question that seemed eminent as far as rail building was concerned was whether or not Cleveland was to use coal and raw materials to become an industrial center or send them out and become a loading dock for the markets of the world.

Quiet voices over the matter were heard occasionally through the 1860s, while the thriving Cleveland & Mahoning hauled coal in two directions, alternating with loads of butter, cheese, and produce from the midwest farmlands. So much commerce passed over the "Butter and Cheese" road that in 1858, Jacob Perkins, the line's prime mover commented, "If I die, you may inscribe on my tombstone, 'Died of the Mahoning Valley Railroad.'"

As business increased, so did prices; and when coal topped $1.50 a ton, Clevelanders woke up. On December 6, 1871, the Cleveland *Leader* commented: "There are millions of tons of coal waiting to be brought to Cleveland over this new route and millions of tons of Lake Superior ore waiting to be smelted here whenever Cleveland can command sufficient cheap fuel to do the work."

---

5. Of course, Youngstown and Pittsburgh were using most of the coal, much to the concern of absolutely no one. But as ore boats piled the best of Mesabi riches at the Cuyahoga docks to be shipped down the C&M rails to the blast furnaces of Youngstown and Pittsburgh, the possibility of coal being brought up from Briar Hill to meet the ore occurred to a great many people. "Why should Youngstown be the great Ohio iron center?" asked a letter to the editor.

The charter for the new line was under the name of the Valley Railroad Company. Unfortunately, the details of the road's construction did not please all the cities along the proposed route.

Akron industrialists wanted broad gauge so that they could load freight and connect at Cleveland with the coast-to-coast railroads without discharging freight and reloading on ordinary gauge lines.

Clevelanders, on the other hand, were interested in the coal the road could bring. They were also interested in freight profits as long as the road never fell into the hands of the big lines. However, that eventually could be offset by building to narrow gauge.

The controversy waged politely in meetings, and the year 1871 closed quietly on a stalemate.

Professor J. S. Newberry, state geologist, offered a suggestion: "... the only way to prevent the Baltimore & Ohio from getting control of the road is to have the stockholders hold onto their stock."

By 1872, every town along the proposed route had sold its share of stock in the enterprise, all except Cleveland.

On February 23, the *Leader*, almost with a sigh of relief, but certainly without enthusiasm, reported the decision of 300 men "representing the capital of the city" who met at City Hall. Standard gauge would be built, which "closes definitely, we suppose, all the debate on the question."

In April, the newspapers were still prodding. Cleveland businessmen just wouldn't get off their wallets. By November, a bond issue was proposed to finance Cleveland's share of the road. And the citizens voted No.

Finally the panic of 1873 crimped business money in an unrelenting grip and the Valley Railroad project silently closed its books and temporarily drifted into history's file of abandoned projects.

But it was not the end. After seven more years of rising coal prices, private capitalists gathered enough money. On February 2, 1880, ten years after its charter was granted, the first train rolled over the Valley Railroad overlooking the banks of the Cuyahoga.

That railroad finally brought the coal to Cleveland blast furnaces. It stirred the great hearths and fanned the flames which marked Cleveland as one of the great cities of the world during the '80s and '90s.[6]

Today, time has forgotten the little railway along the Cuyahoga. But against the sky stands the silent silhouette of the steelmaking it fueled.

---

6. It seems anticlimactic also that so much time and argument was wasted on the question of gauge and whether or not the road would ultimately be absorbed by the sprawling Baltimore & Ohio. The private capitalists who finally built the road voted in favor of the wider tracks which could eventually connect the road's traffic with the rest of the nation's, but they did so with the stipulation that they would do all they could to keep the road from the hands of the big lines. Yet, all breathed a sigh of relief on January 12, 1890, when the story of the acquisition of the Valley Railroad by the B&O appeared in the Cleveland *Leader*. During its ten-year existence as an independent short line, the Valley Road was a loser. It never earned more than its fixed charges.

23

The Cuyahoga River's Greatest Love Story

The Home Place

THERE'S A HOUSE by the side of the river in Bath, that's been building for 141 years. It's the way a house should be built, and I hope it's not finished in my lifetime. They call the house "Old Brick."

Five windows across, three stories high, red brick with white trim, it compels that second and third look. But everyone sees it a little differently. With the sun glancing off rippled glass, it gives back to every man a reflection of what he set out to be.

Having outlived many builders, it's a house which should be studied by all architects and builders who want to know what their business is all about, and by anyone who wants to know the architecture of a love story.

The next to last builder on the job was a lady named Clara Belle Ritchie. Her first move in 1938 was to buy some more of the land around the house. Then she had some workmen replace some bricks that were crumbling, and replace the old stone floor in the basement. The basement mantelpiece was rotting. She had that replaced.

Some newcomers around town thought Miss Ritchie would do better to tear it down and build a modern new ranch. Easier to heat.

"She'll put a lot of money in it."

At first very few knew she was putting back together a love story. She was a single woman for whom love was a fresh and wonderful thing, and she had a lot left over.

The story is there in the structure today to read. It starts with the river road in front of the house, which looks as if a thousand miles of tributary roads were built only to bring someone to this door.

On August 14, 1810, Jonathan Hale, an eagle-faced giant, wrote a letter from this valley back to Glastonbury, Connecticut.

Dear Wife,

This is my fourth letter that I have wrote you since I left home ... and the last one was dated 30th stating my safe arrival, my success, of my Land, etc.

Purchase such articles as you want for yourself in wareing apparel ... medicines, Essences of peppermint, opium which is good in fever & ague. Get a Copper Kettle and get a Plow Share ... a few pounds of nails ...

The best way for you to come, to take Lenox Turnpike to Albany from there to Skenectady & then on to Utica & then to Canandaigue, & then to Buffaloe & put your things on Board a vessel, and come on the shores of Lake Erie ...

Send us word if you can when you get to Buffaloe we will come with oxen and horses (to the mouth of the Cuyahoga) to help you. I'll try to write again before you set out if I can ...

Adieu
J. Hale

To my beloved wife, Mercy Hale

So Jonathan Hale needed a road into his clearing. He went to the county seat at Ravenna.

The record in the county books contains the item:

Jonathan Hale presented a petition signed by Timothy Bishop and others praying for a road beginning at Pontey's Camp on Columbia Road, thence on the most eligible ground to the Cuyahoga Portage ... and said Jonathan having given bond to pay costs ...

277

The road they cut came down along the river and is called River Road; it turned off to become the present Oak Hill Road that runs past the house now called Old Brick, then turned back to the river at Botzum, which at this writing (1998) is the name of a road.

The road was ready in time for the three wagons which were coming on from Glastonbury, Connecticut.

Mercy Hale was in one ox-drawn wagon with Sophronia, six; William, four; and one on lap, Pamelia, two. Jonathan's sister, Sarah, was along and her husband (and cousin), Elijah Hale, with two children, Eveline and Mary. And there were three chickens.

The third wagon held Jason Hammond, his wife and their children, Rachel, Mary, Lewis, and Horatio.

Jonathan had a cabin ready for them. The cabin has quite a lot to do with the construction of Old Brick — and why it is made of brick.

Out of a snug house in Connecticut with a store close by, Mercy came into a wilderness where she must raise five children with just what she found on the land, with her hands and the copper kettle and needles and thread she had brought. A year from her arrival her son, Andrew, was born, the first child born to settlers at this place. In 1813, she had a daughter named Abigail who lived only ten days, and in 1815 she had a son named James Madison.

That translated into fast deepening lines in a soft complexion and premature stiffening of the fingers and swelling of the knuckles of a gentle young woman lugging a huge copper kettle of water and acting as if her husband had brought her to the kind of paradise he had described.

She did not register the shock of seeing her husband thinned down by the ague, with his Connecticut clothes already worn out, and his friends needing clothes and looking to her to make them out of brittle strings of flax they brought her.

She acted very pleased when things improved by 1817 to where she could get imported cloth, a little of it. She was good

with the needle and shears and the valley needed her and kept
her bent over her sewing many hours; for example:

a great coat for Mrs. Miller — $1.25
a jacet for a squatter's son — $3.00
a wedding coat for a groom — $2.50
two pairs pantaloons @ $1.00
two jacets @ $1.50

She was good to the Indians and the squatters and the
neighbors and taught her children some reading, but she lost
weight.

She saw her husband working from sunup to sundown. In
addition to farming for survival food, he had found limestone
on the place, a deposit of lime-bearing rocks washed down by
the streams that fed Hale Run. John J. Horton, the author who
knows this story best, writes that Jonathan piled these rocks up,
covered them with dead timber cut by himself and his boys; then
he burned the rick for 24 hours, pulled off the debris, sifted the
lime from the ashes, packed it in tierces and swapped these
casks of lime up and down the river for cloth for Mercy and for
iron nails and bar iron, and for glass, some livestock, and for
hard money when he could get it or when he was willing to sell
that cheap.

Translated into dollars he was doing this work for about
three dollars a barrel, and delivering up to Hudson and beyond.
But he was better off than most of his neighbors because he was
getting a little cash ahead.

All the while he was watching his wife go from a handsome young woman in 1810 to a work-brittle invalid by 1825.

He wrote her a note:

Mrs. Mercy Hale, she is my true and loving wife
She's been a slave to me a great part of my life.
I hope she'll be rewarded here before she dies
And then receive a mansion in Heaven above the skies.

But actually he meant the mansion to be under the skies right there in Bath by the Cuyahoga River. Therefore at a time when it was a big thing just to plaster between the logs of a cabin and puncheon the floor and plank the loft, Jonathan Hale set out to build a mansion.

In 1825, at a time when there was not a brick house on the Cuyahoga south of Cleveland and many people were moving back east, Jonathan Hale took his sons across Oak Hill Road to dig clay.

Jonathan had built only log sheds. But there was a Colonel Lemuel Porter going to build a brick building up at the school in Hudson. It would be nice if Hale could wait until he could afford to hire a contractor like Porter. But if Mercy Hale was ever to have a mansion on earth ...

Well, Jonathan and his sons, Andrew and James soaked the clay, puddled it into large frames, let it partly dry then sliced it and fired it.

Some of these bricks came out light and powdery, some glassy blue and brittle from too much fire. But a few out of each batch seemed all right. The sides of some bricks bowed out, many had cracks where the clay pulled apart when wet. But the mortar could cover a lot of learning.

Meanwhile, up on the slope they thinned out the woods, cutting large timbers that they squared up with the ax. The family's cash money went to a sawmill on Yellow Creek for sawed planks for flooring.

For heavy jobs like cutting stone for the cellar walls, Jonathan hired some neighbors.

They cut a cellar into the side of the hill, put four great cornerstones in place, and laid up stone to the grade level. Then the heavy timbers went into place.

Because of the slope of the hill, the front of this excavation required no digging. To observers who didn't know Jonathan's pretensions, it looked merely like a one-story house cut into the side of the hill to get the warmth of the ground on three sides.

"Jonathan, you're putting too much weight in those ceiling beams. You don't need it to support the roof."

"They're not roof supports. They're foundation timber."

Then a surprised settlement saw the frame go up two stories, then three.

Jonathan traded lime to Captain Thorndike of Tallmadge for iron nails. And he traded to Dudley Griswold and Mr. Jerrod for raw iron. He had some iron hinges cast in Tallmadge.

The canal came by and Jonathan was able to sell a lot of lime to Samuel Cozad, the lock contractor, for Johnnycake Lock and the Double Lock and the Pancake Lock. And the Irish canal workers had to be fed, from Hale's farm. It was to become important in time that one of the contractors was a man named Cozad from Cleveland, who had a sister, Sarah.

Jonathan Hale erected a three-story brick mansion. Even before it was finished, land jobbers took new settlers by it on Oak Hill Road.

It stood out in the valley like a man's declaration.

Jonathan Hale took Mercy Hale out of the cabin into the mansion. It had the clean unnatural smell of wood shavings and slaked lime.

The second and third floors were still building. But the "cellar," which wasn't really a cellar but the first floor, was livable. It was a giant stone-floored room, with a cooking fireplace, a dining room and living room area, and a root cellar cut into the hillside in back. The back wall, of course, was blind, cut into the hill. But the front had four large windows and a door opening to the valley.

John Horton's book supposes the whole family moved into that floor the first year. It would not have been too crowded because Sophronia moved out. She married Ward K. Hammond of the Hammond family who had driven with the Hales from Glastonbury and worked beside them for 17 years in this clearing.

Meanwhile a small section of the canal opened for business between Akron and Cleveland. What most settlers had not been able to see came true overnight; a steady commerce opened immediately from Akron to New York City.

A bushel of corn jumped from 25 cents to 75 cents.

More important, a heavy export traffic floated north carrying Hale's lime. And there was some call for brick, special kinds of timber, and for flax and wool and whiskey. Hale produced these.

There was even a call for some homemade money, which was being manufactured a half mile from the Hale farm by Hale's friends, the Mallett Brothers and Latta and Brown at Moneyshop Hill.

The wall of hardship was breaking down. But Mercy Hale had a feeling about herself.

"Jonathan, I would like to see our kin in Glastonbury once more."

Hale went out and watched his son, William, at work. He was grown now.

To Mercy, he said one day, "I'll finish off the upstairs parlor for William's marriage and we'll go."

So today in the Hale house one sees a small upstairs parlor. Jonathan Hale could now afford milled boards from Yellow Creek. Mercy liked the room. That's how you design a house.

They liked sparkling Sally Upson whom William was to marry.

"She'll sit and talk with us, Jonathan, but not as a guest. She'll want to be hostess."

"I'll build a family living room that belongs to all." So at the rear of the house, the walls of the root cellar were raised with brick. A living room was built above grade with a small attic over it.

Jonathan Hale went to see Captain Thorndike about transportation to the east. He came back to the house to explain to Mercy. She answered, "But Pamelia and William Oviatt will be married."

"I'll plaster the upstairs parlor and partition a bedroom on the third floor."

That's how a house is designed.

Sally and William Hale moved to the basement. They had now been married long enough to be out among the rest of the family, and the basement was a rather public place. The whole family cooked and dined there. And Sally was the kind who could be hostess all day to the whole family. Pamelia and William Oviatt had the privacy of upstairs.

Jonathan and Mercy packed the new clothes which Mercy had tailored. As the settlers watched, he took her by the arm and stepped aboard the canal packet to Cleveland. There they transferred to the schooner *Eclipse*. Jonathan wrote back to his son-in-law, "Mr. Oviatt" —

> My dear children:
> Your mother has stood this journey better than I expected. Still she is subject to those painful turns. She is impatient to get into the salt water country which I hope by the day after tomorrow ... We feel very troubled about Sally (illness) and the rest of our children. I hope they will see to all things. I know not how they will manage affairs, but have reason to believe they will get along ...
> Jona. Hale

Jonathan and Mercy Hale reached Glastonbury apparently on the 15th of June. Near the end of July, he received the letter from his son, William, announcing Sally's death. It was a sad letter; but in the way of the eldest son in charge of the home place, he felt it important to report: "The wheat looks very well, but the corn, oats and grass will be very high. Our meadows are light." When Jonathan broke the news to Mercy, she wanted to go back to Bath. On the way she worsened. They were coming across the New York canal when Mercy needed some water in the night. Jonathan went topside to fetch it, slipped on the deck and gashed his thigh on an iron boat hook so seriously that, when they transferred off Lake Erie onto a southbound Ohio Canal packet down the Cuyahoga valley, both were ailing.

In October, Mercy died. Jonathan could not get up to attend her funeral.

As you look at Old Brick, you find some interesting reeded mantelpieces. They are there because the house had a prematurely old man in it, puttering around.

Six-foot, 180-pound Jonathan Hale stopped being the driving force in this part of the Cuyahoga valley. Right in front of everyone he grew old; and they all knew he was planning to leave the valley.

And if you look at the land titles to Old Brick, you see that two months after Mercy's death Jonathan Hale sold all of his Lot 13 to Sophronia, his eldest, and her husband, Ward K. Hammond, for $400.

Then Lots 11 and 12, the main farm and meadow and orchard, to his oldest boy, William, the young widower. Jonathan took a trip to Cleveland. The construction of the house would seem to be finished.

But as you look at Old Brick today you'll find a wonderful inconsistency. Even the ornate parts are frontier built from wood and clay and lime and stone right off the land.

But here and there is a carved molding where you can't detect knifemarks at all, a more perfect piece, a milled piece from the city, or a carved pillar head, called for by someone who wouldn't seem to be a Hale or a Hammond.

That brings Sarah.

You'll remember that back when the canal was building a Cleveland contractor named Samuel Cozad built the Johnnycake Lock near the Hale house. He bought lime of Jonathan Hale, and he brought with him his sister, the widowed Sarah Mather, who boarded and kept house for his Irish construction crew. Her presence brightened the town.

When the lock was finished, Sarah went back to Cleveland with her three children, George, Jane, and Betsey, all carrying-size, plus an adopted niece, Harriet.

Back in Cleveland at Doan's Corners Sarah taught school and raised her family.

She was still there when the widowed Jonathan Hale arrived. To our knowledge there is no record of the next events, but we do know that in the parlor of Sarah's father's house, on what is now Western Reserve University, Jonathan Hale and Sarah Cozad Mather were married.

They returned to Old Brick.

Today, visitors note that the bedrooms upstairs in the Hale House are strangely partitioned. But it's not really strange at all. You see, Old Brick tried hard to welcome the new couple. But this was not an easy homecoming.

Old Brick was now more of a men's barracks — the widowed William, and the maturing Andrew. Even young James Madison Hale was four years older than Sarah's oldest child, George Mather. Jane and Betsey Mather were nine and seven.

These were difficult ages under one roof; but even more difficult was Sarah Mather Hale. Frankly accustomed to the sophistication of Cleveland society, a now quite real and exhilarating one, she was a city woman. And she was surrounded by the sons of Mercy Hale, a hard woman to follow.

Jonathan Hale was aware of Sarah's loneliness at Old Brick and the reason for her coolness. He wrote her a poem:

To A Stranger
Far from the land that gave the (e) birth!
Oh! Cans't thou find a spot on earth,
So fondly dear to the (e)
As the heart-woven land thou left behind?

Thou'st left behind thy social train;
Will thy fond spirit rest again,
And feel security
In the bosom of strangers thou ne'er has tried,
By the ebb and flow of prosperity's tide
Or will it retreat on the soft wings of regret
To that frequent bower where so lovingly met
All by friendship made sacred to me.

Believe me here are friends as kind
As those whom thou has left behind.
But cans't thou not the fairy chase
Which binds the (e) to thy native place;
Rather than be unblest,
To the friends of thy children — thy country — thy home
Go — go and be happy, tis folly to roam.

Then something happened. William Hale fell in love with Sarah's niece. They were married in the parlor; then as man and wife they moved to the "cellar" which had been the bridal suite twice before. Within two years they had two children.

Jonathan Hale and Sarah also had two boys and a girl. And now we see what a woman Sarah was. She named the girl Mercy.

Jonathan Hale's powerful body healed. He worked the farm with the strong help of Andrew. Andrew, he could see, was the one who would stay.

In 1836, something stranger still. Andrew Hale married Sarah's daughter Jane — in the parlor. It was Andrew's turn to have the bridal suite. William and Harriet built a frame house across the road. Andrew and Jane moved into the basement.

And Sarah Hale, now deeply involved with both her families became actively the matriarch of the house. Old Brick was back in order. But construction wasn't finished.

In Old Brick is a set of ledgers. Young Andrew gradually took over the farm, and changed the accent. He hired more hands and changed some of the crops from large staples to smaller, higher-priced specialties: honey, vinegar, wool, onions, in addition to the old staples — corn, beef, potatoes, apples, flour, and a decided bent toward apples.

Andrew's family was outgrowing the basement. Therefore, he built a story and a half clapboard wing onto the basement on the south.

Old Jonathan meanwhile had moved heavily into wool. He built a large barn across the road to house their increasing flock of sheep.

In 1854, at the age of 77, Jonathan Hale wrote to Sophronia that he didn't think he would stay much longer, and he died. Sarah followed him.

Construction of Old Brick would seem to be over. Old Jonathan had felt he must divide up his land among his sons and daughters fairly. He left the heart of it to Andrew who had stayed on the farm and was working it. But he willed land to the other sons and daughters.

Therefore Andrew began to buy back these lands and put Old Brick back together again. He loved this place.

He moved the wooden wing he'd built around to the rear of the house, attaching it to the living room. He built a wooden north wing for storage of coal, with a corn room above it, and on the front a delicate, highly trimmed porch with a hipped roof. On this porch, his family watched the valley develop in the evenings. The Valley Railroad came snorting down by the Hale House.

Years rolled. Andrew grew sick with a painful illness. A series of operations failed to relieve the pain. One day Jane found him trying to shoot himself, and was able to stop him. In a second attempt in 1884, be wounded himself seriously, and died soon after. Jane lived on in the front room for 20 years to see the century turn.

Like Jonathan, Andrew divided up the farm in his will.

Old Brick was quiet and lonely. Grass grew up in the driveway. Older people in town watched it ruefully, "Shame to see it run down like that."

"Yes. But it's too big. A fortune just to heat it."

The Hales were strong men. Although they indulged in flashes of humor and some music, they were for the most part hawkfaced earnest pioneers, hard-working, effective leaders. Life was work.

Suddenly, unexpectedly, came a happy-hearted Hale.

Andrew's son, Charles Oviatt Hale, inherited the heartland of Old Brick. Like Andrew, he began to buy back the fringes from his brothers and sisters and cousins.

Now C.O., as he was called, was not a man to make life hard; and he was not a working farmer. He was a hobby farmer, flowers and the like. For the real staple crops, he brought onto the home place his wife's nephew, Carl Cranz, a man who knew what the land was about.

C.O., with more formal education than any Hale thus far, went into the affairs, politics and industry of the valley.

But he loved the home place.

So viewing Old Brick today one wonders about the large number of small rooms in it. Well, C.O. began to turn Old Brick into the showplace of the valley. He planted the grounds beautifully and he invited paying guests from Akron and Cleveland for weekends.

Then families began coming for summer vacations from Cleveland. It was a fashionable thing to do.

C.O.'s wife, Pauline Cranz Hale, cooked and served

meals in the south wing with the help of her daughters, home from college.

As the crowds increased in the summer, the stove had to be moved to the adjoining north wing in summer and back in winter.

The place had an easy manner. It was hard to tell the proprietor's family from the guests. And, in fact, the host and hostesses seemed to be the ones on vacation.

The affection for the place was amazing and the guests distinguished: W. T. Holliday, Seiberling of tires, Hoover of vacuum cleaners, Severance of Severance Hall, Judge Day, Victor Morgan, Rabbi Gries.

A tally-ho party of horses from Akron would be likely to charge in for breakfast at 7:00 a.m. of a Sunday.

C.O. Hale sold timber to an aggressive young man named Samuel J. Ritchie, who cut it himself off the Hale slopes. Watching him was Andrew's daughter, Sophronia. They married, but did not move into the basement. Ritchie went on out into the world to great lumber enterprises, then copper, iron, land. He became wealthy. Ultimately they settled in Tallmadge. But he was away a lot. That's important to this story, because it meant that his daughter Clara Belle Ritchie was home with her mother, Sophronia, listening to stories of life at Old Brick.

When C.O. Hale, "The Squire," died, Clara Belle bought Old Brick. She named it The Hale Farm, and she began to repair it. People said it was too much house for a single woman. She'd find it hard to heat.

But Clara Belle Ritchie was putting back together a love story.

In the middle of her work on it, she died in 1956. In her will she gave the house to the Western Reserve Historical Society to be open to the public.

To many it is a museum of the frontier.

But actually Old Brick is a love story ... which the reader can see.

24

The River's Genial Monster

IF YOU CAN imagine riding on a dinosaur's head while he's feeding, you can imagine how it feels to operate a Hulett. In repose, this monster is the ugliest, ungainliest machine ever made. In action, it is sheer poetry.

A small Hulett chomps ten tons in a mouthful. The adult of the species can slurp up 17 tons of ore from the hold of a ship in a single bite. An occasional Hulett with the right rider will often grab 20 tons in its maw. More than 2,200,000,000 tons of iron ore have come to Lake Erie ports since the first shipment in 1852 on the brigantine *Columbia*. Of this amount, the four Hulett unloaders at the mouth of the Cuyahoga's old riverbed handled over 175,000,000 tons by 1985.

At one time Huletts were the dominant species of ore unloaders along the Cuyahoga. Their towering necks arched over ships whose bows and sterns came close to scraping their paint on the river bends. They looked like rows of prehistoric mechanosaurs dipping their ore-reddened beaks deep into the whalelike ships. They smacked their steel lips with a clatter that shook the whole of Whiskey Island, which is the island of land between the old riverbed and the new.

A Hulett's main action is often described as a monstrous grasshopper's leg, which is very descriptive if you can picture a 500-ton grasshopper leg with very neat knees. But that's only the top part of a Hulett. The knee action part rests on another 500 tons of machinery. It is a massive leviathan standing ten stories high, its legs straddling several hopper car freight trains, while its neck juts out over water and ships. At feeding time, a herd of four of them bobbing their beaks deep into the holds of a ship looked like an outsized flock of those toy birds that sit on the rim of a glass, incessantly tipping forward to drink then upright again; but they are ten stories high.

The Hulett is a mechanical impossibility surrounded by disbelief, yet it reigned supreme as the fastest, most efficient ore unloader in the trade.

Unloading iron ore used to be the bottleneck on the Cuyahoga. In the heyday of the Marquette and Mesabi, when mountains of ore piled into the mouth of the little river, the problem of getting down into that hull to get out that iron became a nightmare.

They tried shovels and buckets, hoists and cables, steamshovels and weird contraptions. But for 50 years, the river remained a bottleneck. Once you dropped ten or 15-thousand tons of dirt into the hold of a ship, you had the devil's own time getting it out again.

The mind that conceived the Hulett monster, which eventually dug out this bottleneck, could only have been a genius. Engineers say it must have been dreamed up by a man with nightmares. Those who knew him say that George Hulett was, well, eccentric.

One thing is certain; he was a kind of mystery, and no

fame seeker. Only the barest biographical traces are recorded about this man who revolutionized ore transportation. The very few men still living who knew him personally are themselves oldtimers with memories dimmed to detail, but they all remember one thing. Hulett was a brilliant engineer with a fantastically inventive mind ... and eccentric.

The stories they tell give the impression of a man who would sit down to a high-level conference table with a Carnegie or a Rockefeller, fish a plug of tobacco from his stained waistcoat and chaw throughout the meeting like a general-store patriarch.

He looked like a bullfrog in a baggy suit, wore steel-rimmed spectacles, and talked as if he were still driving a team of draft horses back on the farm in Conneaut where he was raised. He was a practical farmboy genius whose inventiveness was born of getting the job done, and he didn't care what his inventions or his person looked like as long as they both did the job.

Hulett came to Cleveland with his parents in 1860. On the occasional trips to the city from his boyhood farm, Hulett had become familiar with the sweat and strain of ore unloading, but Cleveland was a revelation. In those days Whiskey Island (the narrow strip of land sheared off from the Flats by the old riverbed and the new channel which cut the Cuyahoga's new course to the lake) was nothing but a great cloud of red dust, filled with men, mules, and dirt. The infant mills on the Cuyahoga were squalling for ore like tiger cubs, while the Marquette was packing boats and piling them through the Soo like floating sausage links. They filled them to the decklines, deepened the canal, enlarged the locks and then built new ships. All this was done just to send ore into a bottleneck of aching backs and wheelbarrows.

The way they tackled a boatful of ore in those days was to put rock-muscled men with shovels into the dirt and they heaved it into wheelbarrows; then more iron-backed men wheeled it to the waiting railroad cars. And when the shovelers got too deep in the hold to throw it out, they built a platform and shoveled to that, while still more men reshoveled it to the decks.

George Hulett wasn't the first one with an idea to unplug the bottleneck. The first was a man who rigged a block and tackle from the mast into the ship's hold. After that, it was a short step to hitching a horse to the block and tackle.

By 1867, they had 40 horses employed with the shovelers on the south bank's Nypano Docks, and possibly no one will ever know how many more horses contributed to the melee of Whiskey Island just across the river to the north. The Cleveland firm of Bothwell and Ferris ran the Nypano and it was J. D. Bothwell himself who first stuck the corkscrew into the bottle's neck by replacing the horses with a steam engine.

The little donkey engines began to multiply along the wharves at Whiskey Island. The neck of the bottle began to clear. It looked as if the 50,000 tons of ore a year cramming through the Soo could at last be handled with relative ease.

Now although the neck of the bottle had been unplugged, the inevitable happened. The bottle got bigger. Youngstown and Pittsburgh added their demand for ore and the 50,000-ton torrent soon swelled to an 831,000-ton deluge. The bottleneck was right back where it started, only tighter.

Captain Thew of the steamer *William P. Thew* was next to design an ore unloader. The device that he outlined was a long-armed steam shovel. The cab of the shovel where the operator controlled the beast, swiveled around like a big giraffe on a turntable. Instead of a block and tackle attached to the mast of the ship, Captain Thew designed a self-contained shovel that took the ore directly from the hold to the dock. This was the day of the whirleys.

As steam was replacing horsepower along the unloading docks, George Hulett embarked upon a career as proprietor of a general store. Later, he went into the commission business where he began to apply his ingenuity to unloading shiploads of grain.

Another young man, however, was applying his talents directly to the ore industry. Alexander Brown's father, Fayette Brown, was one of the original financial backers who tapped the Marquette iron ore range. So the boy, Alex, had a good education as an ivy-league engineer plus firsthand knowledge of the drama that was taking place along the Cuyahoga's docks.

Brown's nimble mind eliminated the whirleys by envisioning a fantastic skeleton of steel girders that straddled the entire railroad yard on one side and jutted out over the ships at the other. The bucket could now be lowered from the "hoist," into the vessel's hold, filled, raised, carried along the skeleton to any one of several tracks and dumped directly into the selected car.

For the next 20 years, the Brownhoist was the marvel of the Cuyahoga. Ore boats grew still bigger, the Soo got bigger, and the demand for more ore never stopped getting bigger. Self-closing buckets were added to the rigs so they could bite out their own ore rather than needing shovelmen to fill their buckets.

The Hoover-Mason bucket came out with an ingenious set of blades that could scrape ships' holds clean. But it wasn't enough to calm the clamor for more ore.

All this while George H. Hulett was the manager of the Cleveland Steam Cooked Food Company.

That was 1886. Two years later, Hulett switched from food to manufacturing derricks. As the skeleton-like Brownhoists were breeding all along the waterfront, Hulett was playing with coal, literally playing. One of his first inventions was a gargantuan machine that clamped an entire railroad car in a viselike hand, lifted it like a toy and upended it to spill 120 tons of coal into a mammoth funnel. Hulett was always pretty direct in his approach. His methods usually followed suit.

To Hulett, unloading an ore boat would be a simple matter of building a thousand-ton posthole digger — and then putting a man in the shovel.

No one really knows whether or not Hulett was influenced by the post hole digger of his farm days, but there is a certain similarity in the way the giant leg jams the clamshell shovel down into the ore, clamps it shut and lifts it out, opens its jaws to release the ore.

With the designs under his arm, Hulett began the rounds of engineering companies and financiers. He was asking them to gamble on an unproved nightmare, and no one was buying. Hulett was well into his second and third calls when he approached Sam Wellman of the Wellman Seaver Company. Hulett hiked a chair up to the machinery tycoon's desk and fished out his lint-encrusted tobacco plug.

"Sam, you build this machine, it'll make you." Hulett usually dispensed with the time-consuming preliminaries.

A smile tickled the mouth of prosperous Sam Wellman.

"I've seen the plans, George. It looks like a monstrosity."

"But it works."

"How do you know?"

"The coal unloader worked, didn't it?"

"How much would it take to build one?"

"Forty-six thousand dollars."

"All right, George. If it works, we'll buy all you can build. If it doesn't, you get nothing."

"Fine, Sam."

It took two years to put the monstrosity together. If boat captains profaned the horses, steam engines, and Brownhoists at their introduction, they were speechless at the sight of this incredible beast that reared its head along the docks.

In 1898, it devoured its first boat of ore.

By 1900 it was king of the Cuyahoga.

The first Huletts were steam operated. In a cab the size of a phone booth there were pipes over the operator's head, dripping constantly, making a steambox in the wintertime and an impossible torrid zone in summer. It was like a Turkish bath with a leaky faucet.

By 1912 the Huletts had been converted to electricity. Since then, the basic design of the monsters has remained unchanged.

In 1985, we walked out on the Cleveland docks at the western tip of Whiskey Island to watch the agile monsters feeding on one of the modern 20,000-ton ore boats. They were all that history and the veterans of the docks claimed. But a siren sounded across the railroad yard — one blast, then two short ones. A clattery little pig skimmed over the tracks to number two Hulett, its massive beak frozen in the hold of the ship. An electrician was already clammering up the ricketty old ladder to the control house.

"The Hulett's are getting old," he commented later. "There's nothing to do the job as fast or as well. But they're getting old and stiff in the joints." The original $46,000 price rocketed to $2,000,000. There were no new Huletts on the river.

The old monsters were growing extinct. The ones that remained would reign supreme until the cost of their maintenance outweighed their ability to create time.

A new breed of ships was coming, with holds built as hoppers; to unload, they open the bottoms and let the ore flow onto built-in conveyor belts swung ashore.

Now, in 1998, the towering hulks of the Huletts sit silently, arms and legs frozen against the darkening sky.

Every man and woman should go down to the Cuyahoga and see the monsters before the species disappears.

When the Huletts go, there'll be an empty place against the Cuyahoga sky.

25

Men at Work

THERE'S A marine population on the Cuyahoga working just below the public eye level. It's a race of great skill and anonymity and professional pride. They're visible only from the water or occasionally in the all-night restaurants alongshore. A few know about them, however. You can see men and women in tuxedos and evening gowns there some early mornings who have come down to view marine life — respectfully, not as a sideshow.

There are salvage men, Coast Guard men, longshoremen, warehousemen, tugmen, bridgemen, crane operators, and ship chandlers.

At work on the Cuyahoga is a precision artist whose job is to thread a needle-straight ship through a crooked river. It's a thing of beauty to watch a Cuyahoga tug use the ship's momentum jujitsu fashion to bend it around the U-turns.

Because of the cramped waters, a Great Lakes tug is essentially an enormous engine packed into the smallest practical hull. When it moves, the thrust is immediate. That's essential, of course, because when the stern of an $8-or-9-million ship is swinging toward the shore, with perhaps ten feet to play with, the action needs to be fast. When the tug pushes the stern around, the bow may be heading for the opposite bank, so the tug moves forward fast to work the bow.

In the early days many independent tugs fought for the available business, racing each other to each approaching bow. In the event of a tie, a battle resulted and towing prices were cut. Falling prices prevented tug owners from maintaining their equipment.

The delays suffered by the shippers from cobbled-up tugs became so costly that they stepped in to form Great Lakes Towing Company, merging the more efficient tug operators. Great Lakes Towing covered all the Great Lakes iron ore ports. The tugs were named for states.

But today the vessels need less help from tugs because bow thrusters are being installed by several fleets. The thruster is a transverse propeller in a hollow tube in the bow of an ore boat. It pushes water left or right so the captain can swing his bow fast, giving him back a lot of control of his own vessel.

A tug veteran waiting for a call explained, "With the new variable-pitch main propulsion propellers in the rear, the captain can reverse the ship, too, without changing the turn of the engine shaft. It's a lot quicker than the old way; gives 'em better maneuvering, too.

"If a ship's got both of these, it stands a fair chance of getting up the river on its own."

There was a awkward silence while he listened apparently to some echo of his own words.

"'Course we've got progress on the tugs, too. All diesel now. And ... why even coming aboard is different. Time was when the tug just slowed down and came close to the shore. The old crew jumped off and the new one on.

"Some missed the boat and couldn't swim. After that we used taxicabs. At seven in the morning, three in the afternoon and 11 o'clock at night he'd take us to what bridge was nearest our boat and we'd change crews at the bridge."

"That's changed though now?"

"We've got our own dock right here. You just step aboard, like you'd go in an office in the morning and out at night. It's a better life now ... I guess."

The Cuyahoga Bridges

Another part of this 'round-the-clock river population are the bridge operators.

Traveling 23 miles upriver from the mouth you pass under 84 bridges to reach Akron — over three and a half bridges per mile. Twenty-one of these are concentrated in the navigable section of the river where both water and land traffic is high, so many of them are movable. The variety of action in the first 21 bridges is interesting. There are vertical-lift bridges, of course, and drawbridges, but the jackknife, side-swing and rotary bridges are worth a trip just to watch.

Every day, without fanfare, a kind of drama goes on at the movable bridges. It starts with an ore boat steaming toward the Cuyahoga. The captain checks down from about 14 miles an hour to about four at the wall, and winds her around a quarter turn at the lighthouse and breakwater. He picks up his tugs and heads upriver. About 300 yards from each bridge he blows it open with one long blast that rattles windows all the way to Public Square.

Then he listens very closely for a long and a short from the bridge. He has 132,000 tons in motion and if the bridge isn't going to open he must put on full reverse soon enough, or carry away the bridge. If the bridge can't open, it answers with three shorts. The captain can't wait long for the answer.

But the bridge operator has multiple safeguard systems. Before the bridge can swing open — or tilt up or lift — traffic lights turn red and a gong rings. Warning gates with flashing lights lower, and, finally, a cable-net barrier blocks the road. Safety still depends on the bridge operator's judgment. But if he should have a stroke or faint, the whistle signal may be safeguard enough. It's up to the ship to leave enough time for stopping if the bridge doesn't blow back. If the operator is incapacitated after the bridge begins to open, however, it will lift all the way open until a limit switch stops it. If the operator can't bring it down, it stays up until help arrives.

In an emergency, road traffic can turn around and use some other crossing, but the ships have only one road.

In heavy storms, a power failure can be a threat. So two power lines run to each bridge. If both lines are out, there is an engine-generator set to operate the bridge. If this fails, a direct gasoline drive comes into play or a compressed air motor. Some Cuyahoga bridges have gears for manual operation with a hand crank. Despite the tremendous weight of the bridges, counterbalancing makes hand operation possible. A measure of the systems' effectiveness is the fact that, outside of a railroad watchman, bridge tenders were the only men down on the river during the great storm of 1913.

Some bridges go unscathed, but during the 1913 spring flood the steamer *Mack* knocked the south span off the lower West Third Street bridge into the Cuyahoga. Inventive engineers replaced it with a secondhand span from Michigan. Three years later the north span was clipped by a runaway streetcar and knocked over onto the B & O tracks. Not to be stopped by lack of a bridge section, the railroad adapted a girder span, only slightly used, which it cut down to length and installed.

This bridge, lashed up wholly of secondhand and jury-rigged parts, lasted without further repair until replacement 24 years later.

When it was time for old bridges to come down, corporate executives and government officials discovered that the bridges had a place in the hearts of the people.

Several years after the Lorain-Carnegie bridge was in use, the 52-year-old Central Viaduct was closed, even to pedestrian traffic. A Reverend Mr. Stark of the Viaduct's west end made it plain that "This community was developed as a result of that bridge and there is a definite need for it."

The old bridges doomed by a 1944 project (with the exception of one swing bridge) were all of the Bascule or jackknife design. Counterweights shoreward of the bridge helped pivot the span up into the air.

Small boys of all ages were sorry when they were torn down. On a hot summer day, you could sit by the river and watch those graceful Bascules by the hour. But sentiment will not widen the river, and captains needed room for bigger boats.

Crews felt differently. Wives and sweethearts of lake sailors were sorry when wreckers took away that little swing bridge near the harbor mouth. The central pier stood right in the river so that ships had to glide within 12 feet of the east bank. At this spot was a park area like a giant widow's walk. There the women waited, to see their men pass by or to welcome them home from the inland seas.

Today, in addition to the tugmen and dock personnel at work on the river, there is a contingent of U.S. Coast Guardsmen stationed at the mouth who worry about the safety of vessels and inspect them on a regular basis.

These are the men at work ... on the Cuyahoga.

26

The Noonday Club — and the Nation

THE MOST exclusive lunch club in the world met at 1200 hours sharp daily at the mouth of the Cuyahoga.

The food was good, but very plain, and the men were neither rich nor especially sociable (how would you like to eat with the same fellows five days a week for decades?). But it was highly exclusive in membership: A man must know the shipping business backwards and forward, and his word must be his company's bond — because at the lunch table he may buy $300,000 worth of coal just with the spoken word; and his company must pay the invoice when it comes, or this lunch club could not work.

In 1985, we watched them function just as they had since World War I days and World War II and the Korean War. These men were the Ore and Coal Exchange. They carryied out the Cuyahoga's role as schedule boss of the Great Lakes fleet from Duluth to Buffalo. Despite the fact that the Ore and Coal Exchange held their final noonday meeting earlier this decade, we include their story here. These men helped shape the history of Cleveland industry and this river.

No Guests

The men who ran the vessel-coal-and-iron-ore complex long ago developed a cold stony eye for laymen who wanted to hear about "the romance of the business," because while they're talking romance they could lose their shirts. And anyway, the interviewer was not likely to understand the split-second tension in a business where ships moved 18 miles per hour.

Besides, the chessboard they played on like the back of their hands was so big nobody really believed it, and the names they named, nobody recognized. I went to this lunch club only because for years I had been scrivening around the Great Lakes marine world, including editing *Inland Seas®* for the Great Lakes Historical Society.

Though the lunch club was exclusive, the intricate and crucial chess game these men played affected the lives and income and well-being of thousands of people in a seven-state belt from Minnesota to Pennsylvania and south to West Virginia and Kentucky.

You see, the most ticklish rendezvous in this geographic iron-coal world was the moment when a train was scheduled to meet a ship at the mouth of the Cuyahoga or anywhere along the south shore of the Great Lakes. If either was late, the cost was gigantic. If early, same problem.

Then when a ship started downlakes from Duluth, Minnesota, to discharge iron ore at the month of the Cuyahoga and meet a train that was rolling north with a hundred cars of coal from Beckley, West Virginia, you had a precision high wire act that kept 50 men on nervous alert for 72 hours.

They planned this meeting precisely, because if the train reached the dock and sat idle, somebody paid. Likewise, if the ship sat empty, or waited for dockage, it was eating raw money.

Despite this planning, though, the ship captain could not control a storm on Lake Superior, a delay at the Soo Locks, a strike on the dock unloading equipment, or an eight-hour fog in the Cuyahoga. The railroader could not control a bridge out or a burnt-out journal. And one of these things or something like it was bound to happen.

But the train and the vessel continued relentlessly toward the original meeting place, even after it was impossible for them to connect.

With telephone and radio, obviously traffic management could get on the phones and re-coordinate this rendezvous with the dock, the shipper, the customer, the vessel, and the train. But if eight docks, seven railroads, four vessel fleets and 90 shippers tried to do this in a 190-million-ton year, it would jam every switchboard in the Great Lakes trade.

They needed a man sitting up so high he could get an eagle's-eye view of the railroads from West Virginia, and all the vessels from Lake Superior to Ontario. He should also be able to see the stevedores and docks to know if they're ready, and which kinds of empty cars they have. In the case of iron ore, some mills accepted ore from hoppers, others from flat-bottoms. This perch sitter had to be able to scan the whole south shore of the Great Lakes to see from where the right kinds of cars came.

Well, there was such an eagle's nest on the 11th floor of the Terminal Tower at the mouth of the Cuyahoga. "Room 1101" was all it said on the door. It was known as The Ore and Coal Exchange, Gordon Walker, Manager, in the early days.

Here we return to 1984, the last time I visited.

Three dispatchers behind a glass window are locked to their desks by telephone and ship-shore radio. They each have a complex ledger in front of them. The way these three dispatchers keep the midwest economy coordinated is this: each shipment of coal gets a consignment name (i.e., "Holiday," "Red Dog," "Blue Sky," etc.). The coal is usually to be transferred from a train from West Virginia to a vessel upbound for the electric power stations on the upper lakes. Coal from West Virginia powers electric motors in Minnesota.

So the shipper at lunch tells the Exchange the plans for each consignment. It's a code language all its own, but in English it tells: what is in the consignment by grade; when depart mine; over what rails; to which dock; for which customer; how mix at dock when loading in ship.

The vessel company then tells the dispatcher which of its ships will pick up this coal.

When the train and the ship are 72 hours away from the rendezvous, the dispatcher receives calls from the shipper and/or railroad and vessel company as to the location of each. At 60 hours, another call. Again at 36; again at 24, 12, and three hours away from port.

The dispatcher is the one man who can see whether or not they're going to connect.

Since it does not always work that neatly, the dispatcher also uses other sources of information. Every morning, his first calls are to Detroit, Buffalo, Port Colborne to see if any of his named-in ships cleared these points last night, and at what times. And which ships did not clear those points. He's familiar with the speed of each vessel, loaded and light.

Vessel operators also need to minimize demurrage ... which begins on each car of coal after 120 hours on the dock. The space is needed by a relentless column of coal coming up behind from the south. The whole secret in coal is to keep it in constant motion. Never let it rest — from the mine face to the customer's furnace blower — or it costs like gold.

By midmorning, every company vessel dispatcher on the Cuyahoga, every railroad, every dock and coal shipper may have a white hot slip of paper in his pocket — an emergency getting closer by the minute. A dispatcher in a vessel company is somebody you don't chat with casually while he's on duty. While you're talking to him he is dying to see the clock over your shoulder, and watching the three buttons light up on his phone. He hopes they are three solutions to problems he just sent out; but he suspects they are three more problems.

At 1145 hours, these company dispatchers each walk out of their offices and go down to the Cuyahoga to the Noonday Club. There, among 90 others, each hopes to find a man who has an emergency which fits with his like the other half of a solution. So you'll see men get up and circulate to other tables, working the room. They are men looking for solutions — before one o'clock. The problem they're seeking to solve has probably been building up all morning, and they have possibly called or visited the Exchange in person previously this morning.

We will follow Mike Bonnard, bulk vessel dispatcher from Ardco Fleet.

He had been down here early this morning to see the chief dispatcher at the Ore and Coal Exchange. "Al, will the *Orion* have a clear dock today when she gets in?"

The chief dispatcher, here for 100 years, smiles and consults his vessel sheets. Although he sits in the ulcer chair, and he's watching six major problems graduate into top grade emergencies, he approaches Bonnard's problem as if it were absurd even to think that everything won't come out all right.

Anyone not used to his job would be sweating bullets. But the three Exchange dispatchers stay calm by assuming the best laid plans will fail, and by having in their minds alternate plans for nearly every situation.

Right at this moment, the chief dispatcher has an alternate plan for Bonnard's big vessel. But before the morning is over, his alternate may have alternates on it.

"Can't say for sure yet, Mike. She might, if the sun comes out in Toledo."

"When can you give us a firm answer, Al?"

"I hope by eleven a.m."

Bonnard leaves.

The dispatcher's phone stops ringing 30 seconds, so we ask a fast question: "What's the sun got to do with it, Al?"

"You see, if the sun comes out," Al explains, "it may loosen up that frozen coal so they can start dumping fifteen-twenty cars per hour instead of seven, which would mean that boat can clear the dock in about half the time."

"But what if the sun doesn't come out"

"Well, if we can't straighten out by noon, then maybe he can make a deal at Noonday Club today with some other shippers or receivers."

Not all those who come to Noonday Club bring a problem. But they come anyway. That's part of a bargain made in 1913 when they organized the Exchange to mobilize all the iron and coal in the midwest against the Kaiser.

The Ore and Coal Exchange organized to solve World War I's traffic jam, served the same role — accelerated — for World War II and again in the continuing wars — Korea and Viet Nam and the flooding civilian demand between wars.

It controlled traffic until 1995 including the new thousand footers like *Columbia Star*, direct descendant of the brig *Columbia* of 1852.

27

Whiskey Island

MR. COHALAN would not recognize the island at this writing (1998). The accurate drawing of its classic age is by Kinley Shogren, distinguished artist of the Great Lakes region.

On Shogren's famous scene has now been superimposed a color photograph of apartments, rows of cabin cruisers and sailboats and chic saloons.

While the Island is totally changed, many readers wrote that it was their "favorite chapter" or "best chapter." Therefore, and since a major mission of this River of America series is history of the rivers, we repeat it here.

Mr. Cohalan, who dominates the chapter, was no longer available. The first interview was set up for me (1966) by a relative of J. C. Dare of the J. C. Dare Café. It was difficult to arrange, as Mr. Cohalan had no interest in it. To prepare for the interview, I asked, "What is his first name?" The answer, "Mister to you."

And so it was.

I did not bring out the tape recorder until it became obvious to him I could not keep up with my pen and paper.

The high-rent island in coastal United States, except for Manhattan, is at the mouth of the Cuyahoga. It grows no crop of high-rise hotels and no reef of cabanas or marinas. It has Huletts, mountains of raw material, and a considerable glory. In fact it would be no exaggeration to say that in one sense the gangs of men who worked Whiskey Island built the modern iron complex just as Lorenzo Carter, on the same site, built Cleveland.

You can hear the story of Whiskey Island in the Greenbrier Room of the Terminal Tower and at the Union Club in Cleveland. But if you have better connections and if you can stand the snobbery of Flanagan's Lookout or Old Angle Bar, it's better to get the story there.

"I'll bet you've listened your ears off trying to find out sumpin' about Whiskey Island. I've seen you around here a week or so. But people here don't talk about it unless they know you."

The gray stubble hunched toward me over his coffee. His grin was battered, but it was also a badge, membership in a quite exclusive group.

Mr. Cohalan matched his surroundings. The double-breasted wide-lapeled pin stripe ran to wrinkles very like the rippled paint on the cafe walls. He wore a new tie and a white shirt with collar tips forced up like butterfly wings by a rugged neck.

However, I was able to show him enough proficiency in Whiskey Islandia — good names like Mr. Kilbain, Mr. O'Mara, Mr. McGranahan — that he considered having a beer with me, but not enough that he'd let me buy.

Mr. Cohalan nodded. He indicated the bundled overcoat across the room. "And you should talk to Mr. Tom Mallory over there."

With outsiders, the islanders used such formality and often the Irish had a formality among themselves.

Whiskey Island in one way *made* this river. It served as terminal for Indian canoes, ore boats, and railroad trains. The Cuyahoga canyon itself is hostile to shipping with its narrow valley shelf and steep escarpment. But Whiskey Island was flat and accessible, making it possible for ships to drop cargo without attempting the trip up past Collision Bend and Irish Town Bend.

Today, Whiskey Island is a 500-foot wide strip from the mouth of the Cuyahoga to West Fortieth Street, 30 blocks paved nearly solid with dock surface.

Whiskey Island is man-made, created in the 1820s. The Cuyahoga flows under Superior bridge bound straight toward

Lake Erie, but a hundred yards before reaching open water, it veers sharply west, cutting a deep bed parallel to the lakeshore as far as West Fortieth Street, where it finally flows north to the lake. This is the old river bed.

But man changed that, as we'll see.

The Cuyahoga looped in a series of S's as it approached the Erie shore. Within 500 feet of open water, it makes a last huge loop to the west. This loop was holding up midwestern commerce. It effectually dammed the entire Cuyahoga. Sluggish waters piled sand around the entrance to frustrate the most ingenious captains, and the torturous channel along the lakefront denied navigation to anything much larger than an Indian canoe.

In 1825, however, the leading men in Cleveland went to the state legislature and hammered through an appropriation of $5,000 to cut the river straight through from the beginning of its last big loop to the lake.

Although this meant the creation of only a 500-foot passage, it demanded more work than could be done for $5,000 even in 1825. When you remember that you had to have width and depth, you're suddenly talking about moving a million cubic feet of dirt.

But the U.S. Engineering Corps officer in charge of the work was Major T. W. Maurice, and a man who knew how to use his imagination.

During the dry season, the Major constructed a dam at the angle, cutting off the unnecessary loop. This forced the waters to flood, building up pressure against the land toward the lake. When the rains came, softening the earth, the pent-up river tore its way through the last few yards to the lake, by the shortest route, gouging a straight ten-foot channel to open water.

That created an island — Whiskey Island.

Widened by 500 feet of fill to create more land, Whiskey Island thus became the transfer point between lake and land transport.

In the 1850s, it gave birth to a world of dockwallopers and

mules surrounded by mountains of ore and studded in succession over the next 60 years with a fantasy of ore unloading mechanisms ranging from the simple wheelbarrows to Huletts.

The men who made their livelihood on Whiskey Island spilled onto the angle of land where the old river bed turns west. That's how the Angle, as it came to be called, grew layers of piled-high dwellings to house their families.

The Angle became the roughhouse of the river, a community of rock-shouldered men who worked together, drank together, and fought together. But they say if you made the grade in this Irish community, your neighbors would never let you go for want.

The Angle was the country of a laconic group who needed no strangers and eyed authority with icy hauteur. Old-timers from the tugs and docks and shore installations met in dim cafés like this one at the west end of Superior bridge topping the Willow Street hill where it dips down into the Angle.

This is where Mr. Cohalan received me over 13 years ago.

"You'll hear a lot of people say Whiskey Island got its name from the bootleggers and rumrunners that landed there during prohibition," he said. "And it is true — lotta people made their living through the depression that way, but that isn't how Whiskey Island became Whiskey Island.

"You'll hear the railroaders say Whiskey Island got its name cause there's no *water* here. That's a fact; but nobody who worked on the island drank water anyways.

"Twenty-four hours a day, the ore was unloaded and the trains were loaded. They had five saloons on that hunka land. Sold thirty-two barrels of beer a day. When we were makin' up trains, we'd send a kid over to Fat Jack's or Corrigan's four times a day to bring back beer in buckets slung on a yoke around his neck.

"Still, that's not why Whiskey Island got its name. Man named Carter had a store here on the Cuyahoga mor'n a hundred years ago, when the Indians were here. And right across the river, right on the tip of Whiskey Island, was where they

311

had the still. It was there for a helluva long time. *That's why they call it Whiskey Island.* "

When the ore boats were smaller and coming in faster, Whiskey Island practically made the city. In those days, the island looked as if a couple of kids had gone wild with a giant Erector set. There were Brownhoists, Hoover-Mason buckets, and whirleys all sticking their skeletons up in the sky. Everywhere you looked, the piles of ore were crisscrossed with wooden catwalks for the men to trundle their wheelbarrows. Inbetween were railroad tracks. It was hard to tell where the island left off and the man-made part began. The railroads put in fill dirt to extend the island. Then they covered it with tracks.

Mr. Cohalan described the most distinguished saloon on the island, "You walk down Willow Street hill outside here, and you'll come to Willow Street bridge. It's brand-new steel now. Back then it was wood. You cross it now and there's nothing. You cross that bridge back then, and there was Fat Jack's.

"J.C. Dare was his real name, but nobody called him that. He was a good-lookin' fellow and not exactly fat. Just stocky. Jack ran the only place on the island where you could pick up your change and have a fair chance of getting out with it. Nobody fooled with Fat Jack.

"About a hundred feet down from the J. C. Dare Café, right on the river, was Mother Carey's place. Now that was a place I can't tell you about. I was tough back then, but Mother was tougher.

"The poison she served was iron ore and ammonia. But her place was very interesting.

"I'd say Mother Carey was about forty or forty-fivish when I saw her. Good-lookin' woman in a rough sort of way. She sure did get along with men. She pulled the roughest bunch this side of Sandusky. I say Sandusky 'cause that's how far the Lake Shore Gang operated. The gang had a thriving business on Whiskey Island back in the nineteen hundreds. They had nothing to do with the main business of the island, unloading ships. They were ... well, crooks. They'd bomb a safe in Sandusky

312

and time it so they could follow a freight on a handcar. It was impossible to catch them. Their hangout was Mother Carey's.

"Mother was kind of a recruiting agent for the boats, too. Those days it took a little time to clear the holds, so the crews would take off for Mother Carey's and Fat Jack's. I guess Mother had some more exciting entertainment for the crews, too.

"Lotta times some of the crews didn't come back, and a vessel was left short-handed. So Mother Carey unofficially helped out with this recruiting problem.

"The other saloons on the island never equaled Fat Jack's and Mother's place. There was Sweeney's — and Corrigan's where the dockmen got their soup. And there was Kilbane's.

"I don't think this Kilbane was any relation to Johnny Kilbane who got to be featherweight champ, although both of them were Irish and both came out of the Angle.

"In a way you had to be something of a fighter on Whiskey Island. Generally nobody'd bother a guy with a lamp in his

hand. That's a railroad man. But even when we were switchin' and had to walk from one end of the train to the other, we went with a buddy. Either that, or you got to be a helluva good fighter.

"Johnny Kilbane was the most famous of the Whiskey

Island fighters. I remember him when he was just fresh out of the Angle. His job was to man the big puzzle switch in the center of the island. We had about ten tracks comin' into this puzzle, so it was pretty important to have someone there all the time. But that Johnny Kilbane, he was always jiggin' and dancin' around, throwin' punches at the moths that used to gather 'round his lantern on summer nights.

"I remember plenty times the yardmaster, Tom Corrigan, would holler at Johnny, 'Yuh gonna take care of those switches 'r keep shadowboxing?'

"Johnny'd fling back, without missing a punch, 'Corrigan! One day ye'll pay tuh see me fight!'

"I know for a fact that when Johnny got to be featherweight champ, Corrigan personally went all the way to California to see him fight. I'd read about his fights in the newspapers, but I couldn't help laughin'.

Later, Johnny went into politics. That's a different story.

"Lotta important people come outa the Angle. They live up in big houses now in Shaker Heights and Pepper Pike and other parts of town."

"Could you name me a few?"

"Could — but I wouldn't care to."

"Why is that?"

"We-ll, it's a kind of a-unspoken deal. They're not eager for people to know they cut their knuckles on Whiskey Island."

"Isn't that kind of irritating?"

Mr. Cohalan looked at me to see if I'd understand. He wasn't sure. "It isn't quite like that. The other half of the deal is — we need something, we ask. They come back and help. I mean real big help."

"But I also hear some big men brag that they came from Whiskey Island."

"True. But those are the medium-sized big shots. And not ones that stayed in the iron business. And that kind didn't really work here. More like sons of men who did. Or men that only spent a year or so here.

"There are a lot of guys you never heard of, too, and probably never will. But there was one — Doughbelly Garlock — was boomer on a line of cars we was feeding into the switch-back one time. The switchback is a kind of dip in the tracks with a switch at the bottom. The engine shoves boxcars one at a time down the incline, and the momentum carries it up the other side aways. Before it rolls back down, the switcher throws the track over so it coasts onto the other track to the coal unloader.

"Well, Doughbelly's riding the first car down the dip, but this time the engine coupling breaks. Before you know it, Doughbelly and twelve cars is riding down the dip and up the other side. They've got more momentum this time and the whole string goes over the top headed straight for the river.

"There's not awful much you can do with twelve runaway boxcars but watch 'em. We just stood there looking at the bubbles comin' up from where all those cars had disappeared in the river. Then someone pipes, 'Gee, Dough's a good old plug. We oughta dive down and see if we can find him.'

"None of us were too willin' to jump into that river and pull him up, but it was a kind of bond among islanders.

"Turns out we didn't have to. Here comes Dough, crawlin' outa the weeds alongside the switchback, his pants all slits and slavers and mouthin' language fit to boil that river.

"That was railroadin' Whiskey Island in the ore-unloadin' days. It lasted about twenty years, until the Huletts beat out the Brownhoists and the Hoover-Masons.

"Me? I got bounced out with the wildcat strike in nineteen twenty. I always felt like Whiskey Island was my home, though. Lotta guys felt that way during the depression. That hobo jungle? Well, after railroading moved out and the island started to fall apart some, a lotta guys moved in there. That whole strip fronting the lake was a jumble of boards and corrugated iron scrounged outa junk piles. The guys put together shacks, open on the side away from the lake with the backs and sides banked with dirt. Hooverville.

"The smells on Whiskey Island never were choice, but

whenever I smell liver and onions frying, it brings back those days with the tin cans over the open fires. There's something about outdoor cooking, right?

"We even had a mayor. John Grady. He elected himself.

"Couple guys used to spot a hunk of scrap at the same time and there'd be all kinds of cussin' and fightin. Grady'd step in and settle the argument. 'Arbitrate' is what he called it. I think he just liked to argue louder. He used to make three hundred dollars a week as a lake diver. But he'd get paid on Friday and be broke by Monday. That was Grady.

"Grady was kind of a last-ditch stand for Hooverville. The city police and the railroads got together one day in nineteen hundred and thirty and marched down on the shacks like an armored tank division — with bulldozers. I heard Grady was right out in front, throwing bottles like he was fighting for his life. They say the language he used soured the ground. Why not? They were destroying a way of life. After they wiped out Hooverville, he just hung around the cafés. It took twenty years more before he really died.

"Whiskey Island had a couple of mayors, but after Hooverville there were no people. Mickey Kane lived on a houseboat, called the *Titanic*, underneath the old Willow Street bridge. Mickey practically had to duck his head every time they swung the bridge open. He left when they announced they were going to put a garbage incinerator on the island. All the waste from every factory south of Cleveland flowing right underneath his house, sea gulls perching on his clothesline, but the thing that makes him move is the thought of a garbage incinerator in his front yard.

"Bill Hoey struck oil. He was pumpin' crude outa Whiskey Island. It was nineteen fifty-two before anyone found out about it. Funny part was that Bill had been pumpin' oil for fifteen years.

"They say for all those fifteen years, Standard Oil was sendin' a truck around to pick up something like a hundred twenty barrels a month. That guy was pullin' over five thousand bucks' worth of oil a year outa that junk pile."

316

I left Mr. Cohalan at his club.

The sinking sun was just setting fire to the high level bridge when I hit the open air, so I sauntered down Willow Street for another look at the Island. The Angle has changed since Mr. Cohalan's days when the streets were mud and the houses looked like something a kid might draw on a blackboard.

Now you look up at low, lean apartment houses that give it a thrifty residential atmosphere. Down near the river, the apartments give way to great piles of bluestone, sand, and ore.

The old Willow Street swing bridge is gone now. In its place is a towering lift bridge so new it's still structural-iron orange.

I stood looking over the loneliness that is now Whiskey Island after quitting time. To my left, stretching west, is an old dirt road running alongside the old river bed, which is really a deep and navigable channel. Wasn't that where Mother Carey's used to be? And Kilbane's and Sweeney's? All I could see now were weeds.

I wondered if Mr. Cohalon could have embellished all those stories.

I walked back to the little cement building in the curve of the road where it angles in front of the new bridge. It stood like an old, lonely guardian of the river's history. And very faintly, in faded paint on the dirty wall, I could make out the peeling letters: "J.C. Dare Café." It stood right across from where Lorenzo Carter had built Carter's Tavern.

Walking off Whiskey Island, I marveled that twice, this strip of land had been the birthplace of the midwest, once when Carter made it the headquarters of the Western Reserve, and again when the steelmen made it the center of the midwest economy — transfer point for iron, coal, ore, and limestone ... foundation of mid-America.

28

Bohn's Palisades

They begin at the mouth, climbing up the slope from the lake, looming above Whiskey Island, and continuing upstream along the west bank, intermittently to the vicinity of the famous West Side Market.

Few who live along the Cuyahoga know that from all over the world, men traveled to see these brick palisades. They brought notebooks and cameras and questions.

You see, these are the nation's pilot model of slum clearance, urban renewal, low-rent public housing, and especially designed housing for the elderly. However, even those who live in these palisades don't yet know that their houses were a pioneering chapter in U.S. history.

Beyond that, these palisades of brick are a story in American politics, an area of startling paradoxes.

The very river that floated millions of tons of ore in to feed the furnaces and families on the Cuyahoga, also washed ashore human problems.

Shantytowns grew, and bars and game rooms, an army of spot labor, overcrowding, disease, crime — and some fairly desperate riverbank poverty.

That is no different from any other industry river. But from the Cuyahoga came a response.

Before Ernest Bohn, the sociology of slums had been relays of bleeders, talkers, planners, writers, who went down yelling, loud and righteous, under waves of advancing slums. What the job needed was a tough and inventive lawyer with a pragmatic understanding about moving ponderous bodies of government, population and attitude coupled to an armor-plated sense of mission.

Bohn's was no simple frontal attack. He hit slums from the flanks and the rear. He was also complex. On the one hand, deeply religious and scholarly. New opponents of his in the Ohio legislature, hearing him argue with quotes from Cicero or the Bible, felt they were contending with a lamb; then discovered it was a battle-scarred ram — cynically tough and tenderly idealistic.

Although held in some degree by many effective men, the two characteristics were in such daily combat in Bohn that they both appear within the same hour. In the same day, the same newspaper quoted him on page one arguing with a contentious committee of divers membership for some unified action on housing for the underprivileged. His tone is gentle, "We've got to get together on this thing, bury our differences and do a little something for God for once. He'll forgive us our trespasses if we forgive those who trespass against us."

Page two: Ernie has just learned the Supreme Court has declared five to two against an Ohio Housing law which Bohn needs to get bond backing for hundreds of new housing units. Bohn: "If those guys think we're going to take that lying down, they've got another think coming!"

Nor did he.

Bohn's victory was the towering bank of Riverview apartments overlooking the Cuyahoga. They rise on the former site of acres of bars, shacks, dumps and misery. And they were being studied by visitors from afar.

That's because they were designed so that there were old people mingled with young people. The tower apartments contain elevators and special rooms for sociability, crafts and the defeat of boredom. The young couples with children were in low buildings with as many as six bedrooms, with playgrounds, easy in-and-out design, off-street parking and recreational buildings.

There was a clinic in one of the high-rise buildings staffed by the nearby Lutheran Hospital, and with someone on duty at night. The U.S. Department of Health, Education and Welfare participated financially in response to the Housing Authority's request. There were public dining areas so the elderly did not need to eat alone.

In the face of all the concern over Medicare and in the face of housing designed especially for segregating old people, reporters for architectural and sociological quarterlies sought out Bohn to get the story. Organizations gave him awards and honorary degrees for vision and sociological pioneering and new concepts.

Actually he appreciated those awards very much; but if it was late in the afternoon and he was petulant, he might explain it with a certain dispatch, "Hell, old people like to be around young people. Is that sociology?

"Young couples need babysitters for their kids. Is that a new concept?

"Young kids got to have a place to dig in the dirt and make castles and stuff, so you put them in apartments near the ground. Is that sociology?"

He would sign a stack of letters for his secretary. She would smile pleasantly at you, but studying to see if you understood. She had worked with Ernie since the days when they called him — not a sociologist — but a Republican socialist.

"Old people have all kinds of sickness; some they don't even know about. So you put in a clinic, not to cure 'em, just for emergencies — like their own daughters should do for them if they were there. Is that a new concept?"

Bohn sat on two single-spaced pages of housing boards and advisory and planning committees and congressional and presidential advisory groups.

But 66 years ago, the name Bohn was contentious.

In 1932, the nation was stunned economically. On the floor of the Cleveland City Council, Bohn had arrived from the Ohio legislature where, like Alfred Kelley, he was the youngest.

His proposition to Council: "Mr. President, my proposal for a council committee to study the housing blight along the Cuyahoga will lead to savings of millions for this city. I am convinced that one particular blighted area which pays us two hundred twenty-five thousand in taxes, costs us nearly two million dollars in fire fighting, crime detection and other services, not counting relief, and sickness from unsanitary, crowded and unsafe housing."

They let Ernie have his harmless little committee, and in fact they made him chairman. Few knew he would use that title to launch a tidal wave that day which would roll from the mouth of the Cuyahoga across the United States.

Bohn immediately began a full-fledged study of slum areas in Cleveland. He held open hearings with architects, investors, labor, renters, landlords, developers, police, realtors.

Alarm set in. At a time when we were faced with a make-or-break depression, Bohn's hearings were stirring up dust. The committee was calling attention to ghettos, parading before Ohioans a horror story.

It would be all right if Bohn were some kind of wild man that you could dismiss. "But this guy's too canny."

He was getting people upset with talk about tearing down slums. Some councilmen naturally would lose voters by removal of constituents they had already won over. Groups of owners of substandard dwellings blinked in the incandescence of open hearings, which recited five dollar fines against major fire and safety violations, with even those costs suspended on promise of repair. And the repairs were never made nor inspected.

Developers didn't like this either, remembering on second thought that they had stated they couldn't possibly build housing for the kind of rent money available in those sections.

Bohn's committee report to city council made 17 recommendations; but the big one was that the council urge the state of Ohio to adopt a housing law for the formation and regulation of limited dividend corporations to sponsor rehousing and with power of eminent domain to condemn and demolish slums under the supervision of a State Housing Board.

Ernie Bohn just happened to have a draft of how he figured such a state law should read. He asked for speed.

"What's the hurry, Ernie?"

"There's an emergency session of state legislature coming up in October. I want to get this bill before them."

The council approved. They might not have if they could have foreseen that Ernie Bohn was about to put together a patchwork quilt of enabling legislation by borrowing some from existing laws, amending some existing laws, and writing some new ones. His trail would be as hard to follow as rabbits through briars.

When the special session of the Ohio legislature convened, it was surprised to be getting pressure from other cities across the state, which Bohn had contacted.

"What's the hurry, Ernie?"

"There's some federal money available for reconstruction projects, now, which will expire June 28, 1934."

Opponents of Bohn's idea were not too alarmed. Bohn was referring to the Federal Emergency Relief and Construction Act of 1932, which made loans available to private limited dividend corporations formed for the purpose of furnishing low rent housing under certain highly controlled conditions. The law intended to stimulate industry and furnish jobs. This money was only a loan, and this federal law had only stimulated one housing project in the entire nation.

Bohn's law to enable the formation of private limited dividend companies passed in Columbus, Ohio, October 3, 1932; but it granted no tax relief to limited dividend companies, which meant no incentive existed to make the law work. So those who were opposed to slum clearance and government getting into it still didn't worry much about Bohn. He was standing there with his bare hands and a law in his pocket that left him a million miles from replacing a hundred acres of slums with good housing.

The old-timers knew that one man against a massive slum is like a woodpecker cutting down redwood trees. For centuries slums have devoured and demolished thousands of bleeding-heart crusaders who died early while the slums grew one block a month. Bohn knew this too.

The job needed not a local voice in the wind; it needed a national uproar. Bohn set out to create one.

He went into his Cleveland Council with a resolution calling for a National Conference on Slum Clearance to be held in Cleveland July 6 and 7, 1933, under the auspices of the government of the City of Cleveland. Councilmen looked at each other, shrugged and voted "Aye."

Ernie Bohn went over to the library. He looked in various kinds of who's who's and professional journals to find the names of 500 men in the country he thought should be interested in slum clearance and low-rent housing. He sent them official invitations, not knowing whether they would come.

Meanwhile, Ernie kept his eyes open for a financial method of getting action. The Ohio limited dividend law would not attract private builders or investors because it gave them no incentive and left them with the same risks that had kept them out of slum districts before.

But on June 16, 1933, the United States Congress enacted the National Industrial Recovery Act. It established the Housing Division of the Public Works Administration and provided for a 30 percent capital grant for housing developments adjudged to stimulate industry. The seeds of a solution seemed to be lurking in here. Of course, there was still no administrative machinery set up to activate it. Even then it would be hard to convince Washington that the place to start was on the shores of the Cuyahoga.

But suddenly, a surprise — 428 men from all over the nation accepted Ernie's invitation to Cuyahoga country and arrived for his National Conference on Slum Clearance. They were welfare people, architects, public officials, and private citizens interested in slum clearance, housing, better cities.

The timing was excellent. They would be Ernie's na-tional uproar — and the noise would come out of Cleveland from the banks of the Cuyahoga.

Ernie lit the opening of the meeting with a short fuse, "Years of academic discussion have reached a climax. The time to strike is now!"

Many good ideas on ways and means to net rehousing came out in the meeting; but out of the meeting also came a set of initials, NAHO, National Association of Housing Officials, first president Ernest J. Bohn.

Now on the second day of the conference, Ernie heard the news that Harold Ickes, PWA Administrator, had appointed the past president of the American Institute of Architecture, Robert Kohn, as Housing Director of PWA.

Ernie excused himself from a meeting saying he was going for a drink of water. Instead he went to a pay station and phoned Kohn in New York. He introduced himself by name and as pres-ident of NAMO, "Wouldn't it be wonderful for the nation, Mr. Kohn, if on your first day on the new job you could announce a big slum clearance and rehousing project."

"Well," Kohn said, "there's nothing like starting off with a success."

I have one that would be a perfect beginning, Mr. Kohn. I'd like to come to see you."

The night his conference closed, Ernie Bohn boarded the B & O with a roll of blueprints under arm.

In PWA headquarters building in Washington, Ernie asked the guard, "Where's the Housing Division?"

"Never heard of it."

A cleaning woman spoke up, "I think I saw it. Follow me."

She led Ernie under the grand stairway to where the brooms were stored. There was a door with a small penciled card on it, misspelled, "Cohen."

Ernie entered and a young woman looked up, studied his face, and said, "Come in, Mr. Kohn. Here's your desk."

So Ernie knew he would be the first in line. He sat down to wait.

The blueprints he had under his arm were for Cleveland Homes, Inc., the limited dividend company created under the wing of Cleveland's Industrial Recovery Commission.

When the Housing Administrator arrived on the job and found Ernie had arrived before him, they had a good laugh and Mr. Kohn told the story with relish for many years.

Even supposing the federal government should act on slum clearance, why would they ever select the Cuyahoga for a start? And even supposing the federal government would lend them 70 percent for the specific projects, where would Bohn get the other 30 percent in a depression-beaten area?

To get action on the shores of the Cuyahoga, Ernie Bohn felt he must offer Washington a model city in slum clearance. If he could offer them a city in which the people were loudly interested in the program, perhaps they would use Cleveland to show the rest of the nation how a massive urban redevelopment could spark recovery across the land, beautify our cities, and effect human rehabilitation.

He called more mass meetings of leaders and also people living in the neighborhoods.

Those opponents who became fully aware of Bohn's intention to use parts of the revised Emergency Relief and Construction Act coupled with the Ohio Limited Dividend Housing Act as a means to housing were somewhat relieved by the massive job it would be to prove to the federal government that part should be spent in Cleveland. And even if that barrier was cracked, "which part of Cleveland" would start an equally tough battle.

But the plans for the project were well regarded in Washington, and would be approved if Cleveland Homes, Inc. could raise only $2,000,000 in private funds. Unfortunately they were unable to do so.

This was discouraging. Ernie Bohn decided that private enterprise was unable to clear slums and furnish rehousing.

The first step was to get the federal government to do the job itself by resorting to the use of the private limited dividend company. So now with a grass fire of commotion started in Cleveland, Ernie Bohn went back to Washington with five specific plans in mind, to ask for action. And he begged for a fast approval for slum clearance in Cleveland and for a shortening of the paperwork.

In his answer to PWA Administrator Ickes and President Roosevelt, Bohn carefully kept sentiment out of it. He knew their problem, and he said, "No form of expenditure spreads its effects for recovery so broadly to every branch of industry as new housing.

"Not just brick, plaster, lumber. But when you put the roof on and the people move in, they buy new furniture. They don't bring only the old." And Bohn was not just talking. He had studied housing so much now that he was truly the national authority on the subject.

"New housing gives business to all material suppliers, but also to appliance manufacturers. And, believe it or not, clothing manufacturers. New housing makes people dress better. New housing makes people want ..."

With unprecedented swiftness, government lawyers cut through the paperwork.

Encouraged, Bohn went on to the next step. He wrote a new law to be introduced in the Ohio legislature, HB 19, Ohio Housing Authority Law. It was to be the turning point in the nation's housing history — the first public housing law in the nation, and the model for other states. All but two states now have such laws modeled on the Ohio law. It made slum clearance and providing housing for low income families a public responsibility.

This law made it possible in 1933 to create The Cleveland Metropolitan Housing Authority, the first in the nation. There are now over 2,000. With such a body created, Bohn then hoped to get it into slum-clearance action by making a financial patchwork of loans and grants from BFC, PWA, and private revenue bond purchasers.

He was starting over again, but now his ways and means were more apparent, and the passage of the Ohio law alerted local opponents of public housing. They could see that Bohn might be getting a little closer to clearing those slums. You couldn't shrug him off.

Ernie felt he would have to be backed up with public opinion.

Returning from the legislative halls in Columbus, he went immediately to a radio station and got on the air, with a challenging thought:

The most important piece of progressive social legislation that was passed by any law-making body in the United States in recent years became law last week. I refer to the state housing act.

Section One says: "It is hereby declared necessary in the public interest to make provisions for housing families of low income and to provide for elimination of congested unsanitary housing conditions which are a menace to ..."

The answer to most social problems is environment.

Bohn then explained his plan for slum removal in Cleveland and the construction of new public housing.

The idea is opposed by conservatives who say it puts government in an additional activity. And on the other hand it is opposed by the more socialistically inclined who say it doesn't go far enough.

I reply to the conservatives that the slums cost most in services and bring least in taxes.

To the others I say, "Though the first spade of dirt has not been turned, *the spade is available!*"

Bohn was issuing a call for broad support to make Cleveland the nation's leader in slum clearance and rehousing. But what he reached first was an alarmed local leadership. "This Bohn is a socialist."

At 30, Bohn was a thousand years old. He knew that before he could get the support of the leadership along the river, he first had to let them all take a crack at him. He called a meeting of the heads of 50 organizations having anything to do with housing in the area. He called for their suggestions, criticisms, ideas. He got all the fights right out in the open.

But what he wanted was enough noise to reach the White House and Congress. He wanted it to look as though a thousand leaders in Cleveland were concerned with slum removal. Well, some were, and some were out for Bohn removal. But the noise was loud, very loud. Bohn intended to make it louder still.

The job of forming the housing authority[1] in Cleveland (authorized by the Ohio law), and then getting the right to condemn a specific slum area, and raising the money from private investors for this new public activity made old pros tired just thinking about it.

Ernie's moves in this direction now generated enormous resistance from some councilmen who did not want their voters to move, land and apartment owners who lived on slum incomes, powerful development and real estate groups.

---

1. This housing authority was in itself a unique animal. It is not government; it is not a private corporation; it is not an individual proprietorship in the law. It's a special public entity, a new kind of being.

An advisory committee was required which would assist the federal government to administer the slum clearance and construction.

Who was chosen would be important. It had to be someone the whole city and Washington would respect and trust with the spending of miles of money. Harold Ickes was a suspicious alumnus of Chicago politics.

I don't know whether it was Ernie Bohn's keen sense of history or just a coincidence. But the man he recommended to head the committee was Leyton E. Carter, 41-year-old direct descendant of Lorenzo Carter, the man who built the mouth of the Cuyahoga in the first place.

Carter was conservative, thoughtful, resourceful and efficient, and an admirer of Bohn.

Oversimply, thus began the first such slum-clearance and public-housing action in the United States. Cedar Apartments in Cleveland were the first, followed closely by the $2,800,000 Lakeview Terrace Apartments just above Whiskey Island, 22 acres of redevelopment at the mouth of the Cuyahoga.

One councilmen moved to stop the action until special guarantees of bi-racial occupancy were built into it by the federal government.

But once things had started, a lot of people with other causes, seeing Bohn's piercing way of getting action, tried to hang their causes onto his. A prominent congressman attacked the plans to install iceless refrigeration, "forcing tenants to accept a type of refrigeration which may be objectionable to them and damaging to their health."

Bohn disposed of these shortly, but then the very people suffering in the slum area above Whiskey Island had pangs of tenderness. Demolition of the old "Angle" and the bars in the Flats where police had to walk in threes now bothered people. "That's where champs John L. Sullivan and Johnny Kilbane trained for their fights," some said. "We got to have slums to build men."

This was boss Brick Masterson country. He ruled from his saloon and dealt with governors and senators in his own establishment. He could deliver votes.

The Sixth District U.S. Court ruled that the U.S. had no power to seize property for housing.

There were warnings to Bohn to hold up the project. Bond buyers backed away quickly at any shadow of legal snarls. But Bohn was by then highly skilled in the art of using the laws of the land.

"We'll keep moving ahead," he said to the government attorneys. "You appeal it to the U.S. Supreme Court. If you lose there, then request local housing authorities to use their unchallengeable condemnation rights over slums. Same result."

The real trial of major leadership is the knowledge that to get your own job done, you have to carry a lot of other people's freight. Bohn bit his tongue and tried to accommodate sentiment, councilmen, manufacturers, U.S. courts. But he would not stop.

There is not time or space to see Bohn fight each fight. The resourcefulness required each time is typically demonstrated by the time he was leading a city council bipartisan coalition opposition to the then-mayor's annual city budget which contained no help for Ernie's programs.

The mayor retaliated with a very effective move. It happened that the muddy Cuyahoga was muddier than usual this season. The siltation was so heavy that ore boats would not be able to get up the Cuyahoga to the docks to bring in ore, stone, and coal for the mills when the thaw came.

The Lake Erie Dredge & Dock Company would not commence dredging the Cuyahoga without a signed contract with the city. The mayor refused to sign a contract giving as his reason, "How can I sign a firm contract with *anyone* when I don't have a budget O.K. from council?"

Mayors had many times let contracts before budget approval, but technically his position was quite correct. The strength of his move was that the Cuyahoga valley is steel country. And anyone holding up the steel business is threatening the livelihood of thousands.

The mayor knew the headline pressure this would bring down upon Bohn: BOHN HOLDS UP STEEL JOBS.

That would get a quick capitulation from many councilmen. But Bohn was gaining the extraordinary powers that come to men with a mission who are asking nothing for themselves. Councilman Bohn went to the United States Government via Senator Bulkley to suggest that rivers and harbors are traditionally a federal concern.

Result: The United States dredged the river. Bohn could go back to his budget battle in peace.

But when Lakeview Terrace was completed, the nation had a model of what could be done. From all over the country, they still came to look.

Bohn became, in the eyes of most, one of the nation's leading authorities on housing.

In 1935, he was one of the young men who helped Senator Robert Wagner of New York write the Public Housing Act, which was finally enacted in 1937, defeating one of the most powerful lobbies in the history of lawmaking. This law gave the Cleveland and other housing authorities the guarantee on their bonds through annual contributions from Congress. This then made it possible for local authorities to function *and the federal government went out of the housing construction business.*

Bohn was then able to move down the river to build Valleyview on 75 acres on the bluff below Walworth Run, a $3,500,000 development. This was the first of a dozen developments subsequently built by the Cleveland Metropolitan Housing Authority.

Years went by with Bohn rebuilding the slums. A man who lives in the world of abstractions, he nevertheless became expert on brick, structural iron, electrical panel boards, concrete, elevators, sinks, financing, and what kind of soap is best for scrubbing floors.

Most of all, he became expert in humanity.

By 1943, the nation was depending upon him so heavily that he had to be much away from his office at the mouth of the river. His own towering reputation now began chipping away at his empty desk.

Ernie was working to construct some kind of shelter along the river for an army of warworkers who had moved in to man the defense factories. They were living in slums, garages, empty stores, or doubled up with others. Now it wasn't that Bohn felt hardship inappropriate in wartime; but sheer roof coverage was needed over the people, and with both parents needed in the factories, there had to be safe places to leave children.

Bohn was also trying to provide for returning veterans who would need 150,000 homes. Private construction could initially furnish only 3,000 dwellings per year, and the area would rapidly build new slums with the intensified doubling up that would occur.

At the same time, he was haunted day and night by a horrible vision recurring more and more in his dreams. Lonely old men and women, sitting in single rooms in the river valley slums, hour after hour in unutterable boredom and squalor, some hoping to die before pains became worse. He saw them in life. He saw them in his sleep.

Bohn can dress down a legislator in a public hearing with a rapier intellect that will leave the victim bleeding. But he cannot square eyes with an old man staring out a broken window.

So he was already working on his biggest dream — beautiful high-rise apartments on the west bank of the river looking over the Cuyahoga valley, a proper view for elderly men and women. He planned to call it Riverview; it would rise, he hoped, halfway between Lakeview and Valleyview.

This is less than half the story. At one time, Bohn was:
- Chairman, Civilian Defense Housing Committee
- Director, Regional Association (citizen's planning organization)

332

- Chairman, City Planning Commission
- Agent for Federal Housing Authority
- President, NAHO's Regional Housing Officials

That gave him a strong position. He was planning housing for war workers and returning war veterans and the growing families of both.

Despite the strong position, he would still have to battle.

While he was away from the river helping the President with national war-housing emergencies, a news story broke back home:

> President of Mortgage Bankers Association says the city needs to put a new watchdog on Bohn to see that he doesn't socialize all residential property.
>
> Bohn's method only *moves* slums, it doesn't *remove* them. We must watch the city planning commission (of which he is chairman) closely. It is controlled by the outstanding public houser in the nation.

So the battles would continue.

Politics being the constant milieu of construction, Washington sent in a gang, and out-of-state contractors moved in as well.

Ernest Bohn continued his plan drawing on his political network and using the same skills we witnessed.

Importantly, he continued his humanity emphasis. In his bullhorn voice, he lectured visiting sociologists.

"Say an old widower has a little trouble remembering one of his ten grandchildren when they come to call the first time in three years. Right away the family says, 'his mind is going.' We should pack him off right away to some institution.

"Baloney. When you get old, you forget. I couldn't even remember *your* name 'til you crossed the threshold. So am I crazy? We let him stay. Is that sociology?"

As I left Ernie Bohn in '85 he and the governor were at work on housing for the nonpsychotic elderly.

The Cuyahoga is a man-made river; even the palisades along its shore.

The Cuyahoga is a man-made river. There was no reason, by virtue of length, width, current, or location, for this red creek to become headquarters of mid-America's steel, oil, and rubber economy. But men leveled it out with the great canal, straightened it with the cut at the mouth, dredged it to let in deep draft ore bulkers, dammed it to take off power and build empires of rubber and flour.

Some rivers are so mighty and overpowering they force conclusions on men and nations — the Ohio, the Columbia, the Mississippi — and diminish the men.

However, the crooked little Cuyahoga, no larger than many a good fishing stream, required of men their best effort and magnified them. It turned them into giants who forced the valley into the pivotal position in mid-America's economy. Sailing out of her mouth, they opened first the Upper Peninsula mines in Michigan, then the Mesabi. Digging upstream alongside with a flat track of slack water, the Ohio Canal made this valley the main freight road from New Orleans to New York.

The little river is still challenging men to works so vast that mile for mile it can't be matched by any river I have ever heard of in the world.

Bibliography

Album, Wilfred Henry, *This Cleveland of Ours*. Cleveland: S. J. Clarke Publishing Company, 1933.

American Monthly Magazine, The. Vol. 38, Jan.-June. Edited by Mrs. Elroy M. Avery. New York: The National Society of the Daughters of the American Revolution, 1911.

Annals of Cleveland, 1818-1935. Cleveland: WPA Project 14066, 1937.

Barnholth, William I., *The Cuyahoga-Tuscarawas Portage*. Akron: Summit County Historical Society, 1954.

Cherry, Peter Peterson, *The Portage Path*. Akron: The Western Reserve Company, 1911.

--- *The Western Reserve & Early Ohio*. Akron: R. L. Fouse, 1921.

Cleveland Topics. Cleveland Topics Company.

Clipping File. *The Cleveland Plain Dealer*.

Clipping File. *The Cleveland Press*.

Coates, William R., *A History of Cuyahoga County*, Vol. 1. (3 vol series) Chicago and New York: The American Historical Society, 1924.

"Cuyahoga River," "Moses Cleaveland," "Cleveland, Ohio— Morgana Run." Clipping File, Cleveland Public Library. History, Biography and Travel Department.

Downes, Randolph Chandler, *History of Lake Shore Ohio*. Vol.1. New York: Lewis Historical Publishing Co., Inc., 1952.

Doyle, William B., *Centennial History of Summit County, Ohio*. Chicago: Biographical Publishing Company, 1908.

Early Settlers' Association of the Western Reserve, Annals, Vol. I, III, and VI. Cleveland, Ohio. (Published by order of the Executive Committee.) n.d.

Fairchild, Thomas B. (Reverend), *Cuyahoga Falls*. Cleveland: Cleveland Herald Print, 1876. (A history of the town of

Cuyahoga Falls, Summit County, Ohio. An address delivered by Mr. Fairchild, July 4, 1876.)

Fowke, Gerald, *Archeological History of Ohio.* n.d.

Grismer, Karl Hiram, *Akron & Summit County.* Akron: Summit County Historical Society, 1952 (?)

Hatcher, Harlan Henthorne, *The Western Reserve.* Indianapolis: Bobbs-Merrill, 1949.

Havighurst, Walter, *The Heartland.* New York: Harper & Row, 1962.

--- *Wilderness for Sale.* New York: Hastings House, 1956. *History of Portage County.* (General history by R. C. Brown; local history, J. E. Norris). Chicago: Warner, Beers & Co., 1885.

Hodges, Orlando John, *Reminiscences* Vol. II. Cleveland: The Imperial Press, 1902-10.

Horton, John J. *The Jonathan Hale Farm. A Chronicle of the Cuyahoga Valley.* Cleveland: Western Reserve Historial Society, 1961.

Howe, Henry, *Historical Collections of Ohio.* Vol. I (Published by the State of Ohio.) Norwalk, Ohio: The Laning Printing Co. Public Printers, 1898.

Inland Seas, ® Quarterly Journal of the Great Lakes Historical Society, 1955-56.

Johnson, Crisfield, *History of Cuyahoga County, Ohio.* Philadelphia: D. W. Ensign & Co., 1879.

Kelley, S. J., "Clippings from Cleveland Plain Dealer, Vol. I & II," Cleveland Public Library. History, Biography and Travel Department.

Kennedy, James Henry, *A History of Cleveland.* Cleveland: The Cleveland Printing and Publishing Company, 1889.

--- *A History of the City of Cleveland.* Cleveland: The Imperial Press. MDCCCXCVI (1896).

Lane, Samuel Alanson, *Fifty Years and Over of Akron and Summit County.* Akron: Beacon Job Department.

Magazine of Western History, Vol. II, Cleveland (1884-88). New York: Magazine of Western History Publishing Co. (1888-1891).

Ohio Guide, The. Compiled by workers of the Writers' Program of the Work Projects Administration in the State of Ohio. American Guide Series sponsored by The Ohio State Archaeological & Historical Society. Oxford University Press, New York: First published in October 1940.

Pioneer & General History of Geauga Co., Ohio. Burton (?) Ohio: Historical Society of Geauga Co., 1880.

Post, Charles Asa, *The Cuyahoga: The Crooked River That Made A City Great* . . . Cleveland (?): Privately printed 1941.

Rose, William Ganson. *Cleveland: The Making of a City.* Cleveland: The World Publishing Company, 1950.

Siebert, Henry Wilbur. *The Underground Railroad From Slavery to Freedom.* New York and London: The Macmillan Co., 1898.

--- *The Mysteries of Ohio's Underground Railroads.* Columbus, Ohio: Long's College Book Co., 1951.

Vietzen, Raymond C., *The Immortal Eries.* Elyria, Ohio: Wilmot Printing Company, 1945.

Whittlesey, Charles, *Early History of Cleveland.* Cleveland: Fairbanks, Benedict & Co., Printers, 1867.

Wilcox, Frank N., *Ohio Indian Trails.* Cleveland: The Gates Press, 1933.

Index